Roswell C. Smith

Smith's New Grammar

English grammar, on the productive system - a method of instruction recently

adopted in Germany and Switzerland - Vol. 3

Roswell C. Smith

Smith's New Grammar
English grammar, on the productive system - a method of instruction recently adopted in Germany and Switzerland - Vol. 3

ISBN/EAN: 9783337191580

Printed in Europe, USA, Canada, Australia, Japan

Cover: Foto ©Paul-Georg Meister /pixelio.de

More available books at **www.hansebooks.com**

ON THE

PRODUCTIVE SYSTEM:

A

METHOD OF INSTRUCTION RECENTLY ADOPTED

IN

GERMANY AND SWITZERLAND.

Designed for Schools and Academies.

BY ROSWELL C. SMITH,

AUTHOR OF "PRACTICAL AND MENTAL ARITHMETIC," "INTELLECTUAL AND PRACTICAL GRAMMAR," AND "INTRODUCTORY ARITHMETIC."

NEW STEREOTYPE EDITION.

PHILADELPHIA:
PUBLISHED BY E. H. BUTLER & CO.
1865.

Entered, according to Act of Congress, in the year 1860, by ROSWELL C. SMITH, in the Clerk's Office of the District Court of the United States, in and for the District of Connecticut.
Entered, according to Act of Congress, in the year 1860, by ROSWELL C. SMITH, in the Clerk's Office of the District Court of the United States, in and for the District of Massachusetts.

THE PRODUCTIVE GRAMMAR.

ENGLISH GRAMMAR

ON THE

PRODUCTIVE SYSTEM:

A

METHOD OF INSTRUCTION RECENTLY ADOPTED.

IN

GERMANY AND SWITZERLAND,

IN THE PLACE OF

THE INDUCTIVE SYSTEM.

Designed for Schools and Academies.

Entered, according to Act of Congress, in the year 1859, by ROSWELL C. SMITH, in the Clerk's Office of the District Court of the District of Connecticut.

PREFACE.

The following work was composed, as is indicated by the title, on what is styled in Germany and Switzerland the "Productive System of Instruction." It is in these countries that the subject of Education has been deemed a matter of paramount importance. The art of teaching, particularly, has there been most ably and minutely investigated. To give a brief account of the different systems which have prevailed there, may not be irrelevant on the present occasion, as they assist in forming an opinion of the comparative merits of the "Productive System," on which this work is principally based.

"In reference to intellectual education, the persons who were instrumental in producing the reformation in schools, in the last century, in these countries, may be divided into four classes—the Humanists, Philanthropists, Pestalozzian and the Productive Schools.

"At the restoration of learning, in the fifteenth and sixteenth centuries, the classics were brought out from the libraries of the cloisters in which they had been buried. As they presented the only examples of exalted sentiments and elevated style which the secular literature of the age afforded, they were regarded as the only means of acquiring enlarged views and a liberal education; the study of them received the proud title of *Humanity;* and the zealous and meritorious men who employed this means for the revival of learning, were subsequently termed *Humanists*.

"The rigid Humanists maintained that 'the Greek and Latin authors are the only source of sound learning, whether in philosophy or rhetoric, in poetry or history, in medicine or law, even in the elements of religion; all has come to us from Greece and Rome.' 'The learning of the Greek and Latin languages is the only foundation of a thorough education;' the knowledge of the grammar ought to precede all other knowledge; 'and philologists are the only thoroughly learned men.'

"The Humanists maintained the entire sway of the learned world until about the middle of the last century, when the school of the *Philanthropists* arose. Disgusted with the extravagant manner in which the ancient languages were extolled, they were led to examine into the foundations of their pretensions. While they yielded the palm to the ancients in all that relates to matters of taste and beauty, they maintained that this superiority arose from the fact, that the ancients derived their views directly from the inspection of nature and the observation of man, instead of occupying themselves, as we do, with the mere pictures of them drawn by others;—they pointed to the obvious truth, that the world is older and vastly more experienced than it was two thousand years ago; that in regard to all that relates to human knowledge, the present generation are really the ancients. They believed that much time was lost by the *indiscriminate* and exclusive use of the classics as the foundation of education, which ought to be spent in acquisition of practical knowledge; and that by this tedious and laborious task, without any perceptible advantage to the pupil, they were often disgusted with every species of intellectual effort. They also pointed out the moral corruption which arises from many of the examples and sentiments of the ancients, and especially disapproved that discipline of compulsion and violence, by which children have been forced to this ungrateful employment. They urged the importance of leading by the attraction of knowledge itself, rather than by force. They paid much attention to the developement of the bodily constitution and powers, and professed to aim at forming men, and not mere scholars.

"But, with the ordinary weakness of human nature, in avoiding one extreme, they ran into the opposite. They forgot the valuable influence of these studies, properly regulated, upon the faculties and habits of the mind.

"Notwithstanding their error, the Philanthropists unquestionably exerted much influence on the improvement of education. The extravagant views of the Humanists were considerably modified; and although many still retain the exclusive maxims of their predecessors, many admit, as stated in the German 'Conversations Lexicon,' that '*all* should be embraced in education which can *promote the formation of the man, and prepare him for the eternal destiny of his spirit.*' The Philanthropists also prepared the way for their successors of the *School of Pestalozzi*. This remarkable man adopted many of the opinions of his predecessors of the Philanthropic school, especially those which related to the developement of the bodily powers, and the methods of discipline, and religious instruction. He perceived, however, that, in assuming practical utility as the *exclusive test* of the value of particular objects of instruction, they had too much neglected the *developement of the mind itself*. In seeking to avoid this error, however, he did not entirely escape the other extreme. He assumed, as a fundamental principle, that a certain developement of mind was necessary for every rank and every occupation. The means of this developement he supposed himself to have found, so far as the intellectual faculties were concerned, in the *elements of form* and *number*, which are combined in the science of *Mathematics*, in *Language*, and in *Natural History*. The Mathematics appear to have assumed a preponderance in practice, which was unfavorable to the regular and harmonious cultivation of other powers. The senses and the bodily powers he endeavored to develope, in accordance with the views of the Philanthropic school, by the careful examination of the various objects of nature and art, which surround the pupil, by means of music, and by gymnastic exercises, alternated or combined with labor. Pestalozzi himself was remarkably the creature of powerful impulses, which were usually of the most mild and benevolent kind, and preserved a child-like character in this respect, even to old age. It was probably this temperament which led him to estimate at a low rate the importance of positive religious truth in the education of children, and to maintain that the mere habit of faith and love, if cultivated towards earthly parents and benefactors, would of course be transferred to our heavenly Father, whenever his character should be exhibited to the mind of the child. The fundamental error of this view was established by the unhappy experience of his own institution: and his own example afforded the most striking evidence that the noblest impulses, not directed by established principles, may lead to imprudence and ruin, and thus defeat their own ends.* This principle, combined

---

* As an example of this, it may be mentioned that, on one of those occasions (frequently occurring) on which he was reduced to extremity for want of the means of supplying his large family, he borrowed $400 from a friend for this purpose. In going home, he met a peasant wringing his hands in despair for the loss of his cow. Pestalozzi put the entire bag of money into his hands, and ran off to escape his thanks.

with the want of tact in reference to the affairs of common life, materially impaired his powers of usefulness as a practical instructer of youth. The rapid progress of his ideas rarely allowed him to execute his own plans; and, according to his own system, too much time was employed in the profound developement of principles to admit of much attention to their practical application. But, as one of his admirers observed, he seemed destined to educate ideas and not children. He combated, with unshrinking boldness, and untiring perseverance, through a long life, both by his example and by his numerous publications, the prejudices and abuses of the age, in reference to education. He attacked, with great vigor and no small degree of success, that favorite maxim of bigotry and tyranny, that obedience and devotion are the legitimate offspring of ignorance. He denounced that degrading system which considers it enough to enable man to procure a subsistence for himself and his offspring — and in this manner to merely place him on a level with the beast of the forest; and which deems every thing lost whose value cannot be estimated in money. He urged upon the consciences of parents and of rulers, with an energy approaching that of the ancient prophets, the solemn duties which Divine Providence had imposed upon them, in committing to their charge the present and future destinies of their fellow beings. In this way he produced an impulse, which pervaded the continent of Europe, and which, by means of his popular and theoretical works, reached the cottages of the poor and palaces of the great. His institution at Yverdun was crowded with men of every nation, not merely those who were led by the same benevolence which inspired him, but by the agents of kings, and noblemen, and public institutions, who came to make themselves acquainted with his principles, in order to become fellow-laborers in his plans of benevolence.

"It is to these companions of his labors, most of whom resided in Germany or Switzerland, that we owe the formation of another school, which has been styled the *Productive School*, and which now predominates in Germany and Switzerland. It might, perhaps, with equal propriety, be termed the *Eclectic School;* for it aims at embodying all the valuable principles of previous systems, without adhering slavishly to the dictates of any master, or the views of any party. It rejects alike the idolatrous homage to the classics, which was paid by the Humanists—the unreasonable prejudices of the Philanthropists against classical and merely literary pursuits — and the undue predilection for the mere expansion of mind, to the neglect of positive knowledge and practical application, which characterized too many of the Pestalozzian School.

"The leading principle of this system, is that which its name indicates —that the child should be regarded not as a mere recipient of the ideas of others, but as an agent capable of collecting, and originating, and producing most of the ideas which are necessary for its education, when presented with the objects or the facts from which they may be derived. While, on the one hand, they are careful not to reduce the pupil to a mere machine, to be moved by the will of his instructer in an assigned direction, or a mass of passive matter, to be formed by him according to his own favorite model, they are equally careful to avoid the extreme, into which some of the preceding school have fallen, of leaving him to wander indefinitely, in a wrong direction in search of truth, in order to secure to him the merit of discovery. They consider a course of education as divided into two parts—*the period of developement* and *the period of acquisition*. In the first period, which they consider as *particularly* devoted to *developing the faculties and forming the habits of the mind*, in order to *prepare it as an instrument for future operations*, they employ the inductive process chiefly. Time is not here of so much importance as the habit of investigation and effort, which can only be acquired by meeting and overcoming difficulties. This period, which must be made longer or shorter according to the character of the pupil, or the necessity that his circumstances in life may impose, is succeeded by the *period of acquisition,* in which *the mind* is more especially *called upon to exercise the powers which have been previously developed and cultivated,* in the acquisition *of such positive knowledge as may prepare the individual for life and action.* The inductive process is still employed as much as possible, not only because it has become, for many cases, the shortest and most agreeable, but because it is important to maintain the habits it has produced, and invigorate the faculties it has served to develope.

" But still it is far less employed than previously, and the pupil is never suffered to waste his time in attempting to create a science for himself, and thus deprived of the benefit of the experience of sages and centuries. On the contrary, they deem his mind capable of being elevated even more rapidly by following the processes of patient investigation, by which the most exalted minds have arrived at results that astonish and delight him, and of thus learning to imitate strides, which seem to him like those of a giant, and to cultivate those habits of untiring attention, which the greatest philosophers have declared to be the principal source of that telescopic glance, that almost unerring power of discrimination, which seems to others so nearly miraculous.

" Such is the Productive System, by which the powers of the pupil are called into complete exercise by requiring him to attempt a task unaided, and then assisting him in correcting his own errors, or returning from his own wanderings, before he is discouraged by the waste of time and the fruitlessness of his efforts. They distinguish carefully between knowledge and the means of obtaining it. To cultivate the senses, and present the objects which they are capable of examining, is to open to the child the *sources of knowledge*—to place before him a book which is ever open, and in which he may every moment read. This, they maintain, is the first and most obvious part of education, according to the dictates of common sense. It is one in which nothing but truth is presented to him, and which, by calling his powers into constant exercise, ensures their improvement, and cultivates a spirit of investigation."

The preceding extracts are taken from Art. I. Vol. I. No. VI. of the American Journal of Education, New Series. The author avails himself of this opportunity to express his obligations to the conductors of this valuable periodical. A constant perusal of its pages has afforded him many valuable ideas on the subject of education, and he cheerfully acknowledges material assistance derived from it in the preparation of the "Productive System of English Grammar," which is now respectfully submitted to the candid examination of the public.

THE AUTHOR.

ENGLISH GRAMMAR

I. OF THE NOUN.

Q. What is your name?
Q. What is the name of the town in which you live?
Q. What does the word *noun* mean?
Ans. The word *noun* means *name*.
Q. What, then, may your name be called?
1. A NOUN.
Q. What may all names be called?
2. Nouns.
Q. Boston is the name of a place: is *Boston* a noun? and if so, why?
3. *Boston* is a noun, because it is a name.
Q. Hudson is the name of a river: is *Hudson* a noun, and why?
Q. Book is the name of something to read in: is *book* a noun, and why?
Q. Will you now inform me what a noun is?
4. A noun is the name of any person, place, or thing.
Q. Will you mention two nouns the names of persons? two, the names of things? two, the names of different places?
Q. Will you tell me which words are the nouns in the following sentences, as I read them to you?
"Thomas and Joseph are in the house."
"The horse and cow are in the lot."
"The hawk and the eagle have flown to the mountain.'
"Trees, corn, potatoes and apples grow in the fields."

II. NUMBER.

Q. What is the meaning of the word *number;* as, "The number of buttons on your coat?"
5. Number means *one or more.*
Q. What does the word *singular* mean?
6. It means *one.*
Q. When, then, I speak of one thing only, as *chair*, what number is it?
7. Singular number.
Q. What, then, does the singular number of nouns denote?
8. The singular number denotes but one thing.

Q. Of what number is *book*, and why?

9. *Book* is of the singular number, because it means but one.

Q. Of what number is *chair*, and why?
Q. What does the word *plural* mean?

10. It means *more than one*.

Q. Of what number is *lamps*, and why?

11. *Lamps* is of the plural number, because it means more than one.

Q. Of what number is *inkstand*, and why?
Q. By adding *s* to *dove*, we have *doves*, and *es* to *box*, we have *boxes*. How, then, is the plural number of nouns usually formed?

12. By adding *s* or *es* to the singular.

Q. Will you spell the plural of *ounce? glass? window? theatre? antecedent? church? labyrinth?*
Q. How many numbers do nouns appear to have, and what are they?

13. Two, the singular and plural.

Q. Will you name a noun of the singular number? one of the plural number?

III. GENDER.

Q. What does the word *gender* mean?

14. *Gender* signifies *sex*.

Q. What does the word *masculine* mean?

15. It means *male*.

Q. *John* is the name of a male: of what gender or sex, then, is *John?*

16. Of the masculine or male gender.

Q. What nouns, then, are said to be of the masculine gender?

17. The names of males.

Q. What gender, then, is *man*, and why?

18. *Man* is of the masculine gender, because it is the name of a male.

Q. Of what gender is *uncle*, and why? *father?* why?
Q. What does *feminine* mean?

19. It means *female*.

Q. *Susan* is the name of a female: of what gender, then, is *Susan?*

20. Of the feminine gender.

Q. What nouns, then, are said to be of the feminine gender?

21. The names of females.

Q. What gender is *woman*, and why?

22. *Woman* is of the feminine gender, because it is the name of a female.

Q. Of what gender is *aunt*, and why? *daughter?* why?
Q. What does the word *neuter* mean?

23. It means *neither*.

Q. *Chair* is the name neither of a male nor a female: what gender, then, may it properly be called?

24. Neuter gender.

Q. What nouns, then, may be said to be of the neuter gender?

25. The names of objects that are neither males nor females.

Q. Of what gender is *inkstand*, and why?

26. Neuter gender, because it is the name neither of a male nor female.

Q. Of what gender is *bench?* why? *chair?* why?
Q. *Parent*, you know, is the name either of father or mother, that is, it is a name *common* to both: of what gender, then, shall we call such nouns as *parent, bird*, &c.?

27. Common gender.

Q. What nouns, then, may be said to be of the common gender?

28. The names of such animals as may be either males or females.

Q. Of what gender is *sheep*, and why?

29. *Sheep* is of the common gender, because it is the name either of a male or female.

Q. Of what gender is *robin*, and why?
Q. How many genders do nouns appear to have, and what are they?

30. Four—the masculine, the feminine, the neuter, and the common.

Q. Will you name a noun of the masculine gender? one of the feminine? one of the neuter? one of the common?
Q. Will you name the gender and number of each noun in the following sentences, as I read them to you?

"James and William."   "Slate and pencil."
"John and the girls."   "Women and birds."

IV. PROPER AND COMMON NOUNS.

Q. What is the meaning of the word *common;* as, "A common complaint?"

31. *Common* means *general*.

Q. Although there are a vast many male children in the world, each one may be called by the general name of *boy:* what kind of a noun, then, would you call *boy?*

32. A common noun.

Q. When, then, is a noun called common?

33. When it is a general name.

Q. What does the word *proper* mean?

34. It means *fit* or *particular*.

Q. John, you know, is the particular name of a boy: what kind of noun, then, may it be called?

35. A proper noun.

Q. When, then, may a noun be called proper?

36. When it is a particular name.

Q. What kind of a noun is *Susan*, and why?

37. *Susan* is a proper noun, because it is a particular name.

Q. What kind of a noun is *John*, and why?

Q. What kind of a noun is *river,* and why?

38. *River* is a common noun, because it is a general name.

Q. How many kinds of nouns do there appear to be, and what are they?
Q. What kind of a noun is *girls? Mary? town? New York? London? boat? chain?*
Q. Will you now tell me which words are the nouns in the following sentences; which are proper, and which common; also their gender and number?

"Thomas and John."   "King and queen."
"Susan and Mary."   "House and barn."

V. PERSON.

Q. When a person, in speaking, says, "I, John, will do it," what person do grammarians call *John?*

39. The first person.

Q. When, then, is a noun of the first person?

40. When it is the name of the person speaking.

Q. When I say, "James, mind your studies," what person do grammarians call *James?*

41. The second person, being the person spoken to.

Q. When, then, is a noun of the second person?

42. When it is the name of the person spoken to, or addressed.

Q. "William, James has come." What person is *William,* and why?

43. Of the second person, because William is spoken to.

Q. When I say, "William, James has come," I am speaking to William about James: of what person, then, is *James,* and why?

44. Of the third person, because James was spoken of; that is, I was talking about James.

Q. When, then, is a noun of the third person?

45. When it is spoken of.

Q. "Thomas, Rufus is in the garden." What person is *Thomas?* why? Is *Rufus?* why?

Q. How many persons do nouns appear to have, and what are they?

46. Three persons — the first, second, and third.

Q. Will you inform me which of the following nouns are proper, which common; also their gender, number, and person?

"I, James, of Boston."   "Boy and girl."
"Henry, study your book."   "William and his sister."

VI. CASE.

Q. We say of an animal, for instance a horse, when he is fat, that "He is in a good case;" and, when he is lean, that "He is in a bad case;" what therefore, does the word *case* mean?

47. *Case* means *condition, state,* &c.

CASES.

Q. When I say, "Charles strikes William," "William strikes Charles," you may perceive that the state or condition of Charles in the former example is quite different from his state or condition in the latter: in the one, Charles strikes; in the other, he is struck: what, then, is meant by the different cases of nouns?

48. The different condition or position they have in relation to other words in the same sentence.

Q. What does the word *nominative* mean?

49. *Nominative* means *naming*.

Q. When I say, "John strikes," he evidently does something: what, then, may John be called?

50. An actor or doer.

Q. Well, then, as the actor or doer is considered the naming or leading noun, in what case is *John*, when I say, "John strikes?"

51. In the nominative case.

Q. What, then, is the nominative case of nouns?

52. The nominative case is the agent or doer.

Q. When I say, "The dog runs," in what case is *dog*, and why?

53. *Dog* is in the nominative case, because it is the agent, actor, or doer.

Q. "The cat catches mice." In what case is *cat*, and why?

Q. When I say, "Thomas is pursuing the thief," what is the object here which Thomas is pursuing?

54. *Thief.*

Q. What does the word *objective* mean?

55. It means *belonging to the object*.

Q. In what case, then, may *thief* be reckoned, in the phrase, "Thomas pursues the thief?"

56. In the objective case.

Q. What, then, does the objective case denote?

57. The objective case denotes the object.

Q. When I say, "William whips John," in what case is *John*, and why?

58. In the objective case, because *John* is the object.

Q. What does the word *possessive* imply?

59. *Possession, ownership, property,* &c.

Q. When I say, "It is John's slate," I mean to say that John owns the slate: in what case, then, shall we reckon *John's?*

60. In the possessive case.

Q. What, then, does the possessive case of nouns denote?

61. The possessive case denotes possession, property, &c.

Q. When I say, "Peter's knife," who owns or possesses the knife?

Q. In what case, then, is *Peter's*, and why?

62. In the possessive case, because Peter possesses the knife.

Q. In the example "John's slate," you perceive that *John's* ends in *s*, with a comma before it: what is the comma, and what is the *s*, called in grammar?

63. The comma is called an apostrophe, and the *s*, an apostrophic *s*.

Q. You also perceive that *John's* is singular: how, then, do nouns in the singular number usually form their possessive case?

64. By taking after them an apostrophe with the letter *s* following it.

Q. "On eagles' wings." Here *eagles'* is plural, and in the possessive case: how, then, do nouns in the plural usually form their possessive case?

65. Simply by taking the apostrophe without the addition of *s*.

Q. But if the plural noun does not end in *s*, as, "men's concerns," how is the possessive case formed?

66. As the same case in the singular number is formed.

Q. From the foregoing remarks, how many cases do nouns appear to have, and what are they?

67. Three—the nominative, possessive, and objective.

Q. Decline sometimes means *to vary the endings of a word:* what, then, do I mean when I ask you to decline a noun?

68. To tell its different cases or endings.

Q. Will you decline *John?*

69. *Nominative case,*   John.
    Possessive case,   John's.
    Objective case,   John.

Q. Will you decline *boy*, in both numbers?

Singular.		Plural.	
70. *Nom.*	Boy.	*Nom.*	Boys.
Poss.	Boy's.	*Poss.*	Boys'.
Obj.	Boy.	*Obj.*	Boys.

Q. When I say, "William's coat," you perceive that the noun *coat* follows *William's:* by what is *William's* said to be governed, and why?

71. By *coat*, because it follows *William's*.

Q. What, then, may be considered a rule for governing the possessive case?

RULE I.

The possessive case is governed by the following noun.

Q. "William's hat." Is *William's* a proper or common noun? Why? (36.)*

Q. What is its person? why? (45.)* Its number? why? (8.)* Its gender? why? (17.)* Its case? why? (61.)* What noun follows *William's?* What word, then, governs *William's?* What is the rule?

Q. When we mention the several properties of the different words in sentences, in the same manner as we have those of *William's*, above, what is the exercise called?

72. PARSING.

EXERCISES IN PARSING.

"*John's knife.*"

73. *John's* is a NOUN, because it is a name — PROPER, because it is a particular name — MASCULINE GENDER; it is the name of a male — THIRD PERSON; it is spoken of — SINGULAR

---

* Refer back to this number.

NUMBER; it means but one — POSSESSIVE CASE; it implies possession — and it is governed by the noun *knife*, according to

RULE I. *The possessive case is governed by the following noun.*

Knife is a NOUN; it is a name — COMMON; it is a general name — NEUTER GENDER; it is neither male nor female — THIRD PERSON; it is spoken of — SINGULAR NUMBER; it means but one.

☞ *Let the learner parse the foregoing, till the mode of parsing the noun is so familiar to him, that he can do it readily, without looking in the book. He may then take the following exercises, which are to be parsed in a similar manner.*

EXERCISES IN PARSING CONTINUED.

" Peter's cap."   " Stephen's coat."   " Brother's knife."
" John's slate." " Father's house."   " Boys' hats."

VII. OF ARTICLES.

Q. When I say, " Give me a book," I evidently mean no particular book, but when I say, " Give me the book," what do I mean?

74. Some particular book.

Q. Which are the words that make this difference in meaning?

75. *A* and *the*.

Q. What are these little words called?

76. ARTICLES.

Q. What, then, are articles?

77. Articles are words placed before nouns to limit their meaning.

Q. What is the meaning of the word *definite*?

78. *Definite* means *particular*.

Q. " Give me the book." Here a particular book is referred to: what kind of an article, then, shall we call *the*?

79. Definite article.

Q. What, then, is a definite article?

80. It points out what particular thing or things are meant.

Q. The word *in*, when placed before words, frequently signifies *not* : what, then, will *indefinite* mean?

81. *Not definite*.

Q. When I say, " Give me a knife," no particular knife is meant: what kind of an article, then, may *a* be called?

82. Indefinite article.

Q. Why is it so called?

83. Because it is not used before the name of any particular person or thing.

Q. We say, "*an* apple," "*an* inkstand," &c. in preference to "*a* app.e," "*a* inkstand," &c.: why is this?

84. Because it is easier to speak, and also more pleasant to the ear.

Q. What kind of letters do *apple* and *inkstand* begin with?

85. Vowels.

Q. In what cases do we use *an* instead of *a*?

86. Before words beginning with the vowels *a, e, i, o, u*.

Q. In speaking, we say, "*a* man," not "*an* man:" when, then, do we use *a*?

87. Before words beginning with consonants.

Q. Which letters are consonants?

88. All the letters of the alphabet, except the vowels, which are *a, e, i, o, u;* and also *w* and *y,* except at the beginning of words, when they are consonants.

Q. How, then, do *a* and *an* differ?

89. Only in their use *a* being used before consonants, and *an* before vowels: both are called by the same name.

Q. How many articles do there appear to be, and what are they?

90. Two—*a* or *an,* and *the.*

Q. It is customary to say, "a boy," not "a *boys;*" also, "an inkstand," not "an *inkstands:*" of what number, then, must the noun be, before which the indefinite article is placed?

91. The singular number.

Q. What, then, is the rule for the indefinite article?

RULE II.

The indefinite article A *or* AN *belongs to nouns of the singular number.*

Q. We can say, "the boy," and "the boys;" using a noun either of the singular or plural number after *the:* what, then, is the rule for the definite article?

RULE III.

The definite article THE *belongs to nouns in the singular or plural number.*

EXERCISES IN PARSING.
"*The boy.*"

92. *The* is an ARTICLE, a word placed before nouns to limit their meaning—DEFINITE; it means a particular boy—and belongs to *boy,* according to

RULE III. *The definite article.* the *belongs to nouns of the singular or plural number.*

Boy is a NOUN; it is a name—COMMON; it is a general name—MASCULINE GENDER; it is the name of a male—THIRD PERSON; it is spoken of—and SINGULAR NUMBER; it means but one.

ADJECTIVES.

EXERCISES IN PARSING CONTINUED.

"A hand." "An eagle." "The man." "The boys' hats."
"A man." "An insect." "The men." "A man's cap."
"A mite." "An acorn." "The boys." "The girls' room."
"A month." "An ounce." "The mice." "The lady's box."

VIII. OF ADJECTIVES.

Q. When I say, "John is an obedient, industrious, and good boy," I use certain words to describe *boy:* which are they?
93. *Industrious, obedient,* and *good.*
Q. When I say, "a good man," to what word is the describing word *good* joined or added?
94. To the noun *man.*
Q. What does the word *adjective* mean?
95. *Joined* or *added to.*
Q. What, then, shall we call such describing words as *good, obedient, industrious,* &c.?
96. ADJECTIVES.
Q. What, then, are adjectives?
97. Adjectives are words joined to nouns to describe or qualify them.
Q. "A wise man." Which word is the adjective here, and why?
Q. "Rufus is a good boy, but James is a better one." How are Rufus and James spoken of here?
98. In comparison with each other.
Q. The adjectives in the last example are *good* and *better:* can you tell me which of these words denotes a higher degree of excellence than the other?
99. The word *better.*
Q. What degree of comparison, then, shall we call *better?*
100. Comparative degree.
Q. What, then, does the comparative degree imply?
101. A comparison between two.
Q. "William is tall, Thomas is taller, but Rufus is the tallest boy in school." What is meant here by *tallest?*
102. Exceeding all in height.
Q. What does the word *superlative* mean?
103. *Exceeding all; the highest or lowest degree.*
Q. What degree of comparison, then, shall we call *tallest?*
104. Superlative degree.
Q. What, then, does the superlative degree do?
105. It increases or lessens the positive to the highest or lowest degree.
Q. When I say, "James is a good boy," I make no comparison between him and any other; but simply assert in a positive manner, that James is a *good* boy. What kind of a sentence, then, would you call this?
106. A positive sentence.
Q. Of what degree of comparison, then, shall we call *good?*
107. The positive degree.

Q. What, then, does the positive degree do?

108. It merely describes, without any comparison.

Q. Will you compare great?

109. "*Positive*, great; *Comparative*, greater; *Superlative*, greatest."

Q. Will you compare wise in the same manner?

Q. Wise and great are words of one syllable: how, then, are the comparative and superlative degrees of words of this sort formed?

110. By adding *r* or *er*, *st* or *est*, to the positive.

Q. Will you in this manner compare small? high? mean?

Q. Will you compare beautiful?

111. "*Pos.* beautiful; *Comp.* more beautiful; *Sup.* most beautiful."

Q. How many syllables compose the word beautiful?

112. Three.

Q. How, then, are words of three, or more syllables than one, usually compared?

113. By placing *more* and *most* before the positive.

Q. Will you in this manner compare industrious? ingenious? dutiful?

Q. Will you compare wise, by using the words less and least?

114. "*Pos.* wise; *Comp.* less wise; *Sup.* least wise."

Q. Will you in like manner compare benevolent? distinguished? dilatory?

Q. "Good men, better men, best men." Which adjective here is the positive, and why? (108.) Which the comparative? why? (101.) Which the superlative? why? (105.)

Q. Good, you perceive, is not compared regularly, like great, beautiful, &c.; and since there are many words of this description, I will give you a list of the principal ones, together with others, regularly compared: will you repeat the comparative and superlative degrees, as I name the positive?

115. *Positive.*	*Comparative.*	*Superlative.*
Good,	Better,	Best.
Little,	Less,	Least.
Much, *or* many,	More,	Most.
Bad, ill, *or* evil,	Worse,	Worst.
Near,	Nearer,	Nearest, *or* next.
Old,	Older,	Oldest, *or* eldest.
Late,	Later,	Latest, *or* last.

Q. From the foregoing, how many degrees of comparison do there appear to be, and what are they?

116. Three—the positive, comparative, and superlative.

Q. Adjectives, you recollect, describe nouns: to what, then, do they naturally belong?

RULE IV.

Adjectives belong to the nouns which they describe.

EXERCISES IN PARSING.

"A wiser child.

117. *A* is an ARTICLE, a word placed before nouns to limit their meaning — INDEFINITE; it means no particular child — and belongs to *child*, agreeably to

RULE II. *The indefinite article* a *or* an *belongs to nouns of the singular number.*

Wiser is an ADJECTIVE, a word joined with a noun to describe it — "*Pos.* wise; *Comp.* wiser; *Sup.* wisest" — made in the *comparative* degree — and belongs to *child*, by RULE IV. *Adjectives belong to the nouns which they describe.*

Child is a NOUN; it is a name — COMMON; it is a general name — COMMON GENDER; it may be either male or female — THIRD PERSON; it is spoken of — and SINGULAR NUMBER; it means but one.

EXERCISES IN PARSING CONTINUED.

1.
* "A dutiful son."
"An idle boy."
"A foolish son."

2.
"An ugly child."
"An irksome task."
"A mild reply."

3.
"The base man."
"The whiter cloth."
"The milder weather."

4.
"The greatest man."
"The wisest prince."
"The noblest man."

5.
"The more (1) benevolent citizen."
"The most (1) suitable method."
"The least (1) distrustful friend."

6.
"A large, convenient, and (1) airy habitation."
"The intelligent, industrious, obedient, and (1) docile scholar."

7.
"The last choice."
"The best man."
"The nearest relations."
"Johnson's (2) large dictionary."
"Murray's small grammar."

IX. OF PRONOUNS.

Q. When I say, "John goes to school, John learns fast, and John will excel," how can I speak so as to avoid repeating *John* so often?

118. By using the word *he* in its place; thus, "John goes to school, *he* learns fast, and *he* will excel."

Q. What little word, then, may stand for *John?*
119. *He.*
Q. What does the word *pronoun* mean?
120. *Standing for, or instead of, a noun.*
Q. What, then, shall we call the word *he*, above?
121. A PRONOUN.
Q. What, then, is a pronoun?
122. A pronoun is a word used for a noun, to avoid a repetition of the same word.
Q. When James says, "I will study," you perceive that *I* stands for the person speaking: what person, then, is it? (39.)
Q. When I say, "James, you must study," the word *you* evidently is applied to *James,* who is spoken to: what person, then, ought *you* to be?
123. The second person.

---

1. To be omitted in parsing. 2. *Johnson's* is governed by *dictionary*, by Rule I.

Q. When I say, "He (meaning William) should learn," what person ought *he* to be, and why?

124. The third person; because it stands in the place of a noun which is spoken of.

Q. If *I* invariably stands for the first person, *you* for the second, and *he* for the third, how can we tell the different persons of pronouns?

125. By the pronouns themselves.

Q. What have these pronouns been called from this circumstance?

126. Personal pronouns.

☞ I will now give you a list of all the personal pronouns, which you must first examine carefully, and then answer such questions on them as may be asked you.

DECLENSION OF THE PERSONAL PRONOUNS.

FIRST PERSON.

127.

	Sing.	*Plur.*
Nom.	I.	We.
Poss.	My *or* mine.	Ours *or* our.
Obj.	Me.	Us.

SECOND PERSON.

	Sing.	*Sing.*	*Plur.*
Nom.	Thou.	You.	Ye *or* you.
Poss.	Thy *or* thine.	Your *or* yours.	Your *or* yours.
Obj.	Thee.	You.	You.

THIRD PERSON MASCULINE.

	Sing.	*Plur.*
Nom.	He.	They.
Poss.	His.	Theirs *or* their.
Obj.	Him.	Them.

THIRD PERSON FEMININE.

	Sing.	*Plur.*
Nom.	She.	They.
Poss.	Hers *or* her.	Theirs *or* their.
Obj.	Her.	Them.

THIRD PERSON NEUTER.

	Sing.	*Plur.*
Nom.	It.	They.
Poss.	Its.	Theirs *or* their.
Obj.	It.	Them.

Q. Will you decline *I* in both numbers? *thou* or *you*? *he*? *she*? *it*?

Q. In what person, number, and case is *I*? *we*? *my*? *mine*? *ours*? *me*? *us*? *thou*? *ye*? *his*? *they*? *them*?

Q. In what gender, person, number, and case is *he*? *she*? *it*? *his*? *he*? *her*? *him*?

Q. How many numbers do pronouns appear to have, and what are they?

128. Two—the singular and plural.

Q. How many cases, and what are they?

129. Three — the nominative, the possessive, and the objective.

Q. How many persons?
130. Three—the first, second, and third.
Q. How many genders?
131. Three—the masculine, feminine, and neuter.
Q. How many pronouns are there in all, of the first person?
Q. How many of the second, and how many of the third?
Q. The pronouns of the nominative case, singular, are called leading pronouns: how many of these are there?
133. Five—*I, thou* or *you, he, she, it.*
Q. Why are not the possessive and objective cases of the singular and plural numbers, also the nominatives plural, reckoned in the number of the leading pronouns?
134. Because they are all considered as variations of the nominative singular.
Q. To which of the pronouns is it customary to apply gender?
135. To the third person singular, *he, she, it.*
Q. Why are not the first and second persons each made always to represent a different gender?
136. The first and second persons being always present, their genders are supposed to be known.
Q. If, as we have seen, pronouns stand for nouns, what gender, number, and person ought they to have?
137. The same as the nouns for which they stand.
Q. What, then, may be considered a rule for the agreement of the pronouns?

RULE V.

Pronouns must agree with the nouns for which they stand, in gender, number, and person.

QUESTIONS ON PARSING.

Q. How many different sorts of words have we now found, and what are they?
138. Four—the NOUN, the ARTICLE, the ADJECTIVE, and the PRONOUN.
Q. The word *part,* you know, means *division;* and *speech,* the *power of using words,* or *language:* what, therefore, shall we call these grand divisions of words?
139. PARTS OF SPEECH.
Q. When, then, I ask you what part of speech *boy* is, for instance, what do you understand me to mean?
140. The same as to ask me whether *boy* is a noun or not.
Q. What part of speech, then, is *William,* and why? (36.)

    1. " He went to school."
    2. " She went to her task."
    3. " William went to his play."
    4. " John returned from his school."
    5. " I request you to mind your studies."
    6. " The book was mine, but now it is yours."

Q. Will you name the pronouns in the six foregoing examples?
Q. How many are there in all?
Q. What is the gender, number, and person of those in the first? second? third? fourth? fifth? sixth?

Q. What is the gender of *his*, in the fourth sentence? why? (137.) Its number? why? (137.) Its person? why? (137.) Its case? why? (61.)

Q. Will you name the nouns in the first sentence? in the second? third? fourth? fifth? sixth?

X. OF THE VERB.

Q. When I say, "James strikes William," which word tells what James does?

141. *Strikes.*

Q. The word *verb* means *word*; and as the words in all sentences, which tell what the nouns do, are the principal ones, what shall such words be called?

142. VERBS.

Q. If, in the phrase, "William strikes James," we leave out the word *strikes*, you perceive at once that the sense is destroyed: what reason, then, can you give, for calling some words in a sentence *verbs*, and others by a different name?

143. The words which we call verbs are the most important.

Q. "William studies his lesson." Which word is the verb here, and why?

144. *Studies*, because it tells what William does.

Q. When I say, "John dances," which word is the verb, and why?

Q. When I say, "James strikes John," which word shows that an action is performed?

145. *Strikes.*

Q. What kind of a verb, then, shall we call *strikes*?

146. An active verb.

Q. What kind of a verb is *walks*, in this sentence, "John walks," and why?

147. *Walks* is an active verb, because it expresses action.

Q. "He beat William." Which word here is the verb? Is *William* an agent or an object?

148. An object.

Q. When I say, "The child walks," *walks*, it is true, is an active verb, but it has no noun after it for an object, as *beat* has, in the phrase above; neither can we supply one; for we cannot say, "The child walks," any thing: what, therefore, is to be inferred from this fact, in regard to the nature of active verbs?

149. That some active verbs will take nouns after them for objects, and others will not.

Q. We will next notice this difference. The term *transitive* means *passing over*; and when I say, "William whips Charles," the verb *whips* shows that the action which William performs, *passes over* to Charles as the object. What kind of a verb, then, shall we call *whips*?

150. An active-transitive verb.

Q. What, then, is an active-transitive verb?

151. It is one that either has, or may have, an object after it.

Q. Walks, we found, would not take an object after it; and, as *intransitive* means *not passing over*, what shall we call such verbs as *walks*?

VERBS. 21

152. Active-intransitive verbs.

Q. What, then, is an active-intransitive verb?

153. An active-intransitive verb is one that expresses action, but will not take an object after it.

Q. When I say, "He eats it," "He beats him," we immediately determine that *beats* and *eats* are active-transitive verbs by the objects after them: how, then, may transitive and intransitive verbs be distinguished?

154. When we can place *him* or *it* after any active verb, and make sense, it is transitive; otherwise, it is intransitive.

Q. "James remains at home — sleeps at home — is at home." Which words are the verbs here?

155. *Remains, sleeps,* and *is.*

Q. These verbs do not imply action, like *strikes, beats, &c.*: what do they imply?

156. *Existence, rest,* or *being,* in a certain state.

Q. These verbs, and others of similar character, have been called *neuter* (signifying neither) by grammarians, because they are neither active nor passive. On a future occasion, I will make you fully acquainted with a passive verb. It is sufficient for our present purpose, that you perceive the reason of the name of the neuter verb. What is a neuter verb?

157. A neuter verb is one that simply implies being or existence in a certain state.

Q. Will you inform me now, in general terms, what is a correct definition of a verb?

158. A verb is a word which signifies ACTION or BEING.

Q. When I say, "I strike," in what number and person is *strike*, and why?

159. *Strike* is of the first person singular, because its agent, *I,* is of this person and number.

Q. Hence you may perceive, that verbs, in themselves considered, do not have person and number: why, then, are they said to have these properties at all?

160. On account of the connection which they have with their agents or nominatives.

Q. We say, "I write," and "He writes;" hence you perceive that the ending of the verb varies, as its agent or nominative varies: what, then, will be the rule for the nominative case?

RULE VI.

The nominative case governs the verb in number and person.

Q. If the nominative case governs the verb in number and person, in what respect must the verb agree with its nominative case?

RULE VII.

A verb must agree with its nominative case in number and person.

Q. When I say, "James beats him," the pronoun *him* is the object of the action denoted by *beats,* and is, therefore, in the objective case: what, then, will be a good rule for the objective case after active verbs?

RULE VIII.

Active-transitive verbs govern the objective case.

ENGLISH GRAMMAR.

Q. I will now give you the different endings of the verb *love*, in its different numbers and persons. Will you repeat them?

Singular.
161. First person, I love.
Second person, You love.
Third person, He loves.

Plural.
First person, We love.
Second person, You love.
Third person, They love.

Q. Will you repeat the variations of *am?*

Singular.
162. 1 *Pers.* I am.
2 *Pers.* You are.
3 *Pers.* He is.

Plural.
1 *Pers.* We are.
2 *Pers.* You are.
3 *Pers.* They are.

Q. Will you repeat, in the same manner, the variations of *hate? desire? read?*

EXERCISES IN PARSING.
" I study my lesson."

163. *I* is a PRONOUN, a word used instead of a noun—PERSONAL; it always denotes the same person, (the first)—FIRST PERSON; it denotes the speaker—SINGULAR NUMBER; it means but one—"*Nom.* I"—made in the NOMINATIVE CASE to *study*, according to

RULE VI. *The nominative case governs the verb in number and person.*

Study is a VERB; it expresses action—TRANSITIVE; it admits an object after it—"1 *Pers.* I study"—made in the FIRST PERSON—SINGULAR NUMBER, because its nominative *I* is, with which it agrees, agreeably to

RULE VII. *A verb must agree with its nominative case in number and person.*

My is a PRONOUN, a word used for a noun—PERSONAL; it always represents the same person—FIRST PERSON; it represents the person speaking—"*Nom.* I, *Poss.* my, *or* mine"—made in the POSSESSIVE CASE—and governed by the noun *lesson*, according to

RULE I. *The possessive case is governed by the following noun.*

Lesson is a NOUN—COMMON; it is a general name—NEUTER GENDER; it is neither male nor female—THIRD PERSON; it is spoken of—SINGULAR NUMBER; it means but one—and in the OBJECTIVE CASE; it is the object of the verb *study*, and governed by it, according to

RULE VIII. *Active-transitive verbs govern the objective case.*

EXERCISES IN PARSING CONTINUED.
Transitive Verbs.

"I lament my fate."
"You regard your friends."
"We desire your improvement."
"We love our children."
"You make a knife."

"He found a dollar."
"She attends the school."
"It retards the work."
"They shun vice."
"Ye derive comfort."

2.

"I love him." "She forsook you."
"I lament her." "They annoy me."
"You assist them." "We took it."
"He struck her." "She relieved us."

"*John reads his book.*"

His is a PRONOUN, a word used instead of a noun — PERSONAL; it uniformly stands for the same person — MASCULINE GENDER, THIRD PERSON, SINGULAR NUMBER, because the noun *John* is, with which it agrees, agreeably to

RULE V. *Pronouns must agree with the nouns for which they stand, in gender, number, and person.*

"*Nom.* he; *Poss.* his"—made in the POSSESSIVE CASE — and governed by the noun *book*, according to

RULE I. *The possessive case is governed by the following noun.*

☞ The remaining words, *book, reads,* and *John,* are parsed as before.

EXERCISES IN PARSING CONTINUED.
3.

"Mary studies her lesson." "Virtue rewards its followers."
"The girls love their books." "A disobedient son grieves his parents."
"Good children mind their parents."
"Sin deceives its votaries." "The intemperate man loves his dram."

☞ In parsing personal pronouns, we do not apply Rule V. unless the nouns for which they stand are expressed.

Intransitive Verbs.
4.

"I walk." "You smile." "John swims."
"James runs." "They wink." "Birds fly."
"William hops." "We dance." "Lions roar."

Neuter Verbs.

"William is (1.) discreet." (2.) "John's wife is fortunate."
"James is happy." "John's brother is unhappy."
"He was studious." "The eagle's flight was sudden."
"He became intemperate." "The scholar's duty is plain."
"Thou art wise." "The judge's pay is sufficient."

XI. INDICATIVE MOOD—TENSE.

Q. When James says, "I will learn," he evidently means, by his manner of speaking, to express his intention to learn; but when he says, "I can learn," what does he mean?

(1.) *Is* is a VERB; it implies being—NEUTER; it is neither active nor passive, but expresses being, merely—"1 *pers.* I am; 2 *pers.* You are; 3 *pers.* He *or* William is"—made in the THIRD PERSON, SINGULAR, because *William*, its nominative, is, and agrees with *William*, according to

RULE VII. *A verb must agree with its nominative case in number and person.*

(2.) *Discreet* belongs to *William,* by Rule IV.

165. That he has the *ability* to learn.
Q. What does the word mood mean?
166. *Mood* means *manner*.
Q. What, then, does the mood of verbs denote?
167. The different manner of representing actions.
Q. What does the word indicative mean?
168. *Declaring* or *showing*.
Q. When I say, "William has studied," I declare some fact: in what mood, then, shall we class has studied?
169. In the indicative mood.
Q. When I say, "Has William studied?" the only difference between this phrase and the foregoing consists in a change in the order of the words, so as to show that a question is asked: in what mood, then, shall we call has William studied?
170. Indicative mood.
Q. What, then, is the indicative mood used for?
171. The indicative mood is used for asserting, indicating or declaring a thing, or asking a question.
Q. In what mood is, "They do sing?" Why? (171.)
Q. What does the word tense mean?
172. *Tense* means *time*.
Q. What does present mean?
173. *Present* means *now*.
Q. When I say, "The bird sings," I mean that the bird sings now: in what tense, then, is sings?
174. In the present tense.
Q. What, then, is the present tense used for?
175. The present tense is used to express what is **now** taking place.
Q. In what tense is, "The dog runs?" Why? (175.)
Q. "James wrote." "James has written." These phrases denote what is past: in what tense are they?
176. In the past tense.
Q. What does the word future mean; as, "At some future time?"
177. *Future* means *yet to come*.
Q. In what tense are the phrases, "I will come," "I shall have come?"
178. In the future tense.
Q. How many grand divisions of time do there appear to be, and what are they?
179. Three—the present, past, and future.
Q. When I say, "John wrote," is the action here spoken of past and finished?
180. It is.
Q. What does imperfect mean?
181. *Unfinished*, or *incomplete*.
Q. "John was writing when I saw him." This denotes an action unfinished in past time, and corresponds with what is usually denominated in Latin the imperfect tense: hence the origin of the name selected by English grammarians to denote action past and finished; a term not all significant of an action finished in past time: what, then, does the imperfect tense express?
182. The imperfect tense expresses what took place in past time, however distant.
Q. "Peter wrote yesterday, and has written to-day." Here both acts of

VERBS.

writing are past and finished; but which has more immediate reference to the present time?

183. *Has written.*
Q. To distinguish this tense from the imperfect, grammarians have called it the perfect tense: what, then, will the perfect tense express?

184. The perfect tense expresses what has taken place, and also conveys an allusion to the present time.
Q. "James had read before I wrote." Here, both acts are past and finished; but which took place first?

185. The act of reading.
Q. What does the word *pluperfect* mean?

186. *More than the perfect.*
Q. What tense, then, shall we call, "James had read?"

187. The pluperfect tense.
Q. What, then, does the pluperfect tense express?

188. The pluperfect tense expresses what had taken place at or before some past time mentioned.
Q. "John will come." This, you know, was called the future tense: can you tell me why?

189. Because it implies time to come.
Q. What, then, does the future tense express?

190. The future tense expresses what will take place hereafter.
Q. "I shall have learned my lesson by noon." Here, an action is to take place at a future time specified or mentioned; and since we already have one future tense, we will call that the first, and this the second future tense: what, then, will the second future tense express?

191. The second future expresses what will have taken place at or before some future time mentioned.
Q. What does *synopsis* mean?

192. *A concise and general view.*
Q. I will now present you with a synopsis of all the different tenses, illustrated by the verb *learn:* will you repeat it?

SYNOPSIS.

193. *Pres. tense,*   I learn, *or* do learn.
Imp. tense,   I learned, *or* did learn.
Perf. tense,   I have learned.
Plup. tense,   I had learned.
1*st Fut. tense,* I shall *or* will learn.
2*d Fut. tense,* I shall have learned.

☞ You shall next have the different variations of the foregoing verb, in each tense of the indicative mood: these I wish you to study very carefully, that you may be able to answer the questions which will then be asked you.

194. *To learn.*

INDICATIVE MOOD.

PRESENT TENSE.

Singular.   *Plural.*
1 *Pers.* I learn.   1 *Pers.* We learn.
2 *Pers.* You learn.   2 *Pers.* You learn.
3 *Pers.* He, she, or it learns.   3 *Pers.* They learn.

OR,

When we wish to express energy or positiveness, thus—

Singular.	Plural
1. I do learn.	1. We do learn.
2. You do learn.	2. You do learn.
3. He does learn.	3. They do learn.

IMPERFECT TENSE.

Singular.	Plural.
1. I learned.	1. We learned.
2. You learned.	2. You learned.
3. He learned.	3. They learned.

OR,

Singular.	Plural.
1. I did learn.	1. We did learn.
2. You did learn.	2. You did learn.
3. He did learn.	3. They did learn.

PERFECT TENSE.

Singular.	Plural.
1. I have learned.	1. We have learned.
2. You have learned.	2. You have learned.
3. He has learned.	3. They have learned.

PLUPERFECT TENSE.

Singular.	Plural.
1. I had learned.	1. We had learned.
2. You had learned.	2. You had learned.
3. He had learned.	3. They had learned.

FIRST FUTURE TENSE.

Singular.	Plural.
1. I shall *or* will learn.	1. We shall *or* will learn.
2. You shall *or* will learn.	2. You shall *or* will learn.
3. He shall *or* will learn.	3. They shall *or* will learn.

SECOND FUTURE TENSE.

Singular.	Plural.
1. I shall have learned.	1. We shall have learned.
2. You will have learned.	2. You will have learned.
3. He will have learned.	3. They will have learned.

*** For the benefit of those who choose to retain the second person singular, as given in former treatises, the following synopsis is inserted.

SYNOPSIS.

195. 2d Pers. Sing. Pres.   Thou learnest, *or* dost learn.
    2d Pers. Sing. Imp.   Thou learnedst, *or* didst learn.
    2d Pers. Sing. Perf.   Thou hast learned.
    2d Pers. Sing. Plup.   Thou hadst learned.
    2d Pers. Sing. 1st Fut.   Thou shalt *or* wilt learn.
    2d Pers. Sing. 2d Fut.   Thou wilt have learned.

Q. In what mood is, "I learn?" Why? (171.) In what tense? Why? (175.) In what mood and tense is, "He learns?" "We learn?" "I did learn?" "I have learned?" "I had learned?" "I shall *or* will learn?" "I shall have learned?"

Q. In what person and number is, "I learn?" "You learn?" "We learn?" "They had learned?" "He shall learn?" "We had learned?"

Q. What does the word *auxiliary* mean?

196. *Auxiliary* means *helping*.

Q. In the phrase, "I will sing," *will*, you perceive, is used to help form the future tense of *sing : will* is, therefore, called an auxiliary verb, and the verb *sing* is reckoned the principal verb: what, then, are auxiliary verbs ?

197. Auxiliary verbs are those by the help of which are formed the different tenses, moods, &c. of the principal verbs.

Q. The auxiliary verbs are not unfrequently denominated the signs of the tenses, because each tense has, in general, an auxiliary peculiar to itself: what, then, is the sign of the second future ?

198. *Shall* or *will have.*
Q. What is the sign of the first future ?
199. *Shall* or *will.*
Q. What is the sign of the pluperfect ?
200. *Had.*
Q. What is the sign of the perfect ?
201. *Have.*
Q. What is the sign of the imperfect ?
202. *Did.*
Q. We can say, "I did strike yesterday," or, "I struck yesterday !" how, then, can we tell when a verb is in the imperfect tense without the sign *did ?*

203. If we can place *yesterday* after the verb, and make sense, it is in the imperfect tense.
Q. What is the sign of the present tense ?
204. *Do,* or the first form of the verb.
Q. From the foregoing, how many tenses does the indicative mood appear to have, and what are they ?

205. Six — the present, the imperfect, the perfect, the pluperfect, the first and second future tenses.

EXERCISES IN PARSING.

" *They have arrived.*"

206. *They* is a PRONOUN, a word used instead of a noun — PERSONAL ; it always represents the same person — THIRD PERSON; it denotes the persons spoken of — PLURAL ; it means more than one — " *Nom.* he ; *Poss.* his ; *Obj.* him. Plural. *Nom.* they" — made in the NOMINATIVE CASE to *have arrived*, according to

RULE VI. *The nominative case governs the verb.*

Have arrived is a VERB, a word that implies action or being — ACTIVE ; it implies action — INTRANSITIVE ; it does no admit of an object — INDICATIVE MOOD ; it simply indicates or declares a thing — PERFECT TENSE ; it expresses what has just taken place — " 1. I have arrived ; 2. You have arrived ; 3. He has arrived. *Plural,* 1. We have arrived ; 2. You have arrived ; 3. They have arrived" — made in the THIRD PERSON PLURAL, because its nominative *they* is, and agrees with it, according to

RULE VII. *A verb must agree with its nominative case in number and person.*

EXERCISES IN PARSING CONTINUED.

1.

"They had come."
"We did go."
"The bird will return."

"The sun has risen."
"Dogs will fight."
"Lions will roar."

2.

"James loves William."
"Susan beats him."
"I have beaten them."
"She had beaten us."
"You shall assist him."
"It did disturb me."

"Columbus discovered America."
"Piety promotes our happiness."
"He will learn his lesson."
"John did make great progress."
"They do study their lessons."
"Boys love sport."

3.

"Do I disturb you?"
"Did they learn their lessons?"
"Have they recited?"
"Does the instructer teach us?"
"Had he dismissed him?"

"Shall I expect your assistance?"
"Will a virtuous citizen commit such (1.) acts?"
"Have you found your knife?"

XII. POTENTIAL MOOD.

Q. What does, "He may write," imply?
207. Permission or liberty to write.
Q. What does, "He must write," imply?
208. Necessity of writing.
Q. What does, "He can write," imply?
209. Power or ability to write.
Q. What does, "He should write," imply?
210. Duty or obligation to write.
Q. What does, "He would write," imply?
211. Will or inclination to write.
Q. What does the word *potential* mean?
212. *Able,* or *powerful.*
Q. In what mood, then, do grammarians reckon *can learn, may write,* and, also, *must write, should write,* &c.?
213. In the potential mood.
Q. Why are all these different forms of representing actions considered to be in the potential mood, a name, as we have seen, peculiar only to that form of the verb which implies power?
214. To prevent multiplying moods to a great and almost numberless extent.
Q. What, then, does the potential mood imply?
215. The potential mood implies possibility, liberty power, will, obligation, or necessity.
Q. What are the signs of this mood?
216. *May, can, must, might, could, would,* and *should.*
Q. What does the word *conjugation* mean?

(1.) Adjective.

217. *Uniting, combining,* or *joining together.*

Q. You recollect that, in varying the verb, we joined the pronouns with t; hence, this exercise is called *conjugation :* what, then, do you understand by the conjugation of a verb?

218. The conjugation of a verb is the regular combination and arrangement of its several moods, tenses, numbers, and persons.

219. *Conjugation of the verb* LEARN.

POTENTIAL MOOD.

PRESENT TENSE.

Singular.
1. I may, can, *or* must learn.
2. You may, can, *or* must learn.
3. He may, can, *or* must learn.

Plural.
1. We may, can, *or* must learn.
2. You may, can, *or* must learn.
3. They may, can, *or* must learn.

IMPERFECT TENSE.

Singular.
1. I might, could, would, *or* should learn.
2. You might, could, would, *or* should learn.
3. He might, could, would, *or* should learn.

Plural.
1. We might, could, would, *or* should learn.
2. You might, could, would, *or* should learn.
3. They might, could, would, *or* should learn.

PERFECT TENSE.

Singular.
1. I may, can, *or* must have learned.
2. You may, can, *or* must have learned.
3. He may, can, *or* must have learned.

Plural.
1. We may, can, *or* must have learned.
2. You may, can, *or* must have learned.
3. They may, can, *or* must have learned.

PLUPERFECT TENSE.

Singular.
1. I might, could, would, *or* should have learned.
2. You might, could, would, *or* should have learned.
3. He might, could, would, *or* should have learned.

Plural.
1. We might, could, would, *or* should have learned.
2. You might, could, would, *or* should have learned.
3. They might, could, would, *or* should have learned.

Synopsis of the Second Person Singular, with THOU.

220.

Pres. Thou mayst, canst, *or* must learn.
Imp. Thou mightst, couldst, wouldst, *or* shouldst learn.
Perf. Thou mayst, canst, *or* must have learned.
Plup. Thou mightst, couldst, wouldst, *or* shouldst have learned.

Q. In what mood is, "I may learn?" Why? (215.)
Q. Will you repeat the synopsis with *I*? *thou*? *he*? *we*? *ye*? *you*? *they*?
Q. In what mood, tense, number, and person, is, "I can learn?" "You may learn?" "You might assist?" "They could have learned?" "He must study?"

Q. In what mood and tense is, "I have learned?" "He shall run?" "William did sing?"
Q. Won you conjugate *learn* in the present tense, potential mood? Will

you conjugate *love* in the same mood, and imperfect tense? *Strike*, in the perfect tense? *Come*, in the pluperfect tense?

Q. How many tenses has the potential mood?

EXERCISES IN PARSING.
"*He may return.*"

221. *He* is a PRONOUN, a word used instead of a noun—PERSONAL; it invariably represents the same person—MASCULINE GENDER; it represents a male—THIRD PERSON; it denotes the person spoken of—SINGULAR NUMBER; it implies but one—and in the NOMINATIVE CASE; it denotes the agent—"Nom. *he*"—nominative case to *may return*, by

RULE VI. *The nominative case governs the verb.*

May return is a VERB; it implies action or being—ACTIVE; it implies action—INTRANSITIVE; it does not admit an object after it—POTENTIAL MOOD; it implies possibility, liberty, &c.—PRESENT TENSE; it denotes what may be now—"1. I may *or* can return; 2. You may *or* can return; 3. He may *or* can return"—made in the THIRD PERSON, SINGULAR, because its nominative *he* is, with which it agrees, according to

RULE VII. *A verb must agree with its nominative case in number and person.*

EXERCISES IN PARSING CONTINUED.
1.

"He may come."
"He might retire."
"John can assist me."
"William must obey his instructer."
"We may have erred."
"John's father would go."

"Boys may learn arithmetic."
"The wind may have shaken the trees."
"The lady could have procured her fan."
"James may catch the thief."
"They might learn."

2.

"I do rejoice."
"We do learn."
"John will resume his task."
"An industrious boy will be rich."

"The committee will visit the school."
"An idle boy will find poverty."

XIII. CONJUGATION OF THE NEUTER VERB
To be.

222. When I say, "I am at home," you know that *am* is a verb, because it implies being or existence; and since *to be* means *to exist*, the verb *am* has been called the verb *to be*.

223. INDICATIVE MOOD.
PRESENT TENSE.

Singular.
1. I am.
2. You are.
3. He is.

Plural.
1. We are.
2. You are.
3. They are.

VERBS. 31

IMPERFECT TENSE.
Singular. | Plural.
1. I was. | 1. We were.
2. You were. | 2. You were.
3. He was. | 3. They were.

PERFECT TENSE.
Singular. | Plural.
1. I have been. | 1. We have been.
2. You have been. | 2. You have been.
3. He has been. | 3. They have been.

PLUPERFECT TENSE.
Singular. | Plural.
1. I had been. | 1. We had been.
2. You had been. | 2. You had been.
3. He had been. | 3. They had been.

FIRST FUTURE TENSE.
Singular. | Plural.
1. I shall *or* will be. | 1. We shall *or* will be
2. You shall *or* will be. | 2. You shall *or* will be
3. He shall *or* will be. | 3. They shall *or* will be

SECOND FUTURE TENSE.
Singular. | Plural.
1. I shall have been. | 1. We shall have been.
2. You will have been. | 2. You will have been.
3. He will have been. | 3. They will have been.

POTENTIAL MOOD.

PRESENT TENSE.
Singular. | Plural.
1. I may, can, *or* must be. | 1. We may, can, *or* must be.
2. You may, can, *or* must be. | 2. You may, can, *or* must be.
3. He may, can, *or* must be. | 3. They may, can, *or* must be.

IMPERFECT TENSE.
Singular. | Plural.
1. I might, could, would, *or* should be. | 1. We might, could, would, *or* should be.
2. You might, could, would, *or* should be. | 2. You might, could, would, *or* should be.
3. He might, could, would, *or* should be. | 3. They might, could, would, *or* should be.

PERFECT TENSE.
Singular. | Plural.
1. I may, can, *or* must have been. | 1. We may, can, *or* must have been.
2. You may, can, *or* must have been. | 2. You may, can, *or* must have been.
3. He may, can, *or* must have been. | 3. They may, can, *or* must have been.

PLUPERFECT TENSE.
Singular. | Plural.
1. I might, could, would, *or* should have been. | 1. We might, could, would, *or* should have been.
2. You might, could, would, *or* should have been. | 2. You might, could, would, *or* should have been.
3. He might, could, would, *or* should have been. | 3. They might, could, would, *or* should have been.

224. *Synopsis of the Second Person Singular, with* **Thou.**

INDICATIVE MOOD.	POTENTIAL MOOD.
Pres. Thou art.	*Pres.* Thou mayst, canst, *or* must be.
Imp. Thou wast.	*Imp.* Thou mightst, couldst, wouldst, or shouldst be.
Perf. Thou hast been.	
Plup. Thou hadst been.	*Perf.* Thou mayst, canst, *or* must have been.
1 *Fut.* Thou shalt *or* wilt be.	*Plup.* Thou mightst, couldst, wouldst, or shouldst have been.
2 *Fut.* Thou wilt have been.	

XIV. QUESTIONS ON THE FOREGOING CONJUGATION.

Q. Why is *am* a verb? (158.) What is it sometimes called? (222.) Why is it so called? (222.)

Q. Will you give the synopsis of the verb *to be* with *I* through the indicative mood?

Q. Will you conjugate *am* in the present indicative? Imperfect? Perfect? Pluperfect? 1 Future? 2 Future? Present potential? Imperfect? Perfect? Pluperfect?

Q. In what mood, tense, number, and person, is, "I am?" "Am I?" "You were?" "I have been?" "Have you been?" "He may *or* can be?" "We should be?" "He may have been?" "They should have been?" "Thou shouldst have been?" "Thou mayst be?"

Q. Will you repeat the synopsis with *thou?*

EXERCISES IN PARSING.

" The girls were industrious."

225. *Were* is a **verb**; it implies action or being—**neuter**; it is neither active nor passive, expressing simply being—**indicative mood**; it simply indicates or declares a thing—**imperfect tense**; it expresses past time—" 1. I was; 2. You were; 3. He was. *Plur.* 1. We were; 2. You were; 3. They were, or *girls* were"—made in the **third person plural**, because its nominative *girls* is, with which it agrees, agreeably to

Rule VII. *A verb must agree with its nominative case in number and person.*

Industrious is an **adjective**, a word joined with a noun to describe it — " industrious, *more* industrious, *most* industrious" —in the **positive degree**; it describes, without any comparison—and belongs to the noun *girls*, according to

Rule IV. *Adjectives belong to the nouns which they describe.*

☞ For *the* and *girls*, apply **Rules III.** and **VI.**

EXERCISES IN PARSING CONTINUED.

" William is attentive." " Am I young?"
" John is studious." " Was I wrong?"
" We are jealous." " Have we been wicked?"
" Thou art dutiful." " Were they penitent?"

"Mary has been intelligent." "Washington was patriotic."
"The boys will have been dutiful." "Columbus was enterprising."
"Their estate was small." "My wife's mother is sick."

XV. OF THE ADVERB.

Q. When I say, "The bird flies swiftly," I do not mean by *swiftly* to describe *bird*: what does *swiftly* describe?
226. The manner of flying.
Q. To what part of speech is *swiftly* joined in the phrase, "The bird flies swiftly?"
227. To the verb *flies.*
Q. What does the word *adverb* signify
228. *Joined to a verb.*
Q. What, then, shall we call all such words as *swiftly?*
229. ADVERBS.
Q. "John runs very swiftly." Which word here describes or shows how swiftly John runs?
230. *Very.*
Q. What is the word *very* called, and all such words as qualify or describe adverbs?
231. Adverbs.
Q. "Industrious, more industrious, most industrious." What are *more* and *most* called here, and why?
232. Adverbs, because they describe or qualify adjectives.
Q. From the foregoing particulars, what appears to be a proper definition of adverbs?
233. Adverbs are words joined to verbs, adjectives, and other adverbs, to qualify or describe them.
Q. "John visits me *often,* but Thomas *oftener.*" In this example, we see that adverbs may be compared: will you, therefore, compare *soon?*
234. "Soon, sooner, soonest."
Q. Will you compare *wisely?*
235. "Wisely, more wisely, most wisely."
Q. How do adverbs ending in *ly* appear to be compared?
236. By the adverbs *more* and *most.*
Q. Will you in this manner compare *admirably? foolishly?*
Q. Many adverbs are compared like adjectives of one syllable, as *soon* above; but there is a very considerable number, the comparison of which is not regulated by any general rule. The following list embraces adverbs variously compared: will you repeat the comparative and superlative of each, as I name the positive?

237.

Positive.	Comparative.	Superlative.
Often,	oftener,	oftenest.
Much,	more,	most.
Well,	better,	best.
Soon,	sooner,	soonest.
Justly,	more justly,	most justly.
Wisely,	more wisely,	most wisely.
Justly,	less justly,	least justly.
Badly, *or* ill.	worse.	worst.

238. *Note.*— Adverbs, though very numerous, may nevertheless be reduced to a few classes. You will now read with attention the following list, and I will then ask you some questions respecting each class.

1. Of *number:* as, "Once, twice, thrice," &c.
2. Of *order:* as, "First, secondly, thirdly, fourthly, fifthly, lastly, finally," &c.
3. Of *place:* as, "Here, there, where, elsewhere, anywhere, somewhere, nowhere, herein, whither, hither, thither, upward, downward, forward, backward, whence, hence, thence, whithersoever," &c.
4. Of *time.*
Of *time present:* as, "Now, to-day," &c.
Of *time past:* as, "Already, before, lately, yesterday, heretofore, hitherto, ong since, long ago," &c.
Of *time to come:* as, "To-morrow, not yet, hereafter, henceforth, henceforward, by and by, instantly, presently, immediately, straightways," &c.
Of *time indefinite:* as, "Oft, often, ofttimes, oftentimes, sometimes, soon, seldom daily, weekly, monthly, yearly, always, when, then, ever, never, again," &c.
5. Of *quantity:* as, "Much, little, sufficiently, how much, how great, enough abundantly," &c.
6. Of *manner* or *quality:* as, "Wisely, foolishly, justly, unjustly, quickly, slowly," &c. Adverbs of quality are the most numerous kind; and they are generally formed by adding the termination *ly* to an adjective or participle, or changing *le* into *ly:* as, "Bad, badly; cheerful, cheerfully; able, ably; admirable, admirably."
7. Of *doubt:* as, "Perhaps, peradventure, possibly, perchance."
8. Of *affirmation:* as, "Verily, truly, undoubtedly, doubtless, certainly, yea, yes, surely, indeed, really," &c.
9. Of *negation:* as, "Nay, no, not, by no means, not at all, in no wise," &c.
10. Of *interrogation:* as, "How, why, wherefore, whether," &c.
11. Of *comparison:* as, "More, most, better, best, worse, worst, less, least, very, almost, little, alike," &c.

When a preposition suffers no change, but becomes an adverb merely by its application: as, when we say, "He rides *about;*" "He was *near* falling;" "But do not *after* lay the blame on me."

There are also some adverbs, which are composed of nouns, and the letter *a* used instead of *at, on,* &c.: as, "Aside, athirst, afoot, ahead, asleep, aboard, ashore, abed, aground, afloat."

Q. Will you name two adverbs of number? two of order? two of place? two of time present? two of time past? two of time to come? two of time indefinite? two of quantity? two of manner or quality? two of doubt? two of affirmation? two of negation? two of interrogation? two of comparison?

Q. Adjectives describe as well as adverbs: how, then, can you tell one from the other?

239. Adjectives describe nouns, but adverbs describe or qualify verbs, adjectives, and other adverbs.

Q. This fact should be remembered; you shall, therefore, have it in the form of a rule: will you repeat it?

RULE IX.

Adverbs qualify verbs, adjectives, and other adverbs.

Q. From *bad* we form the adverb *badly:* how, then, may a large class of adverbs be formed?

240. By adding *ly* to adjectives.

Q. Will you in this manner form an adverb from *wise?* from *great?* from *sinful?*

EXERCISES IN PARSING.

"*The bird sings sweetly.*"

241. *Sweetly* is an ADVERB, a word used to qualify a verb, adjective, or other adverb; in this example it qualifies the verb *sings,* agreeably to

RULE IX. *Adverbs qualify verbs, adjectives, and other adverbs.*

Sings, bird and *the* are parsed as before.

PREPOSITIONS. 35

EXERCISES IN PARSING CONTINUED.

Adverbs qualifying verbs.

" The soldiers marched slowly."   " They will return soon."
" The girls sing delightfully."   " The boys write admirably."
" Henry improves rapidly."   " Susan dances elegantly."

Adverbs qualifying adjectives.

" He was very attentive."   " James is more studious."
" John is quite busy."   " Walter is most studious."
" William is really studious."   " Ellen is less happy."

Adverbs qualifying verbs and other adverbs.

" You learn grammar very well."   " James writes most elegantly."
" The boys write too fast."   " I will assist you most cheer-
" He will come much oftener."   fully."

Adverbs promiscuously used.

" He has read once."   " John is not happy."
" I will first remind you."   " Whither shall I fly ?"
" I saw him yesterday."   " My brother sends me the paper
" I have eaten sufficiently."   monthly."

XVI. OF THE PREPOSITION

Q. To say, " The cider is — cellar," would make no sense: can you inform me what would make sense ?

242. " The cider is *in* the cellar."

Q. By placing the little word *in* after *cider is*, and before *cellar*, the sentence is rendered complete: what office, then, does *in* perform ?

243. It connects words, and thereby shows the relation between them.

Q. What does the word *preposition* mean ?

244. *Placed before.*

Q. What, then, may those words like *in* be called, as they are placed before other words to connect them with words preceding ?

245. PREPOSITIONS.

Q. What, then, are prepositions ?

246. Prepositions are words used to connect words, and thereby show the relation between them.

247. *List of the principal Prepositions.*

Among	at	concerning	near	throughout
around	by	down	of	touching
amidst	below	except	off	up
athwart	between	excepting	on	upon
after	beneath	for	over	under
about	behind	from	out of	underneath
against	betwixt	in	respecting	unto
across	beside	into	to	with
above	beyond	instead of	towards	within
according to	before	notwithstanding	through	without

Q. Will you mention the prepositions beginning with a? with b? c? d? e? f? i? n? o? r? t? u? w?

Q. Will you now repeat all the prepositions?
Q. Do we say, "He works for I," or, "He works for me"?
Q. In what case is *me*? (127.)
Q. What case, then, follows prepositions?

248. The objective case.

Q. This fact is of sufficient importance to constitute a rule: will you therefore, repeat

RULE X.

Prepositions govern the objective case.

EXERCISES IN PARSING.

"*John found his hat in the road.*"

249. *In* is a PREPOSITION, a word used to connect words and show the relation between them; it here shows the relation between *hat* and *road*.

Road is a NOUN; it is a name—COMMON; it is a general name—NEUTER GENDER; it is neither male nor female—THIRD PERSON; it is spoken of—SINGULAR NUMBER; it means but one—OBJECTIVE CASE; it is the object of the relation denoted by the preposition *in*, and governed by it according to

RULE X. *Prepositions govern the objective case.**

EXERCISES IN PARSING CONTINUED.

"John ran through the house into the garden."
"We have deceived him to our sorrow."
"We came in season."
"You study grammar for your improvement in language."
"From virtue to vice the progress is gradual."
"They travelled into France through Italy."
"He lives within his income."
"Without the aid of charity, he lived very comfortably by his industry."

"I will search the house diligently for him."
"We might learn the lesson before them."
"According to my impression, he is in fault."
"Notwithstanding his poverty, he was the delight of his acquaintances."
"On all occasions she behaved with propriety."
"Of his talents we might say much."
"We may expect a calm after a storm."

XVII. OF THE CONJUNCTION.

Q. When I say, "John —— his book," the sense, you perceive, is incomplete. Can you put a word into the blank which will complete the sense?

250. "John reads his book."

---

* The remaining words are parsed as before.

CONJUNCTIONS. 37

Q. Can you inform me what the foregoing expression is called?
251. A sentence.
Q. What, then, is a sentence?
252. A collection of words, forming a complete sense.
Q. "Life is short." This expression is called a sentence: can you tell me what kind, and why?
253. It is a simple sentence, because it makes sense, and has but one nominative and one verb.
Q. What does the term *compound* mean?
254. It means *composed of two or more things.*
Q. "Life is short, and art is long." This sentence is made up of two simple sentences: what, therefore, may it be called?
255. A compound sentence.
Q. What, then, is a compound sentence?
256. A compound sentence contains two or more simple sentences connected together.
Q. What does the term *conjunction* signify?
257. *Union,* or *joining together.*
Q. In the compound sentence, "John writes, and William learns," the simple sentences are joined together by the word *and:* what word, then, may *and* be called?
258. A CONJUNCTION.
Q. "The king and queen are an amiable pair." In this sentence, words and not sentences are connected by *and:* can you point out the words so connected?
259. *King* and *queen.*
Q. From the foregoing particulars, what appears to be the use of the conjunction?
260. A conjunction is used to connect words and sentences together.
Q. When I say, "Five and four are nine," what do I mean?
261. Five added to four make nine.
Q. What, then, is implied by *and?*
262. Addition.
Q. When I say, "I will go, if you will accompany me," what does the conjunction *if* imply?
263. Condition or supposition.
Q. What does the word *copulative* mean?
264. *Uniting, joining,* or *linking together.*
Q. *And, if,* &c. are called copulative conjunctions: can you tell me why?
265. Because a copulative conjunction connects or continues a sentence by expressing an addition, a supposition, a cause, &c.
Q. The following are the principal conjunctions of this class: will you repeat them?
266. "And, both, because, besides, for, if, provided, since, then, that, therefore, wherefore."
Q. When I say, "James *and* John will come," I mean both will come, but when I say, "James *or* John will come," what do I mean?
267. That either James or John, one of them, will come.

Q. Are the words in this sentence, then, joined or disjoined?

268. Disjoined.

Q. What word is it that expresses the disjoining?

269. Or.

Q. What part of speech is *or?*

270. Conjunction.

Q. What does the word *disjunctive* mean?

271. *Disjoining* or *separating.*

Q. What kind of a conjunction, then, shall we call *or?*

272. A disjunctive conjunction.

Q. "James will come, but Henry will not." Here the two clauses of the sentence are opposed to each other in meaning, and the word *but* separates these two clauses: what, then, does this word imply?

273. Opposition of meaning.

Q. From the foregoing, what appears to be the use of the disjunctive conjunction?

274. The conjunction disjunctive connects sentences, by expressing opposition of meaning in various degrees.

Q. The following are the principal conjunctions of this class: will you repeat them?

275. "But, than, though, either, or, as, unless, neither, nor, less, yet, notwithstanding."

Q. Prepositions, you recollect, connect words, as well as conjunctions; how, then, can you tell the one from the other?

276. Prepositions show the relation between words, but conjunctions express an addition, a supposition, a cause, or an opposition of meaning.

Q. "He and she write." In what case is *he? she?*

Q. The pronouns *he* and *she*, you perceive, are both in the same case and connected by the conjunction *and :* when, then, may nouns and pronouns be connected?

277. When they are in the same case.

Q. "She will sing and dances." How may this sentence be corrected?

278. "She will sing and dance."

Q. In what mood and tense is, "She will sing?"

Q. To say, "She dance," is incorrect; *dance*, then, in this example, cannot be in the present tense: will you, then, inform me what "She will sing and dance" means, when fully expressed?

279. "She will sing and she will dance."

Q. Here *will dance* is in the future tense, as well as *will sing :* when, then, may verbs, in general, be connected?

280. When they are in the same mood and tense.

Q. From the foregoing particulars, what appears to be the rule for the use of conjunctions, in connecting words?

RULE XI.

Conjunctions usually connect verbs of the same mood and tense, and nouns or pronouns of the same case.

EXERCISES IN PARSING.

"*John assists his father and mother.*"

281. *And* is a CONJUNCTION, a word chiefly used to connect words and sentences — COPULATIVE; it connects *father* and *mother*.

Mother is a NOUN; it is a name — COMMON; it is a general name — FEMININE GENDER; it is the name of a female — THIRD PERSON; it is spoken of — SINGULAR NUMBER; it means but one — and it is one of the objects of *assists*, and is, therefore, in the OBJECTIVE CASE, and connected with *father* by the conjunction *and*, according to

RULE XI. *Conjunctions usually connect verbs of the same mood and tense, and nouns or pronouns of the same case.*

EXERCISES IN PARSING CONTINUED.

" I will reward him and them at some future time."
" We in vain (1.) look for a path between virtue and vice."
" Reproof either hardens or softens its object."
" In the morning of life, we eagerly pursue pleasure, but oftentimes meet (2.) with sad disappointments."
" A good scholar never, mutters nor disobeys his instructer."

" She reads well, dances (3.) elegantly, and plays admirably on the piano-forte."
" Intemperance destroys the mind and benumbs the senses of man."
" You may read this sentence first, and then parse it."
" He has equal knowledge, but inferior judgment."
" John rises early in the morning, and pursues his studies."

XVIII. OF INTERJECTIONS.

Q. When I exclaim, " Oh! I have ruined my friend," " Alas! I fear for life," which words here appear to be thrown in between the sentences, to express passion or feeling?

282. *Oh! Alas!*

Q. What does *interjection* mean?

283. *Thrown between.*

Q. What name, then, shall we give such words as *oh! alas!* &c.?

284. INTERJECTIONS.

Q. What, then, are interjections?

285. Interjections are words thrown in between the parts of sentences, to express the passions or sudden feelings of the speaker.

(1.) *In vain* means the same as *vainly*. It may, therefore, be called an adverbial phrase, qualifying *look*, by Rule IX.

(2.) *Meet* agrees with *we* understood, and is, therefore, connected with *pursue* by the conjunction *but*, according to Rule XI.

(3.) *Dances* and *plays* both agree with *she*, understood, and are, therefore, connected the former with *reads*, and the latter with *dances*, by Rule XI.

LIST OF INTERJECTIONS.

1. *Of earnestness or grief;* as, "O! oh! alas! ah!"
2. *Of wonder;* as, "Really! strange!"
3. *Of calling;* as, "Halloo! ho! hem!"
4. *Of attention;* as, "Behold! lo! hark!"
5. *Of disgust;* as, "Foh! fy! fudge! away!"
6. *Of silence;* as, "Hush! hist!"
7. *Of contempt;* as, "Pish! tush!"
8. *Of saluting;* as, "Welcome! hail!"

Q. Will you examine the foregoing list, and then name an interjection of grief? One of wonder? One of calling? One of attention? One of disgust? One of silence? One of saluting?

Q. How may an interjection generally be known?

286. By its taking an exclamation point after it.

EXERCISES IN PARSING.

"*Oh! I have alienated my friend.*"

287. *Oh* is an INTERJECTION, a word used to express passion or feeling.

☞ The remaining words are parsed as before.

EXERCISES IN PARSING CONTINUED.

"Oh! I must go and see (1.) my dear father before (2.) he dies."

"We eagerly pursue pleasure, but, alas! we often mistake the road to its (3.) enjoyment."

"Strange! I did not know you."

"Hush! our instructer is at the door."

"Fy! how angry he is!"

(1.) The sense is, "I must go, and I must see;" the verb *see*, then, agrees with *I*, understood, and is, therefore, connected with *must go*, according to Rule XI.

(2.) *Before*, an adverb.

(3.) Apply, first, Rule V.; then, Rule L.

RECAPITULATION.

CRITICAL REMARKS.

COMPOSITION.

XIX. ENGLISH GRAMMAR.

288. ENGLISH GRAMMAR teaches us to speak and write tne English language correctly.
289. GRAMMAR is divided into four parts, namely,
290.   1. ORTHOGRAPHY,   3. SYNTAX,
       2. ETYMOLOGY,   4. PROSODY.

XX. OF ORTHOGRAPHY.

291. ORTHOGRAPHY includes a knowledge of the nature and power of letters, and teaches how to spell words correctly. This part of grammar is usually learned from spelling-books and dictionaries.
292. *Orthography* means *word-making*, or *spelling*.

XXI. OF ETYMOLOGY.

293. ETYMOLOGY teaches how to form, from all the words in the English language, several grand divisions or sorts, commonly called Parts of Speech.
294. It includes a knowledge of the meaning and use of words — also their different changes and derivations.
295. *Etymology* signifies the *origin* or *pedigree* of words.

XIX. What does English grammar teach? 288.
Into how many parts is it divided? 289. What are they? 290.
XX. What does orthography include and teach? 291.

How is a knowledge of orthography usually obtained? 291.
What does orthography mean? 292.
XXI. What does etymology teach? 293.
What does it include? 294.
What does the word signify? 295.

4*

(41)

XXII. OF SYNTAX.

296. SYNTAX teaches how to arrange or form words into sentences correctly.

297. It includes a knowledge of the rules of composition, formed from the practice of the best writers and speakers.

298. *Syntax* signifies *arranging* or *placing together;* or, as used in grammar, *sentence-making*.

XXIII. ETYMOLOGY AND SYNTAX COMBINED.

299. The words of the English language are usually divided into nine sorts, commonly called Parts of Speech, namely,

NOUN,	PRONOUN,	PREPOSITION,
ARTICLE,	VERB,	CONJUNCTION,
ADJECTIVE,	ADVERB,	INTERJECTION.

XXIV. OF NOUNS.

300. A noun is the name of any person, place or thing; as, *man, London, knife*.

301. Nouns are of two kinds, proper and common.

COMMON nouns are general names; that is, they are names common to *all* individuals of the same kind or sort; as, *house, city, river*.

302. PROPER nouns are particular names; that is, they are the names of particular individuals of the same kind or sort; as, *George, Boston, Mississippi*.

303. When proper names have an article placed before them, they are used as common names; as, "He is the *Cicero* of his age."

304. When a proper noun admits of a plural, it becomes a common noun;

XXII. What does syntax teach? 296.
What does it include? 297.
What does the word signify? 298.
XXIII. How many different sorts of words are there? 299.
What are they? 299.
What are these sorts of words commonly called? 299.
XXIV. What does the word *noun* mean?*
What is a noun? 300. Give an example.
How many different kinds of nouns are there, and what are they? 301.

What does the word *common* mean? 31.
What is a common noun? 301. Give an example.
What does *proper* mean? 34.
What is a proper noun? 302. Give an example.
When proper nouns have an article before them, how are they used? 303. Give an example.
Are proper names used as such in the plural? 304.
Why cannot proper names have a plural? 304.

* See L. 1st answer.

NOUNS.

as, "The twelve *Cæsars*," or, "The seven *Jameses.*" This is obvious from the fact, that a proper name is, in its nature, descriptive of one object only, and, therefore, essentially singular. Accordingly, the nouns *Spaniard, European, American,* &c. are common nouns, as well as their plurals, *Spaniards, Europeans, Americans,* &c.*

305. Common nouns may also be used to signify individuals, by the addition of articles or pronouns; as, "The *boy* is studious;" "That *girl* is discreet."

306. When a noun signifies *many*, it is called a noun of multitude, or a collective noun; as, "The *people*," "The *army.*"

307. *Abstract* signifies *taken from:* hence an abstract noun is the name of a quality abstracted from its substance; as, *knowledge, goodness, virtue,* &c.

308. To nouns belong person, gender, number and case.

XXV. PERSON.

309. When any person, in speaking, introduces his own name, it is the first person; as, "I, James, of the city of Boston, do give," &c.

310. The name of the person spoken to, is the second person; as, "James, come to me."

311. The name of the person or thing spoken of, or about, is the third person; as, "James has come."

XXVI. GENDER.

312. Gender is the distinction of sex.

313. Nouns have four genders—the masculine, the feminine, the common, and the neuter.

314. The masculine gender denotes the names of males; as *man, boy,* &c.

315. The feminine gender denotes the names of females; as, *woman, girl.*

What do they become when so used? 304. Give an example.
What kind of nouns are *Spaniard, Americans, Spaniards*? 304.
What effect does the use of articles have on common nouns? 305.
What is a noun of multitude, or a collective noun? 306. Give an example.
What is an abstract noun? 307. Give an example.
What belong to nouns? 308.
XXV. When is a noun of the first person? 309. Give an example.

When is a noun of the second person? 310. Give an example.
When is a noun of the third person? 311. Give an example.
XXVI. What does the word *gender* mean? 14.
What is gender as applied to nouns? 312.
What does the word *masculine* mean? 15. What does the masculine gender of nouns denote? 314. Give an example.
What does *feminine* mean? 19.
What does the feminine gender denote? 315. Give an example.

---

* *Spain* is the proper name of a country, and *Spaniard* has, by some grammarians, been called the proper name of a people; but the latter is a generic term, characterizing any one of a great number of persons, in their connexion with *Spain.*—*Encyclopædia.*

316. The common gender denotes the names of such animals as may be either male or female; as, *parent, bird.*

317. The neuter gender denotes the names of objects which are neither males nor females; as, *chair, table.*

318. Some nouns, naturally neuter, do, by a figure of speech, as it is called, become masculine or feminine; as when we say of the sun, "*He* is setting," and of a ship, "*She* sails well," &c.

319. The English language has three methods of distinguishing sex, viz:

319–1. By different words; as,

Male.	Female.	Male.	Female.
Bachelor,	Maid.	Husband,	Wife.
Boar,	Sow.	King,	Queen.
Boy,	Girl.	Lad,	Lass.
Brother,	Sister.	Lord,	Lady.
Buck,	Doe.	Man,	Woman.
Bull,	Cow.	Master,	Mistress.
Bullock or Steer,	Heifer.	Milter,	Spawner.
		Nephew,	Niece.
Cock,	Hen.	Ram,	Ewe.
Dog,	Bitch.	Singer,	Songstress or Singer.
Drake,	Duck.		
Earl,	Countess	Sir,	Madam.
Father,	Mother	Sloven,	Slut.
Friar,	Nun.	Son,	Daughter.
Gander	Goose.	Stag,	Hind.
Hart,	Roe.	Uncle,	Aunt.
Horse,	Mare.	Wizard,	Witch.

319–2. By a difference of termination; as,

Male.	Female.	Male.	Female.
Abbot,	Abbess.	Enchanter,	Enchantress.
Actor,	Actress.	Executor,	Executrix.
Administrator,	Administratrix.	God,	Goddess.
Adulterer,	Adulteress.	Governor,	Governess.
Ambassador,	Ambassadress.	Heir,	Heiress.
Arbiter,	Arbitress.	Hero,	Heroine.
Baron,	Baroness.	Hunter,	Huntress.
Bridegroom,	Bride.	Host,	Hostess.
Benefactor,	Benefactress.	Instructer,	Instructress.
Caterer,	Cateress.	Jew,	Jewess.
Chanter,	Chantress.	Landgrave,	Landgravine.
Conductor,	Conductress.	Lion,	Lioness.
Count,	Countess.	Marquis,	Marchioness.
Czar,	Czarina.	Mayor,	Mayoress.
Deacon,	Deaconess.	Patron,	Patroness.
Duke,	Duchess.	Peer,	Peeress.
Elector,	Electress.	Poet,	Poetess.
Emperor,	Empress.	Priest,	Priestess.

What does the common gender denote? 316. Give an example.
What does *neuter* mean? 23.
What does the neuter gender denote? 317. Give an example.
What is said of nouns naturally neuter, in respect to gender? 318. Give an example.
How many genders do nouns have, and what are they? 30.
How many methods are there in English of distinguishing sex? 319.
Which is the first; as, *boy? girl?* 319–1.
Will you spell the feminine corresponding to *brother?* 319–1. to *boy? nephew?* wizard? friar? sir? drake? earl? gander? hart? king? lad? man? master? singer? sloven? son? stag? uncle?
Will you spell the masculine corresponding to *maid? girl? madam? daughter? niece?*
What is the second method of distinguishing sex; as, *abbot? abbess?* 319–2.
Will you spell the feminine corresponding to *abbot? actor? administrator? baron? benefactor? bridegroom? conductor? czar? duke? emperor? executor? god? governor? heir? hero? host? hunter? instructer? Jew? lion? marquis? patron? peer? proprietor? shepherd?* &c.

NOUNS.

Male.	Female.	Male.	Female.
Prince,	Princess.	Sultan,	{ Sultaness. Sultana.
Prior,	Prioress.		
Prophet,	Prophetess.	Tiger,	Tigress.
Protector,	Protectress.	Traitor,	Traitress.
Proprietor,	Proprietress.	Tutor,	Tutoress.
Shepherd,	Shepherdess.	Viscount,	Viscountess.
Songster,	Songstress.	Votary,	Votaress.
Sorcerer,	Sorceress.	Widower,	Widow.

319–3. By prefixing a noun, pronoun, or adjective; as,

A cock-sparrow,	A hen-sparrow.
A man-servant,	A maid-servant.
A he-goat,	A she-goat.
A he-bear,	A she-bear.
A male child,	A female child.
Male descendants,	Female descendants.

XXVII. NUMBER.

320. Number shows how many are meant, whether one or more.

321. Nouns have two numbers, the singular and the plural.

322. The singular number expresses but one; as, *boy*.

323. The plural number implies more than one; as, *boys*.

324. Some nouns are used in the singular number only; as *wheat, gold, sloth, pride, dutifulness.*

325. Other nouns are used in the plural number only; as, *bellows, scissors, lungs, riches,* &c.

326. Some nouns are the same in both numbers; as, *deer, sheep, swine.*

327. The plural number of nouns is regularly formed by adding *s* to the singular; as, *sing.* dove, *plur.* doves.

328. The irregular mode of forming the plural is as follows: when the noun singular ends in *x, ch, soft, sh,* or *ss,* we add *es* to form the plural; as, *box, boxes; church, churches; lash, lashes; kiss, kisses.*

329. Nouns ending in *f* or *fe,* change these terminations into *ves* to form the plural; as, *loaf, loaves; wife, wives.*

---

serer? sultan? tiger? tutor? viscount? votary? widower?
Will you spell the masculine corresponding to *abbess? czarina? duchess? ambassadress? heroine? huntress? poetess? prophetess? widow?*
What is the third method of distinguishing sex; as, *a man-servant? a maid-servant?* 319–3.
Will you spell the feminine corresponding to *male child? male descendants?*
XXVII. What does the word *number* mean? 5.
What does the number of nouns show? 320.
What does *singular* mean? 6.

What does the singular number of nouns imply? 322. Give an example.
What does *plural* mean? 10.
What does the plural number of nouns imply? 323. Give an example.
How are *wheat, gold,* &c. used? 324.
How are *bellows, lungs,* &c. used? 325.
What is said of *deer, sheep,* &c.? 326.
How many numbers do nouns have, and what are they? 321.
How is the plural number regularly formed? 327. Give an example.
When do we add *es* to form the plural? 328. Give an example.
What is the plural of *loaf?* 329.
What is the rule for it? 329.

ENGLISH GRAMMAR.

330. When a noun singular ends in *y*, with a vowel before it, the plural is formed regularly; as, *key, keys; delay, delays; valley, valleys*. But if the *y* does not have a vowel before it, the plural is formed by changing *y* into *ies*; as, *fly, flies; beauty, beauties*.

321. The following nouns form their plurals not according to any general rules:—

Sing.	Plur.	Sing.	Plur.	Sing.	Plur.
Man,	Men.	Mouse,	Mice.	Fish,	Fishes. (3.)
Woman,	Women.	Louse,	Lice.	Cupful,	Cupfuls.
Child,	Children.	Cow,	Cows *or* Kine.	Spoonful,	Spoonfuls.
Ox,	Oxen.			Brother-in-law,	Brothers-in-law.
Tooth,	Teeth.	Penny,	Pence. (1.)	Court-martial,	Courts-martial.
Foot,	Feet.	Die,	Dice. (2.)	Brother,	Brothers *or* Brethren.
Goose,	Geese	Pea,	Peas. (3.)		

332. *Mathematics, metaphysics, pneumatics, ethics, politics,* &c. are reckoned either as singular or plural nouns. The same is equally true of *means, alms, amends. Antipodes, credenda, minutiæ, literati,* &c. are always plural. *Bandit* is now considered the singular of *banditti*. The noun *news* is always singular. Many nouns form their plurals according to the laws of the language from which they are derived. The following are of this class:—

Singular.	Plural.	Singular.	Plural.
Antithesis,	Antitheses.	Genius,	Genii. (4.)
Appendix,	Appendixes *or* Appendices.	Genus,	Genera.
		Hypothesis,	Hypotheses.
Apex,	Apices.	Ignis fatuus,	Ignes fatui.
Arcanum,	Arcana.	Index,	Indices *or* Indexes. (5.)
Automaton,	Automata.		
Axis,	Axes.	Lamina,	Laminæ.
Beau,	Beaux *or* Beaus.	Magnus,	Magi.
Basis,	Bases.	Memorandum,	Memoranda *or* Memorandums.
Calx,	Calces.		
Cherub,	Cherubim *or* Cherubs.	Metamorphosis,	Metamorphoses.
		Parenthesis,	Parentheses.
Crisis,	Crises.	Phenomenon,	Phenomena.
Criterion,	Criteria.	Radius,	Radii *or* Radiuses.
Datum,	Data.	Stamen,	Stamina.
Diæresis,	Diæreses.	Seraph,	Seraphim *or* Seraphs.
Desideratum,	Desiderata.		
Effluvium,	Effluvia.	Stimulus,	Stimuli.
Ellipsis,	Ellipses.	Stratum,	Strata.
Emphasis,	Emphases.	Thesis,	Theses.
Encomium,	Encomia *or* Encomiums.	Vertex,	Vertices.
Erratum,	Errata.	Vortex,	Vortices *or* Vortexes.

Will you spell the plural of *delay*? 330. *valley*? What is the rule for forming these plurals? 330. Will you spell the plural of *fly*? 330. *beauty*? Rule for the plural? Do *man, woman*, form their plurals regularly, or irregularly? 331. Will you spell the plural of *man*? of *woman*? *child*? *ox*? *tooth*? *foot*? *goose*? *mouse*? *louse*? *brother*? *die*? *fish*? *spoonful*? *court-martial*? Will you spell the singular of *live*? *kine*? *cows*? *brethren*? *oxen*? *teeth*? *pence*? *pennies*? *peas*? *fishes*? *cupfuls*? *brothers-in-law*? What is the plural of *pea*, when we refer to quantity? Of *fish*?

What is the singular of *banditti*? 332. In accordance with what laws does *antithesis* form the plural? 332. Will you spell the plural of *apex*? *appendix*? *arcanum*? *automaton*? *axis*? *crisis*? *basis*? *criterion*? *datum*? *desideratum*? *effluvium*? *encomium*? *erratum*? *genius*? *index*? *memorandum*? Will you spell the singular of *bases*? *beaux*? *cherubs*? *ellipses*? *genii*? *theses*? *parentheses*? *stimuli*? *strata*? How are *mathematics, optics,* &c. considered in regard to number? 332. Of what number is *means*? 332. *alms*? *amends*? *antipodes*? *literati*? *news*?

(1.) *Pennies*, when the coin is meant. (2.) *Dies*, for coining. (3.) *Pease* and *fish*, meaning quantities; but *peas* and *fishes*, when number is meant.
(4.) *Genii*, when denoting aerial or imaginary spirits; *geniuses*, when denoting persons of genius. (5.) *Indices*, when denoting pointers or tables of contents; *indexes*, when referring to algebraic quantities.

NOUNS. 47

XXVIII. CASE.

333. Case means the different state, condition, or relation which nouns have to other words in the same sentence.

334. In English, nouns have three cases — the nominative the possessive, and the objective.

335. The nominative case is usually the agent or doer, and always the subject of the verb.

336. The subject is the thing chiefly spoken of; as, "John assists William:" here, *John* is the subject spoken of, or the nominative case to the verb *assists*.

337. The possessive case denotes possession, ownership, property, &c.; as, "William's book." This case may be distinguished from the other cases by the apostrophe or the letter *s*.

338. A noun in the singular forms its possessive case by taking the apostrophe and the letter *s* after it; as, "John's hat."

339. Plural nouns usually form their possessive case simply by taking the apostrophe; as, "On eagles' wings."

340. When the plural of nouns does not end in *s*, they form their possessive case by taking both the apostrophe and the letter *s;* as, "*Men's* houses."

341. When the singular ends in *ss*, the apostrophe only is added; as, "For *goodness*' sake:" except the noun *witness;* as, "The *witness's* deposition."

342. Nouns ending in *nce* form the possessive by adding the apostrophe only; as, "For *conscience*' sake:" because an additional *s* would occasion too much of the hissing sound, or increase the difficulty of pronunciation.

343. The objective case denotes the object of an action or relation.

344. In the sentence, "John strikes him," *him* is the object of the action denoted by *strikes;* and in the sentence, "He went from London to York' *York* is the object of the relation denoted by the preposition *to*.

345. DECLENSION OF NOUNS.

	Singular.	Plural.	Singular.	Plural.
Nominative case,	Mother,	Mothers.	Man,	Men.
Possessive case,	Mother's,	Mothers'.	Man's,	Men's.
Objective case,	Mother,	Mothers.	Man,	Men.

XXVIII. What is the meaning of the word *case?* 47.
What is meant by the case of nouns? 333.
How many cases have nouns, and what are they? 334.
What does *nominative* mean? 49.
What is the nominative case? 335. Give an example.
What do you understand by the subject of a verb? 336. Illustrate it by an example.
What does *possessive* mean? 59.
What does the possessive case denote? 337. Give an example.
How may this case be distinguished from the other cases? 337.
How do nouns in the singular form their possessive case? 338. Give an example.

How do nouns in the plural? 339.
When the plural noun does not end in *s*, how is its possessive formed? 340. Give an example.
When the singular ends in *ss*, how is the possessive case formed? 341. Give an example.
How is the possessive case of nouns ending in *nce* formed? 342. Give an example.
Why is not the *s* added? 342.
What does the word *objective* mean? 55.
What does the objective case of nouns denote? 343. Give an example.
What does the declension of nouns mean? 68.
Will you decline *mother?* 345. *man, brother? hat?*

RULE I.

The possessive case is governed by the following noun.

EXERCISES IN SYNTAX.

"*John's wife returned.*"

346. *John's* is a PROPER NOUN, of the MASCULINE GENDER, the THIRD PERSON, SINGULAR NUMBER, POSSESSIVE CASE, and governed by *wife*, by RULE I.

Wife is a COMMON NOUN, of the FEMININE GENDER, the THIRD PERSON, SINGULAR NUMBER, and NOMINATIVE CASE to *returned*, by RULE VI.

Returned is an INTRANSITIVE VERB, in the INDICATIVE MOOD, IMPERFECT TENSE — "1. I returned; 2. You returned; 3. He returned, *or* wife returned"—made in the THIRD PERSON, SINGULAR, and agrees with *wife*, by RULE VII.

MORE EXERCISES IN SYNTAX.

"William's son has come."
"John's brother died."
"John makes (1.) boys' hats."
"John lost his knife."
"The boys neglected their lessons."
"Intemperance ruins its votaries."
"William's wife's sister remained in town."
"Rufus studied Johnson's Dictionary."
"Mary's bonnet is old."
"Virtue's reward is sure." (2.)
"Rufus's hat is new."

SENTENCES TO BE PARSED AND CORRECTED.

"*Brothers estate.*"

347. If you examine the foregoing example, you will find it difficult to ascertain whether the estate is the property of one brother or more; if of one only, an apostrophe should precede the *s*, thus; "Brother's estate:" but if it belongs to more than one, an apostrophe should follow the *s*, thus; " Brothers' estate." Mistakes of this sort often occur; hence you perceive the importance in writing, of attending to the subject of grammar.

"*Mans' happiness.*"

348. Incorrect, because *mans'* is in the possessive case, singular number, and, therefore, the apostrophe should be placed before the *s*, according to the observations above, and Art. 338.

Will you repeat the rule for the possessive case? Rule I.
In the sentence, "John's wife returned," will you parse *John's? wife? returned?* 346.
Why is *John's* in the possessive case? 337.
What kind of a verb is *returned?* 346.
Why? 153.
In what case is *wife?* 346.
Why? 335.
☞ *The pupil may next parse the additional exercises in syntax.*
In the phrase, "Brothers estate," does one brother, or more than one, own the estate? 347.

Why cannot you tell?
If only one brother is meant, how should the apostrophe be placed? How, if more than one?
In the phrase, "Mans' happiness," why is it incorrect for the apostrophe to follow the *s?* 348.
What is the rule for forming the possessive case of nouns? 338.
Will you now parse *man's?*
We spell the possessive case of *man* thus, m-a-n-(apostrophe) *s;* will you in like manner spell the possessive of *John? William? Rufus? women? boys?*
☞ *The remaining exercises are to be corrected as well as parsed.*

(1.) Active-transitive verb. (2.) Adjective, and belongs to reward, by Rule IV.

ARTICLES. 49

SENTENCES TO BE PARSED AND CORRECTED, CONTINUED.

"Johns son departed."
"Susans sister will learn."
"Charles task is too difficult."
"I have read Willi's poem."
"I discovered Marias faults."
"Susan made little Harriets bcn net."
"Johnson makes mens shoes."

EXERCISES TO BE WRITTEN.*

349. Will you write down two sentences, each containing a proper noun, as for example, "William learns grammar"? One, containing a common noun? One, containing a noun of the third person singular? One, of the third person plural, and in the nominative case? One, having a noun of the second person singular and of the feminine gender? One, having a noun the name of some article of food? One, having a noun the name of some quality? One, having a noun of multitude? One, having your own name associated with *book;* as, "John Griscom's book"?

XXIX. OF ARTICLES.

350. ARTICLES are words put before nouns, to point them out, or to limit their meaning.

351. There are two articles, *a* or *an*, and *the*.

352. A or AN is called the indefinite article.

353. THE is called the definite article.

354. The article *a* is called indefinite, because it means no particular person or thing; as, "*a* house," "*a* man," that is, *any* house, *any* man. The article *the* is called definite, because it means some particular person or thing; as "*the* house," "*the* man," meaning some particular house, some particular man.

355. *A* becomes *an* before a vowel, and before a silent *h;* as, "*an* acorn," "*an* hour." But if the *h* be sounded, the *a* only is used; as, "*a* hand," "*a* heart:" except when the word before which the article is placed, has its accent on the second syllable; as, "*an* heroic action," "*an* historical account."

356. Before words beginning with *u* long, *a* is used instead of *an;* as, "*a* union," "*a* university," "*a* useful thing."

357. *A* is also used for *an* before the word *one*, because, in pronouncing *one*, we sound it as if written *wun*.

358. The article *a* or *an* means *one;* as, "*an* ounce," "*a* pound,' that is, one ounce, one pound.

XXIX. What is an article? 350.
What does *definite* mean? 78.
What is *the* called? 353. Why? 354. Give an example.
What does *indefinite* mean? 81.
What is *a* or *an* called? 352. Why? 354. Give an example.
How many articles are there? 351. Name them.
When does *a* become *an*? 355. Give an example.

But if the *h* is sounded, which is to be used? 355. Give an example.
What exception to this? 355. Give an example.
Do we say, "*a* union," or "*an* union"?
"*a* university," or "*an* university"? Why? 356.
Do we say, "*a* one," or "*an* one"? Why? 357.
What does the article *a* mean? 358. Give an example.

* Either on a slate or in a small manuscript book kept for the purpose

D

RULE II.

The indefinite article A *or* AN *belongs to nouns of the singular number.*

RULE III.

The definite article THE *belongs to nouns of the singular or plural number.*

359. *Exception.* When the adjectives *few, great many, dozen, hundred thousand,* &c. come between the noun and article, the noun to which the indefinite article belongs, is plural; as, "a few men," "a great many men."

EXERCISES IN SYNTAX.

"The bird flies swiftly."

360. *The* is a DEFINITE ARTICLE, and belongs to *bird,* according to RULE III.

Bird is a COMMON NOUN, of the COMMON GENDER, the THIRD PERSON, SINGULAR NUMBER, and in the NOMINATIVE CASE to *flies,* by RULE VI.

Flies is an ACTIVE-INTRANSITIVE VERB, INDICATIVE MOOD, PRESENT TENSE — "1. I fly; 2. You fly; 3. He flies, *or* bird flies" — made in the THIRD PERSON, SINGULAR, and agrees with *bird,* by RULE VII.

Swiftly is an ADVERB, qualifying *flies,* by RULE IX.

EXERCISES IN SYNTAX CONTINUED.

"The boys have arrived seasonably."
"Galileo invented the telescope."
"The boy had an ulcer."
"William gave an historical account (1.) of the transaction."
"Columbus discovered the continent of America."
"Children attend the school."
"William founded a university."
"The grass is green."
"Farmers carry hay into the barn."
"The good scholar obeys his instructer."

SENTENCES TO BE PARSED AND CORRECTED.

"He had a ulcer."

361. Incorrect, because we use *an* before a vowel, except *u* long: *a* should, therefore be *an;* thus, "an ulcer."

SENTENCES TO BE PARSED AND CORRECTED, CONTINUED.

"A enemy approaches."
"James procured a inkstand."
"He conferred a honour."
"An unit figure occupies the lowest place in whole numbers."
"Three barley corns make a inch."
"Eight drams make a ounce."
"They formed an union."
"He quoted an hard saying."
"Thomas has lost an horse."

What is the rule for the indefinite article? Rule II.
What exception to this rule? 359.
What is the rule for the indefinite article? Rule III.
In the sentence, "the bird flies swiftly," how do you parse *the? bird? flies? swiftly?* 360.

☞ *The remaining exercises are next to be parsed from the book.*
Would you say, "a ulcer," or "an ulcer"? Why? 361.

☞ *The pupil should now take the remaining sentences to be corrected. He should be required to parse as well as correct them.*

(L.) Apply Rule VIII.

ADJECTIVES.

SENTENCES TO BE WRITTEN.

362. Will you write down two sentences, using in one the definite, and in the other the indefinite article? One, containing a correctly used before u long? One, having a definite article correctly used before the consonant h?
Will you write two nouns, the names of different things in the school-room? Two, the names of different cities? One sentence, having a proper noun used as a common noun?

XXX. OF ADJECTIVES.

363. AN ADJECTIVE is a word joined to a noun, to describe or define it; as, "An *obedient* son."

364. In English, an adjective is varied only to express the degrees of comparison. There are three degrees of comparison—the positive, the comparative, and the superlative.

365. The positive degree simply describes an object; as, "John is *good*."

366. The comparative degree increases or lessens the positive in meaning; as, "William is *better* than John." It implies a comparison between two.

367. The superlative degree increases or lessens the positive to the highest or lowest degree; as, "Thomas is the *best*;" "Walter is the *worst*."

368. It implies a comparison between three or more.

369. The simple word, or positive, if a monosyllable, (1.) becomes the comparative by adding *r* or *er*, and the superlative by adding *st* or *est*, to the end of it; as, *wise, wiser, wisest ; great, greater, greatest*.

370. In words of more than one syllable, the comparison is usually made by placing the adverbs *more* and *most* before the positive; as, *benevolent, more benevolent, most benevolent*.

371. The comparison is sometimes formed by the adverbs *less* and *least*, as, *wise, less wise, least wise*.

372. Dissyllables (2.) ending in *y*; as, *happy, lovely*, and in *le*, after a mute; (3.) as, *able, ample*, or accented on the last syllable; as, *discreet, polite*, easily

---

XXX. What is the meaning of the word *adjective*? 95.
What is an adjective? 363. Give an example.
How many degrees of comparison are there? 364.
Will you name them?
What does the positive degree do? 365. Give an example.
What does the comparative degree do? 366. Give an example.
What does it imply? 366.
What does *superlative* mean? 103.
What does the superlative degree do? 367. Give an example.

What does it imply? 368.
What is a monosyllable? 369.
How are monosyllables compared? 369. Give an example.
How are dissyllables compared? 372.
What effect do *less* and *least* have on adjectives? 371.
What is a dissyllable? 372.
Will you spell the comparative and superlative degrees of *able? lovely? ample? discreet? polite?* 372.
Which are the mutes? 372.
How do words of more than two syllables almost invariably form their comparison? 372.

(1.) A word of one syllable.   (2.) A word of two syllables.
(3.) *b, k, p, t*, and *s* and *g* hard, are mutes.

admit of *er* and *est*; as, *happier, happiest; abler, ablest*, &c. Words of more than two syllables hardly ever admit of these terminations.

373. In some words, the superlative is formed by adding the adverb *most* to the end of them; as, *nethermost, uttermost, uppermost.*

374. Some adjectives, having in themselves a superlative signification, do not admit of comparison; as, *extreme, perfect, right, wrong, infinite, ceaseless, supreme, omnipotent, eternal.*

375. By adding *ish* to adjectives, we have a slight degree of comparison below the positive; as, *black, blackish; salt, saltish.*

376. *Very* expresses a degree of quality, but not the highest; as, " good," " *very* good."

377. Words used in counting and numbering are called *numeral adjectives;* as, *one, two, three; first, second, third.* These adjectives are not compared.

378. An adjective put without a noun, with the definite article before it, becomes a noun in sense and meaning, and may be considered as such in parsing; as, "Providence rewards the *good*, and punishes the *bad*."

RULE IV.

Adjectives belong to the nouns which they describe.

EXERCISES IN SYNTAX.

"*John is sincere.*"

379. *John* is a PROPER NOUN, of the THIRD PERSON, SINGULAR NUMBER, MASCULINE GENDER, and in the NOMINATIVE CASE to *is*, by RULE VI.

Is is a NEUTER VERB, in the INDICATIVE MOOD, PRESENT TENSE—"1. I am; 2. You are; 3. He *or* John is,"—made in the THIRD PERSON SINGULAR, and agrees with *John*, according to RULE VII.

Sincere is an ADJECTIVE,—" sincere, more sincere, most sincere,"—made in the POSITIVE DEGREE, and belongs to *John*, by RULE IV.

EXERCISES IN SYNTAX CONTINUED.

"You are studious."
"John is more studious."
"William is most studious."
"Mary is intelligent."
"James is active."
"Thomas is less active."
"Charles is happy."
"Mary is tall. Susan is taller."
"No composition is perfect."
"Religion makes its votaries happy."

"One man has come."
"Two men have departed."
"Twenty men will sail."
"James wrote his name on the first page."
"Here comes a great man."
"Here comes a greater man."
"Here comes the greatest man."
"The first fleet contained five hundred men."

Is *perfect* compared? Why? 374.
Will you name several others that are not compared? 374.
How is the superlative formed in the word *upper*? 373.
What is the effect of *ish* added to adjectives? 375. Give an example.
What is the force of *very* in comparison? 376.
What are numeral adjectives? 377. Give an example. Are they compared? 377.
Will you spell the comparative and superlative degrees of *good? ill? much? little?*
When is an adjective to be considered a noun? 378.
What is the rule for the adjective? IV.
In the phrase, "John is sincere," how do you parse *John? is? sincere?* 379.
Why is *sincere* in the positive degree? 365. Why do you call *is* a neuter verb? 157.

☞ *Let the pupil next take the exercises that follow, and parse as before*

XXXI.

380. Double comparatives and superlatives, since they add nothing to the sense, should be avoided; as, *worser, more wiser*, &c.; also, *lesser, supremest, most infinite*, &c.

SENTENCES TO BE WRITTEN.

Q. Will you write down two sentences, each containing a different adjective in the positive degree? Two, with adjectives in the comparative degree? Two, with adjectives in the superlative degree?

Q. Will you supply such adjectives in the following sentences as will make sense? "A —— boy studies his lesson." "A —— boy deserves punishment." "A —— man helps the —— man." "Merchants own —— ships." "The instructer loves —— scholars." "William is a -- scholar, Rufus is a —— one, but Thomas is the —— one that I ever saw."

XXXII. OF PRONOUNS.

381. A PRONOUN is a word used instead of a noun, to avoid a disagreeable repetition of the noun.

382. A PERSONAL PRONOUN is so called because it invariably represents the same person. There are five personal pronouns— I, THOU or YOU, HE, SHE, IT. They have person, number and case, like nouns; and those of the third person have gender also.

383. *I* is the first person, *thou* the second, *he, she,* or *it,* the third. *He* is masculine, *she* is feminine, and *it* is neuter.

384. Pronouns, like nouns, have three cases — the nominative, the possessive, and the objective; and two numbers — the singular and plural.

385. *Mine* and *thine,* instead of *my* and *thy,* were formerly used in the solemn style, before nouns and adjectives beginning with a vowel or silent *h;* as, "Blot out all mine iniquities."

XXXI. Is it correct to say, "A lesser evil?" Why not? 380.
Will you correct the following inaccuracies in comparison as I read them to you?
"He is intelligenter."
"She is the most wisest."
"A worser evil."
"William is a bad boy; Joseph is a worser one."
"He gave a more stronger proof of the fact than the other."
"The pleasures of the mind are more (1.) preferable than those of the body."
"That table is round, but this is a rounder one, and that is the roundest of the three."
"This is more square."
"A more greater concern."
"The most fairest of all the daughters of Eve."
"His mother's extremest joy."

XXXII. What does the word *pronoun* signify? 120.
What is a pronoun? 381.
Why is a personal pronoun so called? 382.
How many personal pronouns are there, and what are they? 382.
Why is this number said to include all the pronouns? 134.
Which is the first person? the second? the third? 383.
To which of the pronouns do we apply gender? 383.
Why is not gender applied to the first and second persons? 136.
Which is masculine? 383. which feminine? 383. which neuter? 383.
How many cases have pronouns, and what are they? 384.
How many numbers? 384.
Will you decline *I? thou? he? she? it?* 127.

(1.) For *more preferable than*, read *preferable to*.

XXXIII. COMPOUND PERSONAL PRONOUNS.

386. Compound personal pronouns are formed by adding the word *self*, in the plural *selves*, to the simple pronouns; as, *himself, themselves*, &c.

PERSON.	CASE.	SINGULAR.	PLURAL.
First.	Nom.	Myself,	Ourselves.
	Poss.	Wanting.	
	Obj.	Myself,	Ourselves.
Second.	Nom.	Thyself, or Yourself,	Yourselves.
	Poss.		
	Obj.	Thyself, or Yourself,	Yourselves.
Third.	Nom.	Himself,	Themselves.
	Poss.		
	Obj.	Himself,	Themselves.
	Nom.	Herself,	Themselves.
	Poss.		
	Obj.	Herself,	Themselves.
	Nom.	Itself,	Themselves.
	Poss.		
	Obj.	Itself,	Themselves.

RULE V.

Pronouns must agree with the nouns for which they stand, in gender, number and person.

EXERCISES IN SYNTAX.

"*John found his knife.*"

387. *John* is a PROPER NOUN, of the MASCULINE GENDER, the THIRD PERSON, SINGULAR NUMBER, and NOMINATIVE CASE to *found*, by RULE VI.

Found is an ACTIVE-TRANSITIVE VERB, in the INDICATIVE MOOD, IMPERFECT TENSE — "1. I found; 2. You found; 3. He or John found"—made in the THIRD PERSON SINGULAR, and agrees with *John*, by RULE VII.

His is a PERSONAL PRONOUN, of the THIRD PERSON SINGULAR, MASCULINE GENDER, and agrees with *John*, according to RULE V.; in the POSSESSIVE CASE, and governed by *knife*, by RULE I.

Knife is a COMMON NOUN, of the THIRD PERSON SINGULAR, NEUTER GENDER, the OBJECTIVE CASE, and governed by *found*, according to RULE VIII.

Of what number and person is *mine?* *ours? me? we? they? thine? you? yours?* 127.
Of what gender, number and person is *he? she? it?*
Of what number, person and case is *they? ours? his? hers? mine?*
In what style were *mine* and *thine* formerly used? 385.
XXXIII. How are the compound personal pronouns formed? 386.

What is the rule for the agreement of personal pronouns in the phrase, "John found his knife?" V.
How do you parse *John?* 387.
Will you parse *John* in the phrase, "John found his knife?" 387.
Will you parse *found? his? knife?* 387.

☞ *The learner should next parse the remaining exercises in Syntax from the book and then take the exercises to be written.*

PRONOUNS. 55

EXERCISES IN SYNTAX CONTINUED.

1.

"James obtained his request."
"I will assist you."
"He will receive his reward."
"She misused him."
"Sin ruins its votaries."

"Ye despise reproof."
"They mend their pens."
"Mary tore her handkerchief."
"Virtue has its reward."
"She deceived them."

2.

"An indulgent father will reprove his son when (1.) he deserves it."
"A dutiful son gladdens the hearts of his parents."

"John is in distress, and I will assist him."
"I found Mary and her mother in trouble, and (2.) comforted (3.) them."

EXERCISES TO BE WRITTEN.

Q. Will you compose two sentences, each having a different personal pronoun of the first person? One, having a pronoun of the first person plural?

Q. Will you fill up the following sentences with suitable pronouns, so as to make sense? " — lost my hat, but found — again." "Let Harriet have — book, for — will need — to get her lesson." "The travellers lost — way, and the boys conducted — to — homes."

Q. Will you fill up the following broken sentences with suitable words to make sense? "Intemperance —— — evil." "Washington —— father of his ——." "Columbus —— America." "Boston ——— inhabitants." "The —— ocean is —— miles wide." " —— — first man."

XXXIV. OF ADJECTIVE PRONOUNS.

388. In the sentence, "Both wealth and poverty are temptations; *that* tends to excite pride, *this* discontent;" you perceive that the word *that* represents wealth, and the word *this* poverty. *This* and *that* do, therefore, resemble pronouns, and may, for this reason, be called pronouns.

389. When I say, "This house is mine, that barn is yours," the words *this* and *that* are joined to nouns like adjectives, to define or specify them: they may, on this account, be called adjectives.

390. Adjective pronouns, then, are words that resemble both pronouns and adjectives. These pronouns are sometimes called pronominal adjectives, or specifying adjectives.

391. The ADJECTIVE PRONOUNS may be divided into three sorts—the distributive, the demonstrative, and the indefinite.

392. The distributive are those that relate to persons or things, taken separately and singly.

XXXIV. What are adjective pronouns? 390.
Why are they so called? 388, 389.
By what other name have these pronouns been called? 390.
Will you give an example in which these words resemble pronouns? 388.

One in which they resemble adjectives? 389.
Into how many sorts may these pronouns be divided, and what are they? 391.
What is a distributive pronoun? 392.

393. DISTRIBUTIVE (1.) PRONOUNS.

EACH, EVERY, EITHER, and sometimes NEITHER.

394. EACH relates to two or more persons or things, taken separately, as, "*Each* of his brothers is doing well."

395. EVERY relates to several persons or things, and signifies each one of them, taken separately; as, "*Every* man must account for himself."

396. EITHER relates to two persons or things only, taken separately, and signifies the one or the other; as, "I have not seen *either*." Hence, to say, "Either of the three," is incorrect.

397. NEITHER means not either; that is, not one nor the other; as, "*Neither* of my friends was there."

398. The DEMONSTRATIVE (2.) PRONOUNS are those which precisely point out the things to which they relate.

99. DEMONSTRATIVE PRONOUNS.

Sing.	*Plu.*
THIS,	THESE.
THAT,	THOSE.
FORMER,	FORMER.
LATTER,	LATTER.

400. *This* and *these* refer to the nearest persons or things,—*that* and *those* to the most distant; as, "*These* gloves are superior to *those*." "Both wealth and poverty are temptations; *that* tends to excite pride, *this* discontent."

401. The INDEFINITE are those that refer to things in an indefinite or general manner.

INDEFINITE PRONOUNS.

402. SOME, OTHER, ANY, ONE, ALL, SUCH, NONE. Of these pronouns, *one* and *other* are declined like nouns. *Another* declined in the singular, but it wants the plural.

		Sing.	*Plu.*
403.	*Nom.*	Other,	Others.
	Poss.	Other's,	Others'.
	Obj.	Other,	Others.
		Sing.	*Plu.*
404.	*Nom.*	One,	Ones.
	Poss.	One's,	Ones'.
	Obj.	One,	Ones.

We say, "This book," but, "These books;" also, "One man," "Twenty men:" hence,

405. NOTE I. Adjective pronouns and numerals must agree in number with the nouns to which they belong.

Why is it so called? 393.
Which are they? 393.
What does *each* refer to? 394. Give an example.
What does *every* relate to? 395. Give an example.
What does *either* relate to? 396. Give an example.
What does *neither* mean? 397.
What does *demonstrative* mean? 398.
What are demonstrative pronouns? 398.
Which are they? 399.

Which are singular? 399. Which plural? 399.
What do *this* and *these* refer to? 400.
What do *that* and *those* refer to? Give an example. 400.
What does *indefinite* mean? 61.
What is an indefinite pronoun? 401.
Which are they? 402.
Will you decline *other*? 403.
Will you decline *one*? 404.
What note do you apply in parsing adjective pronouns? NOTE I.

(1.) So called from *distribute*, to divide among several.
(2.) So called from *demonstrate*, to point or show precisely.

PRONOUNS.

EXERCISES IN SYNTAX.
"*These two books belong to me.*"

406. *These* is an ADJECTIVE PRONOUN of the DEMONSTRATIVE kind, In the PLURAL NUMBER, and belongs to *books*, according to NOTE I.
Two is a NUMERAL ADJECTIVE, and belongs to *books*, by NOTE I.
Books, belong, &c. are parsed as before.

EXERCISES IN PARSING CONTINUED.

"Every man performs his part in creation."
"Each man arrived at his station."
"Either party can repair the injury."
"Some persons cannot acquire wealth."
"Many people obtain riches with apparently little exertion."
"One boy labors for his improvement."
"This man neglects his affairs."

"These men might remain with us."
"Those men make many pretences to religion."
"All rational beings desire happiness."
"By application almost any boy may acquire an honorable rank in his class."
"Good and virtuous men will, sooner (1.) or later (1.), attain to happiness."

"*The old bird feeds her young ones.*"

407. *Ones* is an INDEFINITE PRONOUN, representing *birds*, in the COMMON GENDER, THIRD PERSON PLURAL, in the OBJECTIVE CASE, and governed by *feeds*, agreeably to RULE VIII.

EXERCISES IN SYNTAX CONTINUED.

"One boy influences many others."
"None act their part too well."
"Some scholars study diligently; the former will receive praise, the latter censure."

others spend their time in idleness;

We cannot say, "Them run," but, "They run;" hence,

NOTE II. When a noun or pronoun is the subject of the verb, it should be in the nominative case.

It is very common for persons in conversation to say, "Them books," "Them knives," &c. instead of "Those books," "Those knives," &c. The incorrectness here alluded to consists in substituting a personal in the place of an adjective pronoun: hence,

NOTE III. The pronoun *them* should not be used in the place of *these* or *those.*

In the phrase, "These two books," &c. will you parse *these? two?* 406.
Will you now take the book, and parse the remaining exercises under Note I.?
In the phrase, "The old bird feeds her young ones," will you parse *ones?* 407.
Will you correct by Note I. the following examples, as I read them to you?
"He will not come this two hours."
"I dislike those sort of books."
"I have two canes; you may have any of them."
Do we say, "*They* run," or, "*Them* run?" Why? Note II.
Will you now correct, by Note II. the following examples as I read them to you?

"Them will go."
"Him and me went to church."
"Art thee well?"
"Him who is diligent will improve."
Would you say, "*Them* knives," or "*These* knives"? Why? III.
In what does the incorrectness consist? III.
Will you correct the following expressions?
"Them boys are very idle."
"Bring me them pens"
"Which of them three things do you prefer?"

☞ *The pupil may next take the exercises to be written.*

SENTENCES TO BE WRITTEN.

Q. Will you compose two sentences, each having a different adjective pronoun? One, having a demonstrative pronoun? One, having an indefinite pronoun used as a noun?

Q. Will you fill up with pronouns suitable to make sense the following phrases? "When Harriet found — book, — tore —, and then flung — away." " — man likes — farm, — merchandise."

Q. Will you compose a proper example under Rule I.? One under Rule II.? Rule III.? Rule IV.? Rule V.? Rule VI.?

XXXV. OF RELATIVE PRONOUNS.

408. In the sentence, "That man is happy, who lives virtuously," the word *who* is a pronoun, because it stands for a noun (the noun *man*), and it is a relative, because it relates or refers to this noun in the same sentence: hence,

409. A relative pronoun is a word that usually stands for some noun before it in the same sentence.

410. There are three relative pronouns, viz.

411. WHO, WHICH, and THAT.

412. *Who* is used in speaking of persons; as, "The man *who* came."

413. *Which* is used in speaking of animals or things; as, "The bird *which* sings," "The tree *which* I planted."

414. *Which*, however, is used in speaking of persons, when we wish to distinguish one of two individuals, or a particular person among many others; as, "Which of the two is he?" "Which of them has gone?"

415. *That*, as a relative, is often used, in speaking either of persons or things, in the place of *who* or *which;* as,
"The boy that reads," or, "The boy who reads;" "The bird that flew," or, "The bird which flew;" "The bench that was made," or, "The bench which was made."

That is used in preference to *who* or *which*, in the following cases: —

1. In speaking both of persons and things; as, "The man and the bear that I saw, perished."
2. In speaking of children; as, "The child that I met."
3. After the adjective *same;* as, "He is the same man that we saw yesterday."
4. After the superlative degree; as, "He is the wisest man that the world ever produced."
5. After the relative *who;* as, "Who that reflects."

415—1. EXCEPTION. *That*, as a relative, cannot take the preposition immediately before it; as, "He is the same man with that you were acquainted." For *with that*, read *with whom.* It is remarkable, however, that, when the arrangement is a little varied, the word *that* admits the preposition; as, "He is the same man *that* you were acquainted with."

XXXV In the sentence, "That man is happy, who lives virtuously," what part of speech is *who*? Why? 408. What kind? Why? 408.
What is a relative pronoun? 409.
Will you name them? 411.
When do we use *who*? Give an example. 412.
When do we use *which*? Give an example. 413.
In what cases do we use *which*, in

speaking of persons? Give an example. 414.
When may *that* be used? 415.
Is it correct to say, "The child who?" Why not? "The same man who?" Why not? "The wisest man which?" Why not? "Who, who reflects?" Why not? 415; 1, 2, 3, 4, 5.
What exception is mentioned? 415—L Give an example. 415—1

PRONOUNS. 59

116—1. We can say, "The man who," or "The men who," using the relative *who* in speaking either of one man or more than one: *who*, then, is of both numbers, and is thus declined:

	Singular.	Plural.
Nom.	Who,	Who.
Poss.	Whose,	Whose.
Obj.	Whom,	Whom.

417. *Which* and *that* are of both numbers, but they are not declined, except that *whose* is sometimes used as the possessive case of *which*; as, "Is there any other doctrine *whose* followers are punished?"

418. *Whose*, used in the manner last described, is made to represent three words; as, "Philosophy whose end," for "the end of which."

419. *Antecedent* signifies *going before*.

420. The noun or pronoun which goes before the relative, and to which the relative refers, is therefore called the antecedent of the relative; as, "John, who has gone." Here, John is the antecedent of *who*.

421. When you are told that *who*, *which*, and *that* are relatives, you should not get the impression that the last two are always relatives; for *that* is a relative only when it is used in the sense of *who* or *which*; that is, when *who* or *which* may be used in its place, without destroying the sense; as, "Here is the knife that I found," which can be altered to "Here is the knife which I found," without injury to the sense.

422. *That*, when it points out or specifies some particular person or thing, is reckoned an adjective pronoun. When not used as a relative, nor as an adjective pronoun, it is reckoned a conjunction; as, "He studies that he may learn."

423. Hence it appears that the word *that* may be used sometimes as a relative pronoun, sometimes as an adjective pronoun, and sometimes as a conjunction.

424. Since relative pronouns stand for nouns, as well as personal pronouns, they should therefore agree with nouns in the same particulars and by the same rule. RULE V. will therefore apply to both.

EXERCISES IN SYNTAX.

"*That man is happy who lives virtuously.*"

425. *That* is a DEMONSTRATIVE PRONOUN, of the SINGULAR NUMBER, and belongs to *man*, by NOTE I.

Who is a RELATIVE PRONOUN, of the MASCULINE GENDER, THIRD PERSON SINGULAR, and agrees with *man* by RULE V. It is in the NOMINATIVE CASE to *lives*, according to RULE VI.

EXERCISES IN SYNTAX CONTINUED.

"That man is fortunate who escapes censure.
"The girl whom I saw, perished."

"I met the same man in the market to-day (1.), that I met yesterday in the street.

How many numbers has *who*? 416.
Will you decline it? 416—1.
How many numbers have *which* and *that*? Are they declined? 417.
What exception to this? 417.
When *whose* is used as the possessive case of *which*, how many words does it represent? Give an example. 418.
What is the meaning of *antecedent*? 419.
What is the antecedent of a pronoun? Give an example. 420.
Is *that* always a relative? 421.
When is it a relative? Give an example. 421.

When is *that* an adjective pronoun? Give an example. 422.
When a conjunction? Give an example. 422.
How many different parts of speech may *that* represent? 423.
What is the rule for the agreement of relative pronouns? 424.
Will you parse *that*, in the phrase, "That man"? 425.
In the sentence, "That man is happy who lives virtuously," will you parse *who*? 425.
Will you now take the book, and parse the remaining exercises?

"You, who came first, should retire first."
"You taught the boy whose hat I found."
"That house, which stands on the hill, once (1.) belonged to me."
"The boy whom I instruct learns well."

SENTENCES TO BE PARSED AND CORRECTED.
"*The man which I saw.*"

426. Incorrect; because, in speaking of persons, *who, whose*, or *whom* is generally to be used. It should therefore read, "The man whom I saw."

SENTENCES TO BE PARSED AND CORRECTED, CONTINUED.
"The bird whom I killed had made her nest."
"The man which visited me has left town."
"That man is happy whom is virtuous."
"Thou who are in prosperity must assist me in adversity."
"He which shuns vice does generally practise virtue."
"I, who lives by your charity, should be grateful."

SENTENCES TO BE WRITTEN.

Q. Will you construct a sentence containing the relative *who?* One, containing *which?* One, containing *that?*

Q. Will you fill up the following sentences with relatives correctly used? "The man —— sins shall die." "The boy —— studies will learn." "The bird —— sung so sweetly has flown." Will you fill up the following with one or more words that will make sense? "Intemperance —— evils." "If —— truth —— sorry."

Q. Will you embrace in different sentences, each of the following words? *Washington,* Columbus, Captain Cook, Indians, Wisdom, Riches, James Monroe.*

XXXVI. OF COMPOUND AND INTERROGATIVE PRONOUNS.

427. "I took *what* you gave me."
"I took *that which* you gave me."
"I took *the thing which* you gave me."
"I took *those things which* you gave me."

428. By examining the foregoing sentences, you will see that the word *what*, in the first example, means the same as the words in italics in the successive ones: the word *what*, then, is clearly a pronoun; and because it stands for more than one word, it is called a compound pronoun. The word before the relative *which*, in the phrase "that which," or "the thing which," is the antecedent of *which*. Hence,

429. WHAT is a compound relative pronoun, including both the antecedent and the relative, and is generally equivalent to THAT WHICH.

Instead of saying, "The man which I saw," what should I say? Why? 426.
Will you correct and parse the remaining exercises, and then take the exercises to be written?
XXXVI. Will you repeat those sentences which mean the same as "I took what you gave me"? 427.
What words, then, does *what* stand for? 428.
Why is *what* a pronoun? 428.
Why a compound pronoun? 429.

(1.) Adverb.

PRONOUNS. 61

430. *Who, which,* and *what* have sometimes the words *ever* or *soever* annexed (1.) to them : and each combination of this sort is called a compound relative; as, *whoever, whosoever, whichever, whichsoever,* &c. They are not often used.

431. *Who, which,* and *what* are called interrogatives, or relatives of the interrogative kind, when they are used in asking questions; as, "Who is he?" "Which is the book?" "What are you doing?" These relatives, you perceive, have no antecedents, but relate to some word or phrase contained in the answer, which is called a *subsequent*, because it follows after the relative; as, "Whom did you see?" *Ans.* "John." Here *John* is the *subsequent* to which *whom* refers.

432. Hence it follows, that *antecedent* and *subsequent* are opposed to each other in meaning; the former signifying *going before,* the latter *following after.*

433. *Whether* was formerly made use of to express interrogation; as, "Whether of these shall I choose?" but it is now seldom used, the interrogative *which* supplying its place.

434. *Which, what,* and, as we have already seen, *that,* when joined to nouns, are adjective pronouns; as, "unto which promise our twelve tribes."

435. When *what* and *which* are joined to nouns in asking questions, they are called interrogative adjective pronouns; as, "Which horse did he take?"

436. In some instances, we find *what* used in the sense of an interjection; as, "What! take my money, and then my life?"

EXERCISES IN SYNTAX.

"*I will leave what is useless.*"

437. *What,* in the example above, means the same as, "that which," or, "the thing which ;" we will, therefore, in parsing it, bear in mind that it has the government and agreement of two separate words. We will first parse it as standing for *thing,* and secondly for *which.*

What is a COMPOUND RELATIVE PRONOUN, and is equivalent to "that which," or, "the thing which." In representing *thing,* it may be considered a PRONOUN of the THIRD PERSON SINGULAR, NEUTER GENDER, in the OBJECTIVE CASE, and governed by *leave,* according to RULE VIII.

What, in representing *which,* may be considered a RELATIVE PRONOUN of the THIRD PERSON SINGULAR, NEUTER GENDER, and relates to *thing* for its antecedent, according to RULE V. and in the NOMINATIVE CASE to *is,* by RULE VI.

Is is a NEUTER VERB, in the INDICATIVE MOOD, PRESENT TENSE — "1. I am ; 2. You are; 3. He or *which* is"—made in the THIRD PERSON SINGULAR, and agrees with *which,* the relative part of the pronoun *what,* according to RULE VII.

Useless is an ADJECTIVE, in the POSITIVE DEGREE, and belongs to *what,* by RULE IV.

How may *what* be described? 429.
Will you give three examples of compound pronouns formed by annexing *ever* or *soever*? 430.
What is the meaning of *annexed*? 430.
When are *who, which,* and *what* called interrogatives? 431.
What are the nouns called, to which interrogatives refer? 431.
What is the meaning of *subsequent*? 432.
Why so called? 431.
In the phrase, "Whom did you see?" *Ans.* "John ;" which word is the subsequent? 431.

When are *what, which,* and *that* adjective pronouns? Give an example. 434.
Which of the relatives are sometimes interrogative adjective pronouns? When? 435.
When I say, "What! rob me of my money, and then take my life?" in what sense is *what* used? 436.
In the sentence, "I will leave what is useless," how do you parse *what*? is *useless*? 437.
What does *what* stand for? 437.
Do you parse it as one word or two? What two? 437.

☞ *The pupil may now parse the remaining exercises on the pronoun* what.

(1.) Placed after.

ENGLISH GRAMMAR.

EXERCISES IN SYNTAX CONTINUED.

"James will do what is proper."
"You heard what I said."
"Whatever improves delights him."
"William demands what I cannot give."
"They advocate what is excellent."

XXXVII. OF THE VERB.

438. A VERB is a word that expresses ACTION or BEING. Verbs are of three kinds—ACTIVE, PASSIVE, and NEUTER.

439. An active verb expresses action, and the actor is always the nominative case; as, "John runs." Active verbs are either transitive or intransitive.

440. An active verb is transitive, when it either has or may have an object after it, on which the action terminates; as, "John beats William."

441. An active verb is intransitive, when it neither has nor can have an object after it.

442. *Passive* means *suffering* or *receiving*.

443. When I say, "John is beaten by William," *is beaten* is a verb, because it expresses action; and it is a passive verb, because it expresses the action received by John; and if John receives the action, then he is the object of it: hence,

444. A passive verb expresses action or effect received.

445. The object is always its subject or nominative case.

446. *Active nominative*, or *actor*, "John strikes William."

447. *Passive nominative*, or *object*, "William is struck by John."

448. By examining the foregoing examples, you will see that when the verb is active, its nominative is likewise active; and when the verb is passive, its nominative is likewise passive.

449. The passive voice is a convenient mode of expression on occasions when we wish to state *what* has been done, without exposing the author, thus, instead of saying, "William struck John," I can, to avoid alluding to William, say, "John was struck."

XXXVII. What is the meaning of *verb*?*
Why so called? 143.
What is a verb? 438.
What is an active verb? 439.
What is always its nominative? Give an example. 439.
What is the meaning of *transitive*?†
of *intransitive*?‡
How may active verbs be divided? 439.
When is an active verb transitive?
Give an example. 440.
When is an active verb intransitive?
Give an example. 441.
What is the meaning of *passive*? 442.

In the example, "John is beaten by William," which is the verb? Why? What kind? Why? 443.
Which word is the object? Why? 443.
What, then, is a passive verb? 444.
Which is the nominative to a passive verb, the agent or the object? 445.
Is the nominative to an active verb active or passive? Give an example. 446.
Is the nominative to a passive verb active or passive? Give an example. 448.
In what particular is the passive voice a convenient form of expression? Give an example. 449.
What is the meaning of *neuter*?§

450. A neuter verb is one that is neither active nor passive, expressing simply either being or existence in a certain state, as, "He sits," "He is at home."

XXXVIII. MOOD, OR MODE.

451. MOOD, or MODE, is the manner of representing action or being.

452. The INDICATIVE MOOD is used simply for indicating or declaring a thing, or asking a question; as, "I walk;" "Do I walk?"

453. The POTENTIAL MOOD is used for expressing possibility, liberty, power, will, or obligation, either with or without asking a question; as, "I may go;" "May I go?" "He must read," &c.

454. Of the SUBJUNCTIVE MOOD. The term *subjunctive* signifies *subjoined* or *added to*.

455. When I say, "I will go, if he desire it," the phrase, "if he desire it," is added on to the one before it: hence, we say, "if he desire it," is in the subjunctive mood. The term, however, is limited to such sentences as are preceded by the conjunctions *if, unless, although, except, lest*, &c., which imply doubt or some uncertainty.

456. The subjunctive mood is used for expressing doubt or uncertainty.

457. A verb in the subjunctive mood may be expressed in two different forms. It is equally correct to say, "If he *is* poor, he is respected," and. "If he *be* studious, he will excel." The verbs *be* and *is* are both in the present tense; and since each has the conjunction *if* before it, each is in the subjunctive mood.

458. The phrase, "If he *be* studious," means the same as, "If he *will* be studious;" it therefore plainly implies future time.

459. On the contrary, in the phrase, "If he *is* poor," the sense plainly is, "If he is now, at the present time, poor," without any reference to future time.

460. Hence it appears, that, in one form of the verb, *doubt* only is implied; and in the other, both *doubt* and *future time*.

What is a neuter verb? Give an example. 450.
How many kinds of verbs are there, and what are they? 438.
XXXVIII. What is the meaning of mood? 166.
What is *mood*? 451.
What is the meaning of *indicative*? 452.
What is the indicative mood used for? Give an example. 452.
What is the meaning of *potential*? 212.
What is the potential mood used for? Give an example. 453.
What is the meaning of *subjunctive*? 454.
In what mood is, "If he desire it?" 455.

How is the term *subjunctive* limited 455.
What is the subjunctive mood used for? 456.
How many different forms has it? 457. Give an example of each. 457.
In what tense are the verbs *be* and *is*? 457.
In what mood is each with the conjunction *if* before it? 457.
What does, "If he be studious," mean, as it respects time? 458.
What tense, then, is referred to? 458
What does, "If he is poor," mean, in respect to time? 459.
What idea, then, is implied in the one form? 460.
What two ideas in the other form? 460

461. The verb *is* corresponds with the common form of the verb *to be*, in the indicative mood, present tense; as, "I am, you are, he is:"— we will, therefore, when the verb is varied as usual, call it the *common* form of the subjunctive mood; and when the verb is not varied in the different persons, we will call it the *subjunctive* form, since this form is peculiar to this mood. You should here be informed that this distinction relates only to the present tense, it being customary to vary the terminations of the verb in the remaining tenses, as usual.

462. The following general rules will direct you in the proper use of the subjunctive mood:

463. When any verb in the subjunctive mood, present tense, has a reference to future time, we should use the

SUBJUNCTIVE FORM.

Present Tense.

464.   *Singular.*   *Plural.*
1. If I love.   1. If we love.
2. If thou *or* you love.   2. If ye *or* you love.
3. If he love.   3. If they love.

465. When a verb in the subjunctive mood, present tense, has no reference to future time, we should use the

COMMON FORM.

Singular.   *Plural.*
1. If I love.   1. If we love.
2. If thou lovest, *or* ⎫   2. If ye love, *or* ⎫
   If you love.   ⎬   If you love.   ⎬
3. If he loves.   3. If they love.

466. Other conjunctions, besides *if*, are used before the subjunctive mood. *If* is perhaps used most frequently, because it implies doubt more strongly than most others.

467. By the foregoing, you may perceive that when the verb is in the subjunctive form, some auxiliary verb is always understood; as, "He will not be pardoned unless he repent," that is, "unless he will repent;" "If thou ever return, thou shouldst be thankful," that is, "if thou shouldst ever return."

468. A verb in the indicative mood is converted into the subjunctive, common form, simply by placing a conjunction, implying doubt, before it; as, "I walk," the indicative mood, becomes subjunctive by prefixing *if;* thus, "If I walk."

469. In like manner, a verb in the potential may be changed to the subjunctive; as, "I can go," is the potential; "If I can go," the subjunctive.

470. Of the IMPERATIVE MOOD. When I say, "John, mind your book," I command John to do something; and because *imperative* means *commanding*, we say that *mind*, in the phrase above, is in the imperative mood.

With what does the verb *is* correspond? 461.
How is the verb varied in the common form of the subjunctive mood? 461.
Why called common? How varied in the subjunctive form? Why called subjunctive? 461.
How is this distinction limited? 461.
How are the remaining tenses varied? 461.
When do we use the subjunctive form? 463.
Will you conjugate the verb *love* in this form, in the present tense? 464.
When do we use the common form? 465.
Why is the conjunction *if* used most frequently in the subjunctive mood? 466.

What does, "He will not be pardoned unless he repent," mean? 467.
What, then, is understood? 467.
"If thou ever return, thou shouldst be thankful:" what does this mean? 467.
What, then, is understood? 467.
What is always understood in this form? 467.
How may a verb in the indicative mood be converted into the subjunctive? 468.
How can the potential be changed to the subjunctive? Give an example. 469.
In what mood is, "John, mind your studies?" Why? 470.
What is the meaning of *imperative*? 470.

MOOD. 65

471. This mood, for reasons assigned before, (214.) embraces the following particulars:

1. *Command;* as, "John, sit up."
2. *Entreaty;* as, "Do visit me."
3. *Exhorting;* as, "Remember my counsel."
4. *Permitting;* as, "Go in peace."

472. The imperative mood, then, is used for commanding, entreating, exhorting, or permitting.

473. The application of this mood is limited to the second person; as, "John, come to me;" because, in uttering a command, making an entreaty, &c. we must necessarily address some one; hence, you can see the reason why this mood has but one person, viz. the second.

474. We cannot, with any propriety, command a person to-day, or in present time, to do any thing in past time, yesterday for instance; consequently a verb in this mood cannot have any past tense.

475. When I command a person to do any thing, the performance of the command must take place in a period of time subsequent to that of the command; that is, in future time; but the command itself must, from the very nature of the case, take place in present time: this mood, therefore, cannot, strictly speaking, have any future tense: hence,

476. A verb in the imperative mood must be in the present tense, and in the second person.

477. Of the INFINITIVE MOOD. In the phrases, "John begins to sing," "The boys begin to sing," "Thou beginnest to sing," you perceive that the verb *to sing* is not varied to correspond with the number and person of its different agents, *John, the boys,* and *thou:* hence, *to sing* is said not to be limited either by person or number.

478. This mood, then, is properly denominated *infinitive*, signifying *not limited:* hence,

479. The infinitive mood is used to express an action not limited either by person or number.

480. *To,* the usual sign of this mood, is sometimes understood; as, "Let me go," instead of, "Let me *to* go;" "I heard him say it," for, "I heard him *to* say it." This little word *to,* when used before verbs in this manner, is not a preposition, but forms a part of the verb, and, in parsing, should be so considered.

481. From the foregoing, it appears that there are five moods — the indicative, the imperative, the potential, the subjunctive, and the infinitive.

How many particulars does this mood embrace? 471. Why so many? 214.
What, then, is the imperative mood used for? 472. Give an example of commanding? one of entreating? one of exhorting? one of permitting? 471.
How many persons has this mood? 473.
What person is it? 473.
Has this mood any past tense? Why? 474.
When I command a person, when, if at all, must the performance of the command take place? 475.
When, or in what time, must the command itself be given? 475.
Has this mood, then, any future tense? 475.
How many tenses, then, has it? How many persons? 476.

What is the meaning of *infinitive*? 478.
In what mood is *sing*, in the phrases "John begins to sing," "The boys begin to sing," "Thou beginnest to sing?" 477, 478.
In what particulars is this mood reckoned not to be limited? 477.
What, then, is the infinitive mood used for? 479.
What is the usual sign of this mood? 480.
Is it always expressed? Give an example. 480
How is the sign *to* to be parsed? 480.
Why parsed with the verb? 480.
How many moods are there, and what are they? 481.

XXXIX. OF TENSE.

482. The *present tense* expresses what is now taking place, as, "John swims."

483. This tense is often employed to express the actions of persons long since dead; as, "Seneca reasons and moralizes well."

484. The present tense, preceded by the words *when, before, after, as won as*, &c., is sometimes used to point out the relative time of a future ction; as, "When he arrives, he will hear the news."

485. This tense is elegantly applied to qualities and things which are in their nature unchangeable; as, "Truth is eternal;" "William boldly asserted there was no God;" properly, "*is* no God."

486. In animated (1.) historical narrations, (2.) this tense is sometimes used for the imperfect; as, "He *enters* the territory of the peaceable inhabitants; he fights and conquers, takes an immense booty, which he divides among his soldiers, and returns home to enjoy an empty triumph."

487. The *imperfect tense* expresses what took place in time past, however distant; as, "John died."

488. The *perfect tense* expresses what has taken place, and conveys an allusion to the present time; as, "I have finished my letter."

489. When any particular period of past time is specified or alluded to, we use the imperfect tense; as, "John wrote yesterday;" but when no particular past time is specified, we use the perfect tense; as, "I have read Virgil many times."

490. The perfect tense and the imperfect tense both denote a thing that is past; but the former denotes it in such a manner that there is still actually remaining some part of the time to slide away, wherein we declare the thing has been done; whereas the imperfect denotes the thing or action past, in such a manner, that nothing remains of that time in which it was done. If we speak of the present century, we say, "Philosophers *have made* great discoveries in the present century;" but if we speak of the last century, we say, "Philosophers *made* great discoveries in the last century." — "He has been much afflicted this year." "I have this week read the king's proclamation." "I have heard great news this morning." In these instances, *He has been, I have read,* and *heard,* denote things that are past;

XXXIX. What is the meaning of *present?* 173.
What does the present tense express? 482. Give an example. 482.
"Seneca reasons well." What tense is employed here? Why? 483.
In the phrase, "When he arrives," future time is alluded to: why, then, is the present employed? 484.
Do we say, "There is," or, "there was no God?" Why? 485.
What is the meaning of *animated?* 486.
Meaning of *narrations?* 486.
"He enters the territory," &c. Why is the present tense used? 486.
What is the meaning of *imperfect?* 181.
How came this term to be used, to denote an action past and finished?*
What does the imperfect tense express? 487. Give an example. 487.
Meaning of *perfect?*†

What does the perfect tense express? Give an example. 488.
"John wrote yesterday." What tense is the verb in here? 489.
Why is this tense used? 489.
"I have read Virgil many times." Why is the perfect tense used here? 489.
What do both the perfect and imperfect denote? 490.
How does the former denote it? 490.
How does the latter? 490.
Do we say, "Philosophers *made*," or. "*have made*, great discoveries in the present century?" Why? 490.
Which tense do we use in speaking of the last century? 490. Give an example. 490.
"I have this week read the king's proclamation." "I have heard great news this morning." Which are the verbs used in these two sentences? 490.

(1.) Lively.
* See question to 182.

(2.) Descriptions, or telling what has been done. Finished, or complete.

but they occurred in this year, in this week, and to-day; and still there remains a part of this year, week, and day, whereof I speak.

490—1. In general, the perfect tense may be applied wherever the action is connected with the present time, by the actual existence, either of the author or of the work, though it may have been performed many centuries ago; but if neither the author nor the work now remains, it cannot be used. We may say, " Cicero *has written* orations;" but we cannot say, " Cicero *has written* poems ;" because the orations are in being, but the poems are lost. Speaking of priests in general, we may say, " They *have*, in all ages, *claimed* great powers;" because the general order of the priesthood still exists: but if we speak of the Druids, as any particular order of priests, which does not now exist, we cannot use this tense. We cannot say, " The Druid priests *have claimed* great powers ;" but must say, " The Druid priests *claimed* great powers ;" because that order is now totally extinct.

491. The *pluperfect tense* expresses what had taken place at some past time mentioned; as, " I had finished my letter before my father returned."

492. The *first future tense* expresses what will take place; as, " John will come."

493. The *second future* expresses what will have taken place, at or before some future time mentioned; as, " I shall have finished my business before the steam-boat starts."

494. Tense is the distinction of time, and admits of six variations, namely—the present, the imperfect, the perfect, the pluperfect, and the first and second future tenses.

XL. OF PARTICIPLES.

495. In the phrase, "I found a man laboring in the field," the word *laboring* shows what the man was doing, and therefore resembles a verb. When I say, "The laboring man should not be wronged," *laboring* is joined to the noun *man*, to describe it, and therefore resembles an adjective.

496. The word *laboring*, then, partakes of the nature of two different parts of speech; and since *participle* signifies *partaking of*, we will call such words as *laboring*, participles.

What do they denote? When did these things occur? 490.
To what may the perfect tense in general be applied? What exception is mentioned? 490—1.
Do we say, " Cicero *wrote*," or, " *has written*, orations?" " Cicero *wrote*," or, " *has written*," poems?" Why? 490—1.
In speaking of priests, in general, why do we say, " They have in all ages claimed great powers?" 490—1.
Can we say, " The Druid priests *have claimed* great powers?" What should we say? Why? 490—1.
What is the meaning of *pluperfect*? 186.
What does the pluperfect tense express? 491. Give an example. 491.
Meaning of *future*? 177.
What does the first future express?

Give an example. 492. Why called first future?*
What does the second future express? Give an example. 493.
How many tenses are there in all, and what are they? 494.
In what mood is, " He runs?" Why? 452. " Does he run?" Why? 452. " I may run?" Why? 453. " Should I have studied?" Why? 453. " If he accept?" Why? 456. " If he accepts?" Why? 456. " To sing?" Why? 479.
In what tense is, " He sings?" Why? 482. ", id he sing?" Why? 487. " He has read?" 488. Why? " Had he written?" 491. Why? " Shall he go?" 492. " I shall have gone?" Why? 493
XL. What parts of speech does *laboring* resemble? Give an example. 495.
What is the meaning of *participle*? 496.

---

* See question to 1-1

497. All participles are derived from verbs; thus, from *labor* comes *laboring ;* from *beat, beating ; rejoice, rejoicing,* &c.: hence,

498. The participle is a word derived from a verb, and partakes of the nature of a verb and adjective.

499. When I say, "John is writing," the participle *writing* shows what John is now doing, but has not finished; *writing,* then, may be called a present participle: hence,

500. The present participle expresses what is now taking place, but not finished.

501—1. This participle always ends in *ing ;* as, *sinning, fighting, weeping, loving,* &c. There are many words of this termination, which are not participles; as, *morning evening,* which are nouns; *uninteresting, unsatisfying,* which are adjectives. The fact that these cannot be formed from verbs will furnish you with a certain rule for distinguishing the participle from all other words of the same termination; as, for instance. *uninteresting,* we know, is not a participle, because there is no such verb as *uninterest,* from which to form it.

501. "The letter is written." Here the participle *written* shows that the act of writing is past and finished; it may then be called a perfect participle: hence,

502. The perfect participle expresses what is past and finished.

502—1. This participle may always be distinguished by its making sense with *having ;* thus, *having written, having sung,* &c. Here *written* and *sung* are perfect participles.

503. "John, having written his letter, sealed it." Here you doubtless perceive that the act of writing took place before that of sealing ; also, that the participle is composed of two words, *having* and *written ;* it may then be called a *compound participle,* and because it denotes also an action past and finished, it may very properly be called a compound perfect participle: hence,

504. The compound perfect participle expresses what took place before something else mentioned.

504—1. This participle is formed by placing the present participle *having* before the perfect participle of any verb ; as, *having fought, having ciphered*

XLI. FORMATION OF THE PASSIVE VERB.

505. *Struck* is a perfect participle. from the verb *strike,* and this you know, because it makes sense joined with *having ;* as, *having struck.*

From what are all participles derived?
497. Give an example. 497.
What is a participle? 498.
When I say, "John is writing," what does *writing* show? 499.
What, then, may it be called? 499.
What, then, is a present participle? 500.
What does this participle always end in? 500—1. Give an example. 500—1.
Are all words ending in *ing* participles? Give an example of nouns of this termination? of adjectives? 500—1.
How, then, can the participle be distinguished? Give an example. 500—1.
"The letter is written." What does the participle *written* show here? What, then, may it be called? 501.
What is a perfect participle? 502.
How may this participle always be known? Give an example. 502—1.

Having written, having sung. Which are the perfect participles here? 502.
"John, having written his letter, sealed it." Which took place first, the writing or sealing? 503.
Of what is this participle composed? 503.
What, then, may it be called? 503.
What does *having written* denote in reference to time and action? 503.
What may it thence be called? 503.
What does a compound perfect participle express? 504.
How is this participle formed? 504. Give an example. 504.
XLI. *Striking, struck, having struck.* Here are three different participles: can you tell which is the present? Why? 500. Perfect? Why? 502. Compound perfect? Why? 503.
What kind of a participle is *struck?* 505. How do you know this? 505.

506. *Is*, you doubtless recollect, is a variation of the verb *to be;* as, "I am, you are, he is:" now, by joining *is* with *struck*, we can form the passive verb *is struck;* "John strikes Joseph," is active; but, "Joseph is struck by John," is passive.

507. In these two examples, you perceive that the sense of each is the same: hence, by means of the passive verb, we are enabled to express, in a different form, the precise meaning of the active, which, you will oftentimes find, contributes not a little to the variety and harmony of the language.

508. By examining the conjugation of the verb *to be,* you will discover that it has, in all, ten variations: viz. *am, art, is, are, was, wast, were, been, be,* and *being.* Every passive verb must be composed of one of these ten variations, and the perfect participle of any active transitive verb. Thus, taking *was,* and joining it with the perfect participle of the verb *beat,* namely, *beaten,* we form the passive verb *was beaten,* to which prefixing an object, or nominative case, we have the phrase, "William was beaten."

509. It is a fact worthy to be remembered, that the passive verb always retains the same mood, tense, number, and person, that the verb *to be* has, before it is incorporated with the participle; thus, "He has been," is the indicative perfect, third person singular; then, "He has been rejected," is likewise the indicative perfect, third person singular, passive. It cannot, therefore, be difficult to tell the mood, tense, number, and person, of any passive verb, if you are familiar with the conjugation of the verb *to be.*

From the foregoing particulars, we derive the following general rule:

510. All passive verbs are formed by adding the perfect participle of any active-transitive verb to the neuter verb *to be.*

XLII. OF THE AUXILIARY VERB.

511. Auxiliary verbs are those by the help of which the principal verbs are conjugated.

512. The auxiliary verbs are *may, can, must, might, could, would, should,* and *shall.* The following are sometimes auxiliaries, and sometimes principal verbs: *do, be, have,* and *will.*

513. When, in the formation of any tense, we use an auxiliary verb, that tense is called a compound one; and the tense formed by the principal verb alone is called a simple tense.

XLIII. SIGNS OF THE MOODS.

514. The indicative mood may be known by the sense, or by its having no sign except in asking a question; as, "Who comes here?"

Of what verb is the verb *is* a variation? 506.
Will you form a passive verb with *is* and *struck?* 506.
"John strikes Joseph." How may the sense of this sentence be expressed by a passive verb? 506.
What advantage does the use of the passive verb often afford us? 507.
To what does it contribute? 507.
How many variations has the verb *to be* in all? 508. What are they? 508.
What will always compose one part of a passive verb? 508. What the other part? 508.

What fact is mentioned as worthy of notice? 509.
What mood, tense, number, and person, is, "He has been?" 509. Is, "He has been rejected?" 509.
What will make the mood, tense, &c. of passive verbs familiar? 509.
How are all passive verbs formed? 510.
XLII. What is the meaning of auxiliary? 196.
What are auxiliary verbs? 511.
Will you name them? 512.
What verbs are used both as auxiliary and principal verbs? 512.
XLIII. What is the sign of the indicative mood? 514. Give an example. 514.

515. The potential mood has for its signs the auxiliaries *may, can, must, might, could, would,* and *should;* as, "I could love," &c.

516. The subjunctive mood has usually for its signs the conjunctions *if, though, unless, except, whether,* and *lest;* as, "Unless he repent," &c.

517. The infinitive mood has usually for its sign the word *to;* as, *to sing.*

518. The imperative mood may be distinguished by its always being in the second person, and by its agreement with *thou,* or *ye,* or *you;* as, "Depart thou," &c.

XLIV. SIGNS OF THE TENSES OF THE INDICATIVE.

519. The present tense has for its sign the first form of the verb; as, *weep, remain,* &c.; excepting the occasional use of *do;* as, "I do learn."

520. The imperfect tense has no auxiliary for a sign, except *did,* which is sometimes used. If, however, the verb is not in the present tense, and has no auxiliary, it follows that it is in the imperfect; as, "I fought."

521. The perfect tense has for its sign the word *have;* as, *have loved.*

522. The pluperfect has for its sign *had;* as, *had loved.*

523. The first future has for its sign *shall* or *will;* as, *shall* or *will love.*

524. The second future has for its sign *shall have* or *will have;* as, *shall have loved,* or *will have loved.*

525. The indicative mood has six tenses.

526. The subjunctive mood has six tenses.

527. The potential mood has four tenses.

528. The infinitive mood has two tenses.

529. The imperative mood has one tense.

What is the sign of the potential mood? 515. Give an example. 515.

What is the sign of the subjunctive mood? 516. Give an example. 516.

What is the sign of the infinitive mood? 517. Give an example. 517.

What is the sign of the imperative? 518. Give an example. 518.

XLIV. What is the sign of the present indicative? 519. Give an example. 519.

Sign of the imperfect? 520. Give an example. 520.

Sign of the perfect? 521. Give an example. 521.

Sign of the pluperfect? 522. Give an example. 522.

Sign of the first future? 523. Give an example. 523.

Sign of the second future? 524. Give an example. 524.

How many tenses has the indicative mood? 525.

How many the subjunctive? 526.

How many the potential? 527.

How many the infinitive? 528.

How many the imperative? 529.

XLV. CONJUGATION OF VERBS.

530. When I ask you to raise your *voice*, in reading, you readily understand what I mean by *voice*; but in grammar, its application is somewhat peculiar. Grammatically considered, it refers to the active and passive nature of verbs.

531. The CONJUGATION of a verb is the regular combination and arrangement of its several numbers, persons, moods, and tenses.

532. The CONJUGATION of an active verb is styled the ACTIVE VOICE, and that of a passive verb the PASSIVE VOICE.

533. Verbs are called REGULAR, when they form their imperfect tense of the indicative mood, and their perfect participle, by the addition of *ed* to the verb in the present tense, or *d* only when the verb ends in *e*; as,

Pres. Tense.	*Imp. Tense.*	*Perf. Participle.*
I favour.	I favoured.	Favoured.
I love.	I loved.	Loved.

534. When a verb does not form its imperfect tense and perfect participle in this manner, it is called an IRREGULAR VERB; as,

Pres. Tense.	*Imp. Tense.*	*Perf. Participle.*
I am.	I was.	Been.

535. The regular verb *love*, and the irregular verb *to be*, are conjugated as follows:—

CONJUGATION.

TO LOVE AND *TO BE.*

ACTIVE AND PASSIVE VOICE CONTRASTED.

INDICATIVE MOOD.

PRESENT TENSE.

ACTIVE VOICE.	PASSIVE VOICE.	NEUTER.
Singular.	*Singular.*	*Singular.*
1 *Pers.* I love.	1 *Pers.* I am loved.	1 *Pers.* I am.
2 *Pers.* You love.	2 *Pers.* You are loved.	2 *Pers.* You are.
3 *Pers.* He loves.	3 *Pers.* He is loved.	3 *Pers.* He is.
Plural.	*Plural.*	*Plural.*
1 *Pers.* We love.	1 *Pers.* We are loved.	1 *Pers.* We are.
2 *Pers.* You love.	2 *Pers.* You are loved.	2 *Pers.* You are.
3 *Pers.* They love.	3 *Pers.* They are loved.	3 *Pers.* They are.

XLV. What does *voice* mean in grammar? 530.
Meaning of *conjugation*? 217.
What is the conjugation of an active verb styled? 532.
What the conjugation of a passive verb? 532.
When are verbs called regular? 533.
Give an example. 533.
Will you repeat after me the present tense, and name the imperfect tense and perfect participle, of the verbs *favour? love?* 533.
When is a verb called irregular? 534.
Give an example. 534.

ENGLISH GRAMMAR

IMPERFECT TENSE.

Singular.
1. I loved.
2. You loved.
3. He loved.
Plural.
1. We loved.
2. You loved.
3. They loved.

Singular.
1. I was loved.
2. You were loved.
3. He was loved.
Plural.
1. We were loved.
2. You were loved.
3. They were loved.

Singular.
1. I was.
2. You were.
3. He was.
Plural.
1. We were.
2. You were.
3. They were.

PERFECT TENSE.

Singular.
1. I have loved.
2. You have loved.
3. He has loved.
Plural.
1. We have loved.
2. You have loved.
3. They have loved.

Singular.
1. I have been loved.
2. You have been loved.
3. He has been loved.
Plural.
1. We have been loved.
2. You have been loved.
3. They have been loved.

Singular.
1. I have been.
2. You have been.
3. He has been.
Plural.
1. We have been.
2. You have been.
3. They have been.

PLUPERFECT TENSE.

Singular.
1. I had loved.
2. You had loved.
3. He had loved.
Plural.
1. We had loved.
2. You had loved.
3. They had loved.

Singular.
1. I had been loved.
2. You had been loved.
3. He had been loved.
Plural.
1. We had been loved.
2. You had been loved.
3. They had been loved.

Singular.
1. I had been.
2. You had been.
3. He had been.
Plural.
1. We had been.
2. You had been.
3. They had been

FIRST FUTURE TENSE.

Singular.
1. I shall *or* will love.
2. You shall *or* will love.
3. He shall *or* will love.
Plural.
1. We shall *or* will love.
2. You shall *or* will love.
3. They shall *or* will love.

Singular.
1. I shall *or* will be loved.
2. You shall *or* will be loved.
3. He shall *or* will be loved.
Plural.
1. We shall *or* will be loved.
2. You shall *or* will be loved.
3. They shall *or* will be loved.

Singular.
1. I shall *or* will be.
2. You shall *or* will be.
3. He shall *or* will be.
Plural.
1. We shall *or* will be.
2. You shall *or* will be.
3. They shall *or* will be.

SECOND FUTURE TENSE.

Singular.
1. I shall have loved.
2. You will have loved.
3. He will have loved.
Plural.
1. We shall have loved.
2. You will have loved.
3. They will have loved.

Singular.
1. I shall have been loved.
2. You will have been loved.
3. He will have been loved.
Plural.
1. We shall have been loved.
2. You will have been loved.
3. They will have been loved.

Singular.
1. I shall have been.
2. You will have been.
3. He will have been.
Plural.
1. We shall have been.
2. You will have been.
3. They will have been.

Will you conjugate *love* in the present tense, active voice, indicative mood? 835. In the imperfect? perfect? plu perfect? first future? second future? present passive? imperfect? perfect? pluperfect? first future? second future?

TENSES.

POTENTIAL MOOD.

PRESENT TENSE.

Singular.
1. I may *or* can love.
2. You may *or* can love.
3. He may *or* can love.

Plural.
1. We may *or* can love.
2. You may *or* can love.
3. They may *or* can love.

Singular.
1. I may *or* can be loved.
2. You may *or* can be loved.
3. He may *or* can be loved.

Plural.
1. We may *or* can be loved.
2. You may *or* can be loved.
3. They may *or* can be loved.

Singular.
1. I may *or* can be.
2. You may *or* can be.
3. He may *or* can be.

Plural.
1. We may *or* can be.
2. You may *or* can be.
3. They may *or* can be.

IMPERFECT TENSE.

Singular.
1. I might, could, would, *or* should love.
2. You might, could, would, *or* should love.
3. He might, could, would, *or* should love.

Plural.
1. We might, could, would, *or* should love.
2. You might, could, would, *or* should love.
3. They might, could, would, *or* should love.

Singular.
1. I might, could, would, *or* should be loved.
2. You might, could, would, *or* should be loved.
3. He might, could, would, *or* should be loved.

Plural.
1. We might, could, would, *or* should be loved.
2. You might, could, would, *or* should be loved.
3. They might, could, would, *or* should be loved.

Singular.
1. I might, could, would, *or* should be.
2. You might, could, would, *or* should be.
3. He might, could, would, *or* should be.

Plural.
1. We might, could, would, *or* should be.
2. You might, could, would, *or* should be.
3. They might, could, would, *or* should be.

PERFECT TENSE.

Singular.
1. I may *or* can have loved.
2. You may *or* can have loved.
3. He may *or* can have loved.

Plural.
1. We may *or* can have loved.
2. You may *or* can have loved.
3. They may *or* can have loved.

Singular.
1. I may *or* can have been loved.
2. You may *or* can have been loved.
3. He may *or* can have been loved.

Plural.
1. We may *or* can have been loved.
2. You may *or* can have been loved.
3. They may *or* can have been loved.

Singular.
1. I may *or* can have been.
2. You may *or* can have been.
3. He may *or* can have been.

Plural.
1. We may *or* can have been.
2. You may *or* can have been.
3. They may *or* can have been.

Will you conjugate the verb *to be*, or *am*, in the present? the imperfect? perfect? pluperfect? first future? second future?

Will you name the first person singular, of the present indicative, active and passive, of *love*, and the first person singular of the verb *to be*?

The second person in like manner? the third? the first person plural? second person plural? third? first person singular, imperfect? second person? third? first person plural? second person plural? third? first person singular, perfect? second person? third? first person plural? second? third?

PLUPERFECT TENSE.

Singular.
1. I might, could, would, or should have loved.
2. You might, could, would, or should have loved.
3. He might, could, would, or should have loved.

Plural.
1. We might, could, would, or should have loved.
2. You might, could, would, or should have loved.
3. They might, could, would, or should have loved.

Singular.
1. I might, could, would, or should have been loved.
2. You might, could, would, or should have been loved.
3. He might, could, would, or should have been loved.

Plural.
1. We might, could, would, or should have been loved.
2. You might, could, would, or should have been loved.
3. They might, could, would, or should have been loved.

Singular.
1. I might, could, would, or should have been.
2. You might, could, would, or should have been.
3. He might, could, would, or should have been.

Plural.
1. We might, could, would, or should have been.
2. You might, could, would, or should have been.
3. They might, could, would, or should have been.

SUBJUNCTIVE MOOD.

PRESENT TENSE.

Common Form.

Singular.
1. If I love.
2. If you love.
3. If he loves.

Plural.
1. If we love.
2. If you love.
3. If they love.

Singular.
1. If I am loved.
2. If you are loved.
3. If he is loved.

Plural.
1. If we are loved.
2. If you are loved.
3. If they are loved.

Singular.
1. If I am.
2. If you are.
3. If he is.

Plural.
1. If we are.
2. If you are.
3. If they are.

Subjunctive Form.

Singular.
1. If I love.
2. If you love.
3. If he love.

Plural.
1. If we love.
2. If you love.
3. If they love.

Singular.
1. If I be loved.
2. If you be loved.
3. If he be loved.

Plural.
1. If we be loved.
2. If you be loved.
3. If they be loved.

Singular.
1. If I be.
2. If you be.
3. If he be.

Plural.
1. If we be.
2. If you be.
3. If they be.

IMPERFECT TENSE.

Common Form.

Singular.
1. If I loved.
2. If you loved.
3. If he loved.

Plural.
1. If we loved.
2. If you loved.
3. If they loved.

Singular.
1. If I was loved.
2. If you were loved.
3. If he was loved.

Plural.
1. If we were loved.
2. If you were loved.
3. If they were loved.

Singular.
1. If I was.
2. If you were.
3. If he was.

Plural.
1. If we were.
2. If you were.
3. If they were.

Will you conjugate *love* in like manner, through each person and voice of the pluperfect? first and second futures? present potential? imperfect? perfect? pluperfect? present subjunctive, common form? subjunctive form? imperfect, common form? subjunctive form? perfect? pluperfect? first and second futures?

Will you conjugate *love* in the present indicative active? imperfect? perfect? pluperfect? first and second futures? present passive? imperfect? perfect? pluperfect? first and second futures? present indicative of *to be*? imperfect? perfect? pluperfect? first and second futures?

TENSES.

Subjunctive Form.

Singular.
1. If I loved.
2. If you loved.
3. If he loved.

Plural.
1. If we loved.
2. If you loved.
3. If they loved.

Singular.
1. If I were loved.
2. If you were loved.
3. If he were loved.

Plural.
1. If we were loved.
2. If you were loved.
3. If they were loved.

Singular.
1. If I were
2. If you were.
3. If he were.

Plural.
1. If we were.
2. If you were.
3. If they were.

The remaining tenses are all of the Common Form.

PERFECT TENSE.

Singular.
1. If I have loved.
2. If you have loved.
3. If he has loved.

Plural.
1. If we have loved.
2. If you have loved.
3. If they have loved.

Singular.
1. If I have been loved.
2. If you have been loved.
3. If he has been loved.

Plural.
1. If we have been loved.
2. If you have been loved.
3. If they have been loved.

Singular.
1. If I have been.
2. If you have been.
3. If he has been.

Plural.
1. If we have been.
2. If you have been.
3. If they have been.

PLUPERFECT TENSE.

Singular.
1. If I had loved.
2. If you had loved.
3. If he had loved.

Plural.
1. If we had loved.
2. If you had loved.
3. If they had loved.

Singular.
1. If I had been loved.
2. If you had been loved.
3. If he had been loved.

Plural.
1. If we had been loved.
2. If you had been loved.
3. If they had been loved.

Singular.
1. If I had been.
2. If you had been.
3. If he had been.

Plural.
1. If we had been.
2. If you had been.
3. If they had been.

FIRST FUTURE TENSE.

Singular.
1. If I shall *or* will love.
2. If you shall *or* will love.
3. If he shall *or* will love.

Singular.
1. If I shall *or* will be loved.
2. If you shall *or* will be loved.
3. If he shall *or* will be loved.

Singular.
1. If I shall *or* will be.
2. If you shall *or* will be.
3. If he shall *or* will be.

Will you conjugate *love* through each person of the present indicative active? passive? the neuter verb *to be?* also in the imperfect? perfect? pluperfect? first and second futures? present potential? imperfect? perfect? pluperfect? present subjunctive, in both forms? perfect? pluperfect? first and second futures? What is the present infinitive active of *love?* present passive? present of *to be?* perfect active of *love?* perfect passive? perfect of *to be?* present participle active of *love?* present passive? perfect of *be?* perfect of *love?* perfect of *to be?* compound perfect of *love*, in the active? in the passive of *to be?*

In what voice and mood is, "I love?" "They love?" "They are loved?" "Are they loved?" "I do love?" What is the force of *do?* In what voice and mood is, "The man loved?" "He has loved?"

"He has been loved?" "Has he been loved?" "She had loved?" "She had been loved?" "We shall love?" "We shall be loved?" "Shall I have been loved?" "May I love?" "May I be loved?" "She may have loved?" "She may have been loved?" "If I love?" "If he be loved?" "If he is loved?" "If I love?" "If I were loved?" "If I was loved?"

In what tense is, "They love?" "Ye are loved?" "She did love?" "We were loved?" "They shall love?" "They shall be loved?" "I may be loved?" "If she has been loved?"

In what number and person is, "I love?" "We love?" "He does love?" "The man did love?" "The men were loved?" "If he love?" "If I was?" "If I were?" "If ye have been?" "If ye have loved?" "You may be loved?"

ENGLISH GRAMMAR

Plural.	*Plural.*	*Plural.*
1. If we shall *or* will love.	1. If we shall *or* will be loved.	1. If we shall *or* will be.
2. If you shall *or* will love.	2. If you shall *or* will be loved.	2. If you shall *or* will be.
3. If they shall *or* will love.	3. If they shall *or* will be loved.	3. If they shall *or* will be.

SECOND FUTURE TENSE.

Singular.	*Singular.*	*Singular.*
1. If I shall have loved.	1. If I shall have been loved.	1. If I shall have been.
2. If you shall have loved.	2. If you shall have been loved.	2. If you shall have been.
3. If he shall have loved.	3. If he shall have been loved.	3. If he shall have been.
Plural.	*Plural.*	*Plural.*
1. If we shall have loved.	1. If we shall have been loved.	1. If we shall have been.
2. If you shall have loved.	2. If you shall have been loved.	2. If you shall have been.
3. If they shall have loved.	3. If they shall have been loved.	3. If they shall have been.

IMPERATIVE MOOD.
PRESENT TENSE.

Singular.	*Singular.*	*Singular.*
2. Love you, *or* do you love.	2. Be you loved, *or* do you be loved.	2. Be you, *or* do you be.
Plural.	*Plural.*	*Plural.*
2. Love you, *or* do you love.	2. Be you loved, *or* do you be loved.	2. Be you, *or* do you be.

INFINITIVE MOOD.

Pres. To love.	*Pres.* To be loved.	*Pres.* To be.
Perf. To have loved.	*Perf.* To have been loved.	*Perf.* To have been.

PARTICIPLES.

Pres. Loving.	*Pres.* Being loved.	*Pres.* Being.
Perf. Loved.	*Perf.* Loved.	*Perf.* Been.
Compound Perf. Having loved.	*Compound Perf.* Having been loved.	*Compound Perf.* Having been.

536. For the benefit of those who wish to retain the pronoun *thou*, in the conjugation of verbs, the following synopsis is given. The pupil can take it separately, or be taught it in connection with the other persons of the verb, by substituting *thou* for *you*, in the foregoing conjugation.

Is *love*, as, "They love," a regular or irregular verb? why? 533. active or passive? 439. What mood is it in? why? 452. tense? why? 482. number? person? What does *love* agree with? Rule VII.

Is *are*, as, "They are," a regular or irregular verb? why? 534. passive or neuter? why? 450. What mood is it in? why? 452. tense? why? 482. number? person? Rule for its agreement? VII.

What is the present imperative of *love*? present infinitive?

What mood and tense is, "Love you?" is, "To have been loved?"

Will you conjugate *learn* in the present indicative active? passive? perfect active? perfect passive? present potential active? passive? imperfect active?

passive? imperative present active? passive? perfect infinitive active? passive? present subjunctive active in both forms? passive? perfect infinitive? future active passive?

What kind of verb (that is, regular or irregular,) what voice, mood, tense, number, and person is, "I sing?" "We are formed?" "He is?" "You are determined?" "It rains?" "It has happened?" "The man was respected?" "The boys did study?" "If he improve?" "Unless he repent?" "Although she be disappointed?" "He may depart?" "Depart now?" "To love?" "To sing?" "To be sung?" "To rejoice?" "To have wept?" "To have been seen?" "To have been found?"

TENSES. 77

Synopsis with THOU.

INDICATIVE MOOD.

Pres. Thou lovest. Thou art loved. Thou art.
Imp. Thou lovedst. Thou wast loved. Thou wast.
Perf. Thou hast loved. Thou hast been loved. Thou hast been.
Plup. Thou hadst loved. Thou hadst been loved. Thou hadst been.
1 *Fut.* Thou shalt or wilt love. Thou shalt or wilt be loved. Thou shalt or wilt be.
2 *Fut.* Thou wilt have loved. Thou wilt have been loved. Thou wilt have been.

537.
POTENTIAL MOOD.

Pres. Thou mayst or canst love. Thou mayst or canst be loved. Thou mayst or canst be.
Imp. Thou mightst, couldst, wouldst, or shouldst love. Thou mightst, couldst, wouldst, or shouldst be loved. Thou mightst, couldst, wouldst, or shouldst be.
Perf. Thou mayst or canst have loved. Thou mayst or canst have been loved. Thou mayst or canst have been.
Plup. Thou mightst, couldst, wouldst, or shouldst have loved. Thou mightst, couldst, wouldst, or shouldst have been loved. Thou mightst, couldst, wouldst, or shouldst have been.

SUBJUNCTIVE MOOD.
538.   *Common Form.*
Pres. If thou lovest. If thou art loved. If thou art.
Imp. If thou lovedst. If thou wast loved. If thou wast.

539.   *Subjunctive Form.*
Pres. If thou love. If thou be loved. If thou be.
Imp. If thou loved. If thou wert loved. If thou wert.

540.   *Common Form.*
Perf. If thou hast loved. If thou hast been loved. If thou hast been.
Plup. If thou hadst loved. If thou hadst been loved. If thou hadst been.
1 *Fut.* If thou shalt or wilt love. If thou shalt or wilt be loved. If thou shalt or wilt be.
2 *Fut.* If thou shalt have loved. If thou shalt have been loved. If thou shalt have been.

Interrogative Form.
541.   INDICATIVE PRESENT.

Singular.   *Singular.*   *Singular.*
1. Do I love?   1. Am I loved?   1. Am I?
2. Do you love?   2. Are you loved?   2. Are you?
3. Does he love?   3. Is he loved?   3. Is he?
Plural.   *Plural.*   *Plural.*
1. Do we love?   1. Are we loved?   1. Are we?
2. Do you love?   2. Are you loved?   2. Are you?
3. Do they love?   3. Are they loved?   3. Are they?

542. You will find, on examination of the foregoing conjugation, that the tenses of the subjunctive are in every respect similar to the corresponding ones of the indicative, except the following, namely, the present and imperfect

Will you give the synopsis of *love* joined with *thou* through the indicative active? passive? Neuter verb *to be*? Will you name the synopsis of *learn* in the first person in the active voice, through each mood and tense? Will you repeat the two tenses of the infinitive and the three participles? Synopsis of *honor* in like manner through the passive? also the synopsis of the verb *to be*? Give the synopsis of *desire* in the active, like *love*; in the passive; verb *to be*; first person plural active; passive; *to be*; third person active; passive; *to be*. What mood does the subjunctive resemble in its tenses? 542

of the verb *to be*; the present and imperfect of the passive, the present and the second future active. The last, however, corresponds in termination, but not in formation. Among the exceptions should be reckoned the use of the conjunction *if*. There are instances, however, of the subjunctive form, when no conjunction is expressed, but in all such cases it is plainly understood; as, "Were I to go, he would not follow;" "Had he known me, he would have treated me differently;" that is, "If I were to go," and, "If he had known." Examples of this description are conjugated as follows:

SUBJUNCTIVE FORM.

543. IMPERFECT TENSE.

Singular.
1. Were I.
2. Were you.
3. Were he.

Plural.
1. Were we.
2. Were you.
3. Were they.

PLUPERFECT TENSE.

Singular.
1. Had I loved.
2. Had you loved.
3. Had he loved.

Plural.
1. Had we loved.
2. Had you loved.
3. Had they loved.

544. The second person singular of all verbs* formerly (1.) ended in *st*; as, "Thou hast," "Thou wast," &c. This form is still retained by that respectable class of persons denominated (2.) Friends, and in the Sacred (3.) Scriptures. (3.)

545. *Eth*, for the termination of the third person singular, obtained (4.) very generally till within a recent (5.) period, especially on grave (6.) and didactic (7.) subjects; as, "He that *hath* ears to hear, let him hear;" "Simple multiplication *teacheth* to repeat," &c. But the custom of the present day is decidedly (8.) against the usage. (9.)

546. The Scriptures abound (10.) with instances of the use of the pronoun *ye* for *you*; as, "Ye are the salt of the earth;" but it is scarcely to be met with in any standard works of modern date.

547. The following conjugation accords with the ancient usage of the verb.

INDICATIVE PRESENT.

Singular.
1. I love.
2. Thou lovest.
3. He loveth *or* loves.

Singular.
1. I am loved.
2. Thou art loved.
3. He is loved.

Singular.
1. I am.
2. Thou art.
3. He is.

What exceptions? 542.
How does the second future differ? 542.
Will you explain the difference? 542.
What is the sign of the subjunctive mood? 516. Is it always expressed? 542. Give an example. 542. Will you supply the conjunction?
Will you conjugate the verb *to be* in the subjunctive mood, imperfect tense, without its usual sign? In like manner conjugate *love* in the pluperfect.
Will you conjugate *love* in the present active, interrogative form? passive? neuter verb *to be*?
In what voice, mood, tense, number and person is, "Do I study?" "Did she study?" "Were they dismissed?" "Are we?"
In what did the second person singular of all verbs formerly end? 544. Give an example. 544.
Meaning of *formerly*? 544.

By whom is this termination still retained? 544. In what writings? 544.
Meaning of *Sacred Scriptures*? 544.
What form of the third person singular obtained till recently? 545. Give an example. 545.
Meaning of *obtained*? 545. Of *recent*? 545.
On what subjects was the termination *eth* used in writing? 545.
Meaning of *grave*? of *didactic*? 545.
In what writings do we find *ye* used for *you*? 546.
Is it common in modern works? 546.
Will you conjugate *love* in the present active, according to the ancient usage? 547. passive? neuter verb *to be*?
In what number and person is, "He hath?" "He hates?" "Thou lovest?" "Thou hast?" "He learneth?" "Ye learn?" "He rejoiceth?" "Thou art rejoiced?" "Thou art?" "He weepeth?"

* Excepting *art*.
(1.) Some time ago. (2.) Called. (3.) The Bible. (4.) Prevailed. (5.) Late. (6.) Serious (7.) Abounding in precepts or instructive. (8.) Positively. (9.) Use. (10.) Have many.

VERBS. 79

Plural.	*Plural.*	*Plural.*
1. We love.	1. We are loved.	1. We are.
2. Ye *or* you love.	2. Ye *or* you are loved.	2. Ye *or* you are.
3. They love.	3. They are loved.	3. They are.

548. ☞ For a further illustration of these obsolete conjugations, the learner is referred to those treatises on grammar in our schools, which *profess* to furnish him with a sure and infallible guide to the true and proper use of the English language.

RULE VI.
The nominative case governs the verb in number and person.

RULE VII.
A verb must agree with its nominative case in number and person.

RULE VIII.
Active-transitive verbs govern the objective case.

EXERCISES IN PARSING.
" *William was admired for his prudence.*"

549. *William* is a PROPER NOUN, of the THIRD PERSON, SINGULAR NUMBER, MASCULINE GENDER, and in the NOMINATIVE CASE to *was admired*, agreeably to RULE VI.
Was admired is a REGULAR PASSIVE VERB, from the verb *to admire* —" *Pres.* admire; *Imp.* admired; *Perf. part.* admired. 1. I was admired; 2. You were admired; 3. He *or* William was admired"— made in the INDICATIVE MOOD, IMPERFECT TENSE, THIRD PERSON, SINGULAR NUMBER, and agrees with *William*, according to RULE VII.
For is a PREPOSITION.
His is a PERSONAL PRONOUN, of the THIRD PERSON, SINGULAR NUMBER, MASCULINE GENDER, and agrees with *William*, according to RULE V. — " *Nom.* he; *Poss.* his"— made in the POSSESSIVE CASE, and governed by *prudence*, by RULE I.
Prudence is a COMMON NOUN, of the THIRD PERSON, SINGULAR NUMBER, NEUTER GENDER, OBJECTIVE CASE, and governed by *for*, by RULE X.

EXERCISES IN PARSING CONTINUED.

" John was applauded for his eloquence."
" The king was crowned at Westminster Abbey."
" Thomas has been esteemed."
" The business will be regulated."

" The girl was ridiculed by her companions."
" Susan was respected for her virtuous conduct."
" James will be rewarded by his instructer."

" Addition teacheth?" "He that hath ears?" "He that sinneth?" "Thou lovedst?" "Thou mightst, couldst, wouldst, *or* shouldst have lamented?"
What is the rule for the agreement of the verb? rule for the nominative? rule by which verbs govern the objective case?
" William was admired for his prudence." Will you parse *William?* 549

was admired? 549. *for?* 549. *his?* 549. *prudence?* 549.
What is a passive verb? 444. How formed? 510. Why is *admired* regular? 533.
Why is *for* a preposition? 246. Why is *his* a pronoun?
Will you now parse the remaining exercises?

2.

"We may be esteemed."
"He might have been promoted."
"William would have been dethroned."

"Justice may have been stayed"
"The task must be performed."
"We should not (1.) be easily (1.) disheartened in a good cause."

"*If he be learned.*"

550. *If* is a COPULATIVE CONJUNCTION. *Be learned* is a REGULAR PASSIVE VERB, from the verb *to learn* — "*Pres.* learn; *Imper.* learned; *Perf. part.* learned. 1. If I be learned; 2. If you be learned; 3. If he be learned"— made in the SUBJUNCTIVE MOOD, SUBJUNCTIVE FORM, PRESENT TENSE, THIRD PERSON, SINGULAR NUMBER, and agrees with *he*, according to RULE VII.

EXERCISES IN SYNTAX CONTINUED.

"If John be rewarded."
"If I am noticed."
"Unless he be punished."
"Although they are respected."
"Columbus discovered America."
"America was discovered by Columbus."
"John wounded his brother."
"John's brother was wounded by him."

"Although you will be disappointed."
"If the man had been elected."
"Except he repent."
"Susan assisted the little girl."
"The little girl was assisted by Susan."
"Pain follows pleasure."
"Pleasure is followed by pain."

2.

"An obedient son is deservedly respected by his friends."
"An idle boy will be punished."
"Without knowledge, a man is commonly (1.) despised."

"Unless great labor had been bestowed on William, he would have disappointed the expectations of his parents."
"He will not (1.) mind without corporal punishment."

3.

"The boy who visited me in September, died in the city of Boston."
"The man whom I found perished in a storm of snow."

"They that seek knowledge will find it."
"That lion which was exhibited in this town has been killed by his keeper."

4.

"I found (2.) John and William (3.) in the garden with their father and mother. (3.)"

"I have assisted him and his sister in many difficulties, to no (4.) purpose."

XLVI. OF IRREGULAR VERBS.

551. Irregular verbs are those which do not form their imperfect tense and perfect participle by adding to the present tense *ed*, or *d* only when the verb ends in *e ;* as,

---

"If he be learned." Will you parse *if?* 550. *be learned?* 550. Why in the subjunctive mood? 456.

Why in the subjunctive form? 463. Will you parse the remaining exercises in these lessons?

(1.) Adverb.   (2.) Irregular verb.   (3.) For *William* and *mother* apply Rule XL.   (4.) Adjective.

IRREGULAR VERBS.

Pres. tense.	*Imperf. tense.*	*Perf. Participle.*
Go,	Went,	Gone,
Begin,	Began,	Begun.

LIST OF IRREGULAR VERBS.

Those marked *r* admit likewise a regular form.

Present.	Imperfect.	Perf. or Pass. Part.	Present.	Imperfect.	Perf. or Pass. Part.
Abide,	abode,	abode.	Hang,	hung, r.	hung, r.
Am,	was,	been.	Hear,	heard,	heard.
Arise,	arose,	arisen.	Hew,	hewed,	hewn. r.
Awake,	awoke, r.	awaked.	Hide,	hid,	hidden, hid.
Bear, to bring forth,	bare,	born.	Hit,	hit,	hit.
			Hold,	held,	held.
Bear, to carry,	bore,	borne.	Hurt,	hurt,	hurt.
Beat,	beat,	beaten, beat.	Keep,	kept,	kept.
Begin,	began,	begun.	Knit,	knit, r.	knit. r.
Bend,	bent,	bent.	Know,	knew,	known.
Bereave,	bereft, r.	bereft. r.	Lade,	laded,	laden.
Beseech,	besought,	besought.	Lay,	laid,	laid.
Bid,	bid, bade,	bidden, bid.	Lead,	led,	led.
Bind,	bound,	bound.	Leave,	left,	left.
Bite,	bit,	bitten, bit.	Lend,	lent,	lent.
Bleed,	bled,	bled.	Let,	let,	let.
Blow,	blew,	blown.	Lie, to lie down,	lay,	lain.
Break,	broke,	broken.	Load,	loaded,	laden. r.
Breed,	bred,	bred.	Lose,	lost,	lost.
Bring,	brought,	brought.	Make,	made,	made.
Build,	built,	built.	Meet,	met,	met.
Burst,	burst,	burst.	Mow,	mowed,	mown. r.
Buy,	bought,	bought.	Pay,	paid,	paid.
Cast,	cast,	cast.	Put,	put,	put.
Catch,	caught, r.	caught. r.	Read,	read,	read.
Chide,	chid,	chidden, chid.	Rend,	rent,	rent.
Choose,	chose,	chosen.	Rid,	rid,	rid.
Cleave, to stick or adhere,	regular.		Ride,	rode,	rode, ridden. †
			Ring,	rung, rang	rung.
Cleave, to split,	clove or cleft,	cleft, cloven.	Rise,	rose,	risen.
Cling,	clung,	clung.	Rive,	rived,	riven.
Clothe,	clothed,	clad. r.	Run,	ran,	run.
Come,	came,	come.	Saw,	sawed,	sawn. r.
Cost,	cost,	cost.	Say,	said,	said.
Crow,	crew, r.	crowed.	See,	saw,	seen.
Creep,	crept,	crept.	Seek,	sought,	sought.
Cut,	cut,	cut.	Sell,	sold,	sold.
Dare, to venture,	durst,	dared.	Send,	sent,	sent.
Dare, to challenge,	r.		Set,	set,	set.
			Shake,	shook,	shaken.
Deal,	dealt, r.	dealt. r.	Shape,	shaped,	shaped, shapen.
Dig,	dug, r.	dug. r.	Shave,	shaved,	shaven. r.
Do,	did,	done.	Shear,	sheared,	shorn.
Draw,	drew,	drawn.	Shed,	shed,	shed.
Drive,	drove,	driven.	Shine,	shone, r.	shone. r.
Drink,	drank,	drunk.	Show,	showed,	shown.
Dwell,	dwelt,	dwelt. r.	Shoe,	shod,	shod.
Eat,	eat or ate,	eaten.	Shoot,	shot,	shot.
Fall,	fell,	fallen.	Shrink,	shrunk,	shrunk.
Feed,	fed,	fed.	Shred,	shred,	shred.
Feel,	felt,	felt.	Shut,	shut,	shut.
Fight,	fought,	fought.	Sing,	sung, sang,	sung.
Find,	found,	found.	Sink,	sunk, sank,	sunk.
Flee,	fled,	fled.	Sit,	sat,	sat.
Fling,	flung,	flung.	Slay,	slew,	slain.
Fly,	flew,	flown.	Sleep,	slept,	slept.
Forget,	forgot,	forgotten, forgot.	Slide,	slid,	slidden.
Forsake,	forsook,	forsaken.	Sling,	slung,	slung.
Freeze,	froze,	frozen.	Slink,	slunk,	slunk.
Get,	got,	got. *	Slit,	slit, r.	slit, or slitted.
Gild,	gilt, r.	gilt. r.	Smite,	smote,	smitten.
Gird,	girt, r.	girt. r.	Sow,	sowed,	sown. r.
Give,	gave,	given.	Speak,	spoke,	spoken.
Go,	went,	gone.	Speed,	sped,	sped.
Grave,	graved,	graven. r.	Spend,	spent,	spent.
Grind,	ground,	ground.	Spill,	spilt, r.	spilt. r.
Grow,	grew,	grown.	Spin,	spun,	spun.
Have,	had,	had.	Spit,	spit, spat,	spit, spitten. ‡

XLVI. When is a verb called irregular? 551.
Will you name the present and imperfect tenses, also the perfect participle of go? begin? am? arise? awake? bear? (to carry.) bid? bite? break? choose? do? drink? eat? forget? have? known? lie? (to lie down.) mow? rise? see? throw? wear? write?

---

* *Gotten* is nearly obsolete. Its compound, *forgotten*, is still in good use.
† *Ridden* is nearly obsolete.
‡ *Spitten* is nearly obsolete.

F

ENGLISH GRAMMAR.

Present.	Imperfect.	Perf. or Pass. Part.	Present.	Imperfect.	Perf. or Pass. Part.
Split,	split,	split. r.	Take,	took,	taken.
Spread,	spread,	spread.	Teach,	taught,	taught.
Spring,	sprung, sp ang,	sprung.	Tear,	tore,	torn.
Stand,	stood,	stood.	Tell,	told,	told.
Steal,	stole,	stolen.	Think,	thought,	thought.
Stick,	stuck,	stuck.	Thrive,	throve, r.	thriven.
Sting,	stung,	stung.	Throw,	threw,	thrown.
Stink,	stunk,	stunk.	Thrust,	thrust,	thrust.
Stride,	strode, or strid,	stridden.	Tread,	trod,	trodden.
Strike,	struck,	struck or stricken.	Wax,	waxed,	waxen. r.
String,	strung,	strung.	Wear,	wore,	worn.
Striv.	strove,	striven.	Weave,	wove,	woven.
Strow or strew,	strowed, or strewed,	strown, strowed, strewed.	Weep,	wept,	wept.
			Win,	won,	won.
Swear,	swore,	sworn.	Wind,	wound,	wound.
Sweat,	swet, r.	swet. r.	Work,	wrought	wrought or worked.
Swell,	swelled,	swollen. r.			
Swim,	swum, swam,	swum.	Wring,	wrung,	wrung.
Owing,	swung,	swung.	Write,	wrote,	written.

553. We say, "I have seen," "I had seen," and "I am seen," using the participle *seen* instead of the verb *saw:* hence,

NOTE VI. We should use participles, only, after *have*, and *had*, and the verb *to be*.

EXERCISES IN SYNTAX.
"*John has written his copy.*"

554. *Has written* is an IRREGULAR ACTIVE-TRANSITIVE VERB, from the verb *to write*—"*Pres.* write; *Imperf.* wrote; *Perf. part.* written. 1. I have written; 2. You have written; 3. He or *John* has written"—found in the INDICATIVE MOOD, PERFECT TENSE, THIRD PERSON, SINGULAR NUMBER, and agrees with *John*, by RULE VII.

John, copy, and *his,* are parsed as before.

EXERCISES IN SYNTAX CONTINUED.
1.

" Job has struck John."
" John has been struck by Job."
" The men caught the thief in the tavern."
" The thief was caught by the men in the tavern."
" A wise son will make a glad father."

" The act was done by William."
" James found his little brother in the boat."
" The instructer makes good pens."
" The farmer ploughs the ground in spring."
" I may spend my time in the country."

Will you correct, in accordance with NOTE VI., the following examples from the *list* above?
" John has wrote."
" He done it well."
" The sun has rose."
" The sun risen yesterday in a cloud."
" I see him yesterday."
" He has did his task."
" The birds have flew away."
" The birds flown or flew."
" The post is drove into the ground."
" He began or begun to write."
" The task is began."
" I had went with him."
" My brother has not spoke."
" The cloth is wove."
' The boys run swiftly."
" The thief has stole my watch."

" His copy was wrote well."
" He was smote on his cheek."
" John was awoke by the noise."
" My father has came."
" He come yesterday."
" Mary has chose the better part."
" He drunk to excess."
" The book was gave to me."
" His friends have forsook him."
" He was not forsook by his children."
" The laborer worked for me forty days."
" He was took and bound."
" John has written his copy." Will you parse *has written?*
Why is *has written* an irregular verb?
551. Why active? 439. Why transitive? 446.

1.

"John is at home."
"Rufus rode into the country."
"The sun will shine."
"The thief was confined in jail."
"The horse ran with great violence."

2.

"He abode in peace."
"They would be cruel."
"We may have been negligent."
"The boys should have been studious."
"William was in town."

3.

If he will assist me, I shall be much (1.) obliged to him."
*If he be virtuous, then he will be happy."
*If he is happy, then I am contented."
"Had he mentioned that circumstance, I should have avoided my present calamities."
"Although he acknowledged his faults, still he would not recompense me."
"I will write him, lest he neglect my business."
"Should I be disappointed, I shall despair."
"Unless he repent, he will not be pardoned."
"Were I* in your place, I would relieve him."

4.

"Thou hast benefited me."
"Ye make no pretensions."
"This doctrine hath no followers."
"If thou love me."
*If thou art more comfortable, I heartily rejoice."
"Dost thou hear me?"
"Hath he many advisers?"
"Ye do always err."
"Thou shalt surely die."
"If thou hadst obeyed me, thou wouldst not have been disappointed."

5.

*If Thomas, who is at school, return in season, I will visit you."
*The boys whom I admonished have reformed."
'The man whose life was in danger returned in safety."
"The task which the instructer imposed was performed with reluctance."
"The measure which he adopts will succeed."
"I have known a little child that exhibited the prudence of mature years."

XLVII. GOVERNMENT OF THE INFINITIVE.

555. When I say, " John begins to read," *to read* is a verb in the infinitive mood; and it follows, as you perceive, the verb *begins :* hence we say that it is governed by *begins.*

" He is beginning to read." Here, the infinitive follows the participle *beginning ;* it is, therefore, governed by *beginning.*

" He is eager to learn." Here, the infinitive follows the adjective *eager;* we therefore say that it is governed by *eager.*

" He has an opportunity to learn." Here, the infinitive, *to learn* is governed by the noun *opportunity,* because it follows the noun.

In like manner the infinitive may be governed by pronouns; as, " There is a fine opportunity for him to learn :" hence,

XLVII. " John begins to read." In what mood is *to read* ? 555. Why ? 479. By what is it governed ? 555. Why ? 555.
" He is beginning to read." What governs *to read* in this case ? 555.
" He is eager to learn." What governs *to learn* in this case ? 555. Why ? 555.

" He has an opportunity to learn?" What part of speech governs *to learn* in this example ? 555. Why ? 555.
—— " opportunity for him to learn." What does the infinitive here follow ? By what, then, is it governed? 555.

(1.) Adverb. * See 643.

RULE XII.

The infinitive mood may be governed by verbs, participles, adjectives, nouns, and pronouns.

EXERCISES IN SYNTAX.

"*James begins to learn.*"

556. *To learn* is a REGULAR TRANSITIVE VERB — "*Pres.* learn, *Imperf.* learned; *Perf. part.* learned"—made in the INFINITIVE MOOD, PRESENT TENSE, and governed by *begins*, agreeably to RULE XII.

James and *begins*, are parsed as before.

EXERCISES IN SYNTAX CONTINUED.

"George desires to learn."
"He is eager to learn."
"He has a desire to study."
"It seems to please John."
"William has come to see us."
"They are determined to excel."

"A knowledge of the rules of grammar teaches us to write correctly."
"He should seek to obtain knowledge."
"We may be taught to write, read, and spell."

Omission of TO, *the usual Sign of the Infinitive.*

"John saw the man strike (1.) the boy."
"The instructer made him submit."
"They need not proceed in such haste."

"I heard the clock strike."
"The tutor bade him do it."
"The soldiers dare not rebel."
"My uncle let the boys play in the garden."
"See (2.) the blind beggar dance."

NOTE VII. The infinitive mood is sometimes governed by conjunctions or adverbs; as, "The summit of a mountain so high as to be invisible."

EXAMPLES.

"They are about (3.) to depart."
"He is wise enough (3.) to study."

"He desired no more (4.) than (5.) to know his duty."

XLVIII.

557. We have before seen, that participles partake of the nature of two parts of speech, namely, verbs and adjectives. One point of resemblance which participles have to adjectives, is in referring to some noun in the sentence in which they are used; as, "The sun is setting:" here, the participle *setting* is said to refer to the noun *sun :* hence,

What, then, may be regarded as a rule for the government of the infinitive? XII.
"John begins to learn." Will you parse *to learn? James? begins?* 556.
Is *to* ever omitted? 480.
Will you now parse the exercises in the lessons which follow?
What is the infinitive mood used for? 479.

"They are about to depart." By what is the infinitive here governed? What is the note for this? VII.
XLVIII. What is a participle? 498.
"The sun is setting." What is *setting?* 557. To what, then, does *setting* refer? 557. Rule? XIII.
Will you now parse *setting* in full?

(1.) *Strike* is governed by Rule XII.
(2.) *See* is in the imperative, agreeing with *thou* or *you*, understood, by Rule VII
(3.) Adverb. (4.) Noun. (5.) Conjunction.

PARTICIPLES.

RULE XIII.
Participles refer to nouns.
EXERCISES IN SYNTAX.
"*The wind is rising.*"

558. *Rising* is a PRESENT ACTIVE PARTICIPLE, from the irregular erb *to rise*—"*Pres.* rise; *Imp.* rose; *Perf. part.* risen"—and it efers to *wind*, according to RULE XIII.

EXERCISES IN SYNTAX CONTINUED.

1.

"The moon is setting."
"The sun is rising."
"The trees are growing."
"John was dancing."

"Mary was playing."
"I have been writing."
"I found him crying."
"I left him rejoicing."

PARTICIPIAL ADJECTIVES.
"*The rising sun cheers us.*"

559. *Rising* is a PARTICIPIAL ADJECTIVE, from the verb *to rise* — "*Pres.* rise; *Imp.* rose; *Perf. part.* risen"— and belongs to *sun*, by RULE IV.

EXERCISES IN SYNTAX CONTINUED.

2.

"The setting sun reminds us of declining years."
"The roaring winds alarm us."
"The rippling stream pleases us."
"The singing-master visited me."

"We view with pleasure the twinkling stars."
"The roaring cataract strikes us with awe."
"The laboring man should not be defrauded."

3.

"Having dined, I returned to school."
"Having fought bravely, they were at last (1.) overcome."
"John, having exercised too violently, fainted."

"Having slept, he recovered his strength."
"Having retired to rest, he was seized with violent pain."
"The thief, having escaped, was never afterwards seen in that region."

4.

"William returned, mortified at his loss."
"The stream, swollen by the rains, overflowed its banks."
"The man accustomed to his glass seldom reforms."

"A child left to follow his own inclinations is most commonly ruined."
"Admired and applauded, he became vain."

Will you parse the next lesson?
Will you parse *rising*, in the sentence, "The rising sun?" 559. Why is it called a participial adjective? *Ans.* Because it describes, like an adjective, and implies action, like a participle.
Will you now parse the next lesson?

What kind of a participle is, "Having dined?" 504. Why? 504.
Who dined, in the phrase, "Having dined, I returned to school?"
To what, then, does *having dined* refer? Rule XIII. Will you now parse the remaining lessons?

(1.) *At last* is an adverbial phrase.

5.

"A dissipated son grieves his parents."
"We must not neglect any known duty."
"My father took the forsaken youth into his own house, and rendered to him deserved assistance."
"William befriended the deserted man."

6.

"The men, being fatigued by labor, sought rest in sleep."
"William, being dismissed from college, retired to the country."
"Thomas, after having been repeatedly admonished to no effect, was severely and justly punished."
"The tree, having been weighed down for a long time by abundance of fruit, at last (1.) fell to the ground."

RULE XIV.

Active participles, from active-transitive verbs, govern the objective case.

"*James is beating John.*"

560. *John* is a PROPER NOUN, of the THIRD PERSON, SINGULAR NUMBER, MASCULINE GENDER, OBJECTIVE CASE, and governed by *beating*, by RULE XIV.

EXERCISES IN SYNTAX CONTINUED.
1.

"John is striking William."
"Susan is studying her lesson."
"Mary has been repeating her lesson to her mother."
"The teamster, seeing the stage upsetting, ran and prevented it."
"Having obtained my request, I immediately set off for Boston."
"I spied the cat watching a mouse."
"Having given directions to his servants, he left his family and took the stage for Washington."

"*He delights in fighting.*"

561. *Fighting* is a PARTICIPIAL NOUN, in the OBJECTIVE CASE, and governed by the preposition *in*, according to RULE X.

EXERCISES IN SYNTAX CONTINUED.
1.

"Job was exhausted by wrestling."
"Mary acquired a livelihood by sewing."
"Walter excels in writing."
"Fishing delights me."
"Job practises fencing daily."
"The instructer teaches reading, writing, and spelling, in his school."
"Whispering is forbidden in school."

"Beating John." Will you parse *John?* 560. *Beating?* 558.

Will you parse the remaining exercises in the lesson above?

"In fighting" Will you parse *fighting?* 561. Why is *fighting* called a participial noun? *Ans.* Because it implies action, like a participle, and has, also, the sense of a noun.

Will you parse the rest of the exercises in this lesson?

(1.) *At last* is an adverbial phrase.

2.

562. "*You will much oblige me by sending those books.*"

Sending is a PARTICIPIAL NOUN, in the OBJECTIVE CASE, and governed by the preposition *by*, according to RULE X.

Books is a COMMON NOUN, of the THIRD PERSON, PLURAL NUMBER, NEUTER GENDER, OBJECTIVE CASE, and governed by the active participle *sending*, according to RULE XIV.

EXERCISES IN SYNTAX CONTINUED.

"James derives pleasure from reading useful books."
"John is above doing a mean action."
"Parents are pleased at seeing the progress of their children."
"Mary's reading has been useful in improving her taste in composition."
"I am discouraged from undertaking this study."
"A good instructer takes no delight in punishing."

The present participle, when used as a noun, often has the definite article *the* before it, and the preposition *of* after it; as, "By the observing of truth, you will command respect." With equal propriety, however, it may be said, "By observing truth," &c., omitting both the article and the preposition. If we use the article without the preposition, or the preposition without the article, the expression will appear awkward: hence,

NOTE VIII. The definite article *the* should be used before, and the preposition *of* after, participial nouns, or they should both be omitted.

EXERCISES TO BE PARSED AND CORRECTED.

"By the observing these rules, he will avoid mistakes."
"He prepared them for the event by the sending to them proper information."
"In writing of his letter, he made some mistakes."
"In the regarding his interests, he neglected the public affairs."
"He was sent to prepare the way by preaching of repentance."
"Keeping of one day in seven (1.) is required of Christians."

PROMISCUOUS EXERCISES IN SYNTAX.

"William calls George."
"John's father will reward his industry."
"George's father's carriage passed the tavern."
"If William return, he will be disappointed."
"John has beaten his little brother most shamefully."
"John will be punished for his insolence."
"We may improve under our instructer, if we choose."
"He who would excel in learning, must be attentive to his books."
"She begins to improve."

"By sending those books." Will you parse *sending*? 562. *books*? 562.
Will you parse the remaining exercises in this lesson?
From what are present participles formed? 497.
How may participles in *ing* be distinguished from other parts of speech of the same termination? 500.

Instead of saying, "By the observing these rules," what should I say? Why? Note VIII.
Will you now parse and correct the exercises under Note VIII.?
Will you parse the promiscuous exercises in Syntax? Next take those to be written.

(1.) *Seven* is a numeral adjective belonging to *days*, understood, by Note 1

SENTENCES TO BE WRITTEN.

563. Will you compose a sentence, containing an active-transitive verb? One, containing a neuter verb? One, containing a passive verb? One, expressing the same sense as the last in an active form? Will you compose a sentence having a verb in the potential mood? One, in the subjunctive mood? One, in the imperative mood? One, in the infinitive mood? One, having an adjective in the superlative degree? One, having the article *an* correctly used before a vowel? One, having an adjective in the positive degree that has in itself a superlative signification? One, containing the relative *whose*? One, containing *which*? One, with *what* used as a compound pronoun? One, having *who* used as an interrogative pronoun? One, having a verb in the subjunctive mood, common form?

Will you construct one or more sentences, which will make sense with the word *truth* contained in them? One, with the word *wisdom* contained in it? One, with the word *knowledge*? One, with the word *learning*? One, with the word *science*?

Will you construct a sentence about *prudence*? One about *history*? One or more on the following subjects, namely, *geography, gardening, farms, orchards*?

Will you fill up the following phrases with suitable words to make sense, namely, "Industry —— health?" "By — we acquire ——?" "In youth —— characters ——?" "Arithmetic —— — business?" "Washington —— live —— hearts of his ——?"

XLIX. OF THE AUXILIARY VERBS.

564. The verbs *have, be, will* and *do*, when they are unconnected with a principal verb, expressed or understood, are not auxiliaries, but principal verbs; as, "We *have* enough;" "I *am* grateful;" "He *wills* it to be so;" "They *do* as they please." In this view, they also have their auxiliaries; as, "I *shall have* enough;" "I *will be* grateful," &c.

565. The peculiar force of the several auxiliaries will appear from the following account of them.

566. *Do* and *did* mark the action itself, or the time of it, with greater energy and positiveness; as, "I *do* speak truth;" "I *did* respect him;" "Here am I, for thou *didst* call me." They are of great use in negative (1.) sentences; as, "I *do not* fear;" "I *did not* write." They are almost universally employed in asking questions; as, "*Does* he learn?" "*Did* he not write?" They sometimes also supply (2.) the place of another verb, and make the repetition of it, in the same or a subsequent sentence, unnecessary; as, "You attend not to your studies as he *does*;" i. e. "as he attends," &c.) "I shall come, if I can; but if I *do not*, please to excuse me;" (i. e. "if I come not.")

567. *May* and *might* express the possibility or liberty of doing a thing; *can* and *could*, the power; as, "It may rain;" "I may write or read;" "He might have improved more than he has;" "He can write much better than he could last year."

XLIX. Which are the auxiliary verbs? 512.
What is an auxiliary verb? 511.
What a principal one?*
When are *have, be, will,* and *do* principal verbs? 564. Give an example of each. 564.

What effect have *do* and *did* in sentences? 566. Give an example. 566.
Will you give an example in which the repetition of the principal verb is unnecessary? 566.
What do *may* and *might* express? 567.

AUXILIARY VERBS. 89

568. *Must* is sometimes called in for a helper, and denotes necessity; as, "We must speak the truth, whenever we do speak, and we must not prevaricate." (1.)

569. *Will*, in the first person singular and plural, intimates (2.) resolution and promising; in the second and third person, it only foretells; as, "I will reward the good, and will punish the wicked;" "We will remember benefits, and be grateful;" "Thou wilt, or he will, repent of that folly;" "You, or they, will have a pleasant walk."

570. *Shall*, on the contrary, in the first person, simply foretells; in the second and third persons, it promises, commands, or threatens; as, "I shall go abroad;" "We shall dine at home;" "Thou shalt, or you shall, inherit the land;" "Ye shall do justice, and love mercy;" "They shall account for their misconduct." The following passage is not translated (3.) according to the distinct and proper meanings of the words *shall* and *will*: "Surely goodness and mercy shall follow me all the days of my life; and I will dwell in the house of the Lord for ever." It ought to be, "*will* follow me," and, "I *shall* dwell."—The foreigner who, as it is said, fell into the Thames, and cried out, "I *will* be drowned! nobody *shall* help me!" made a sad misapplication of these auxiliaries.

571. These observations respecting the import (4.) of the verbs *will* and *shall*, must be understood of explicative sentences; for when the sentence is interrogative, just the reverse, (5.) for the most part, takes place: thus, "I *shall* go," "You *will* go," express event (6.) only; but, "*Will* you go?" imports intention; and, "*Shall* I go?" refers to the will of another. But, "He *shall* go," and, "*Shall* he go?" both imply will; expressing or referring to a command.

572. When the verb is put in the subjunctive mood, the meaning of these auxiliaries likewise undergoes (7.) some alteration; as the learners will readily perceive by a few examples: "He *shall* proceed;" "If he *shall* proceed;" "You *shall* consent;" "If you *shall* consent." These auxiliaries are sometimes interchanged (8.) in the indicative and subjunctive moods; to convey the same meaning of the auxiliary; as, "He *will* not return;" "If he *shall* not return;" "He *shall* not return;" "If he *will* not return."

573. *Would* primarily (9.) denotes inclination of will; and *should*, obligation; but they both vary their import, and are often used to express simple event.

574. *Do* and *have* are sometimes used as principal verbs, according to the following

SYNOPSIS.

INDICATIVE MOOD.

Pres. I do. I have.
Imp. I did. I had.
Perf. I have done. I have had.
Plup. I had done. I had had.
1 *Fut.* I shall *or* will do. I shall *or* will have.
2 *Fut.* I shall have done. I shall have had.

What is the use of *must*? 568. What does *will* intimate in the first person singular? plural? 569. Give an example. 569. In the second and third persons? 569. Give an example. 569. What does *shall* intimate in the first person? 570 Give an example. 570. In what particular is the translation of the following passage incorrect? "Surely goodness and mercy shall follow me all the days of my life; and I will dwell in the house of the Lord for ever." 570. In what consists the mistake in the expression which the foreigner made when he fell into the Thames? 570. What do *shall* and *will* denote in interrogative sentences; as, "Shall I go?" "Will you go?" 571. What do *would* and *should* primarily denote? 573.

(1.) To shun the truth. (2.) Shows. (3.) Expressed. (4.) Meaning (5.) Contrary (6.) What happens. (7.) Suffers. (8.) To exchange one for the other. (9.) In the first place.

575.   POTENTIAL MOOD.
Pres. I may *or* can do.   I may *or* can have.
Imp. I might, could, would, *or* should do.   I might, could, would, *or* should have.
Perf. I may *or* can have done.   I may *or* can have had.
Plup. I might, could, would, *or* should have done.   I might, could, would, *or* should have had.

576.   ‾SUBJUNCTIVE MOOD.
Pres. 1. If I do.   If I have, &c.

576—1.   IMPERATIVE MOOD.
Pres. Do you, *or* Do you do.   Have you, *or* Do you have.

577.   INFINITIVE MOOD.
Pres. To do.   To have.
Perf. To have done.   To have had.

578.   PARTICIPLES.
Pres. Doing.   Having.
Perf. Done.   Had.
Comp. perf. Having done.   Having had.

L. OF DEFECTIVE VERBS.

579. Defective verbs are those which are used only in some of the moods and tenses.

580. The following are the principal ones:

Pres. Tense.	*Imp. Tense.*	*Perf. Participle.*
May,	Might,	(Wanting.)
Can,	Could,	————
Will,	Would,	————
Shall,	Should,	————
Must,	Must,	————
Ought,	Ought,	————
————	Quoth,	

581. Of these, *ought* and *must*, you perceive, are not varied.

582. *Ought* and *quoth* are always used as principal verbs. *Ought* is the same in the imperfect tense as in the present, and is always followed by an infinitive; as, "He ought to study;" "He ought to have read." In this last example, *ought* is in the imperfect; and in the first, it is in the present. This we determine by the infinitive, which follows the verb, thus: when the present infinitive follows *ought*, *ought* is in the present tense; but when the perfect infinitive follows it, it is in the imperfect tense.

583. In English, verbs are often used both in a transitive and intransitive, or neuter signification. Thus, *to flatten*, when it signifies *to make even or level*, is an active-transitive verb; but when it signifies *to grow dull or insipid*, it is an intransitive verb.

Will you repeat the synopsis of *do* through all the moods? of *have*?
Will you conjugate *do* in the present tense? *have* in the perfect tense?
What is the perfect participle of *do*? of *have*? the compound perfect of *do*? of *have*?
L. What are defective verbs? 579.
Will you mention the principal ones with their imperfect tenses? 580.

Which are not varied? 581.
How are *ought* and *quoth* always used? 582.
How can you tell when *ought* is in the present tense? 582.
When is it in the imperfect tense? 582.
Give an example of each tense. 582.
When is *to flatten* transitive, and when intransitive? 583.
How, then, are verbs often used? 583.

DEFECTIVE VERBS.   91

584. A neuter or intransitive verb, by the addition of a preposition, may become a compound active-transitive verb; as, *to smile* is intransitive; it cannot, therefore, be followed by an objective case, nor be changed into the passive form. We cannot say, "She smiled him," or, "He was smiled;" but we say, very properly, "She smiled on him;" "He was smiled on by her."

585. Prepositions affect the meaning of verbs in different ways. *To cast* means *to throw;* as, "He cast a stone at her." *To cast up*, however, means *to compute;* as, "He casts up his accounts." In all instances in which the preposition follows the verb, and modifies its meaning, it should be considered a part of the verb, and be so treated in parsing.

586. There are some verbs, which, although they admit an objective case after them, still do not indicate the least degree of action; as, "I resemble my father." This seeming inconsistency may be easily reconciled by reflecting that, in all such cases, the verb has a direct reference to its object. Of this nature are the verbs *retain, resemble, own, have*, &c.

587. Some neuter or intransitive verbs admit of a passive form, and are thence called neuter passive verbs; as, "John goes home to-night." Here *goes* is an intransitive verb. But in the sentence, "John is gone home," *is gone* is a neuter passive verb. Again, in the phrase, "William comes," *comes* is an intransitive verb; and in the phrase, "William is come," *is come* is a neuter passive verb.

EXERCISES IN SYNTAX.

1.

"William had had many advantages before he improved them in a proper manner."
"A good scholar will not do what (1.) is forbidden by his instructer."

"He has had many precious opportunities."
"John will do as his instructer directs."
"He may have had time."

2.

"I own this book."
"Charles resembles his parents."
"He retains his place."

"I cannot believe him."
"His father does not hesitate to trust him."

3.

"The farmer casts seed into the ground."
"The merchant casts up his accounts often."

"She smiles sweetly."
"She smiled on John."
"John was smiled on by fortune in every undertaking."

4.

"The instructer has come."
"Our instructer has come."
"William has gone to visit his parents."
"Susan has gone."

"Mary was gone before her mother came."
"When they came to town, they made many purchases."

How can an intransitive verb become transitive? 584. Give an example. 584.
What does *to cast* mean? 585.
Meaning of *to cast up?* 585.
When may the preposition be reckoned a part of the verb? 585.
How should it be considered in parsing? 585.

Is *resemble*, strictly speaking, a transitive verb? 586.
Why does it admit an object after it? 586.
There are several verbs of this class; will you name some of them? 586.
What is a neuter passive verb? 587. Give an example. 587.
Will you now parse the next lessons?

LI. OF ADVERBS.

588. Adverbs are words joined to verbs, participles, adjectives, and other adverbs, to qualify them.

589. Expressions like the following, namely, *a few days ago, long since, none at all, at length, in vain, by no means, a great deal,* &c., are denominated *adverbial phrases*, when they are used to qualify verbs or participles, by expressing the manner, time or degree of action.

590. The definite article *the* is frequently placed before adverbs of the comparative and superlative degrees, to give the expression more force; as, "The *more* he walks, the *better* he feels." When the article is used in this sense, both the article and adverb may be reckoned an adverbial phrase, and be so considered in parsing.

591. You have doubtless noticed that most words ending in *ly* are adverbs. The reason of this is that *ly* is a contraction of the adverb *like:* thus, from *manlike* we form *manly:* *gentlemanly* is a contraction of *gentlemanlike.*—Hence,

592. If you meet with a word ending in *ly*, implying in its signification the idea of *like*, you may conclude at once that it is an adverb.

RULE IX.

Adverbs qualify verbs, participles, adjectives, and other adverbs.

EXERCISES IN SYNTAX.

"*In vain we look for perfect happiness.*"

593. *In vain* is an ADVERBIAL PHRASE, and qualifies *look*, according to RULE IX.

EXERCISES IN SYNTAX CONTINUED.

"John has come again, but William has not."
"Very many persons fail of happiness."
"A vast many evils are incident to man in his wearisome journey through life."
"The instructress has at length arrived."
"William acted very nobly."
"I will by no means consent."
"He wrote a long letter a few days ago." (1.)
"John was writing carelessly."
"I have admonished her once and again."
"A few days ago, there was much excitement in town."

LI. What is the meaning of *adverb*? 228.
To what is the adverb joined? 588.
For what purpose? 588.
How many different parts of speech does it qualify? 588.
Which are they? 588.
What is the definition of an adverb? 588.
Are adverbs compared?*
Will you compare *wisely*? 235. *soon*? 234.
How are they compared? 236.
Will you compare the adverbs *much*? *well*? *bad*? *ill*? 237.
Some adverbs are not regular in their comparison, will you name one? 237.
Will you name four or five adverbial phrases? 589.
When are they to be considered adverbial phrases? 589.
Is the article *the* ever joined to an adverb? 590. For what purpose? 590.
What do the article and adverb form in such cases? 590.
How is it to be considered in parsing? 590.
How came most words ending in *ly* to be considered adverbs? 591. Give an example. 591.
How can we determine between words ending in *ly*, whether or not they are adverbs? 592.
What rule do you apply when you parse an adverb? IX.
"In vain we look." Will you parse *in vain*? 593.

NOTE IX. To qualify verbs, participles, adjectives, and other adverbs, we should use adverbs; but to qualify nouns, we should use adjectives.

SENTENCES TO BE PARSED AND CORRECTED.

"William writes good."*
"Susan studies diligent."
"He speaks fluently and reasons correct."
"John writes tolerable well, but readst miserable."
"Harriet dresses neat."
"On conditions suitably to his rank."
"He speaks correct."
"Mary sings admirable."
"He writes elegant."
"He reads and spells very bad."

SENTENCES TO BE WRITTEN.

594. Will you write down a sentence, containing a compound active-transitive verb? One, having a neuter-passive verb?
Will you compose two or more sentences about *a lion*? Two or more, about *sheep*? Two or more, about *a cow*? One, about *an ox*? One, about *a dog*? One, about *a cat*? One, about *Africans*? One, about *Indians*? One, about *fishes*? One, about *steam-boat disasters*? One, about *stage accidents*?

LII. OF PREPOSITIONS.

595. Prepositions are used to connect words, and to show the relation between them.

596. We not unfrequently meet with verbs compounded of a preposition and verb; as, "to *uphold*," "to *invest*," "to *overlook*;" and this composition sometimes gives a new sense to the verb; as, "to *understand*," "to *withdraw*." But the preposition more frequently occurs *after* the verb, and *separate* from it; as, "to cast *up*," "to fall *on*." The sense of the verb, in this case, is also materially affected by the preposition.

598. The prepositions *after, before, above, beneath*, and several others, sometimes appear to be adverbs, and may be so considered; as, "They had their reward soon *after;*" "He died not long *before;*" "He dwells *above;*" but if the noun *time* or *place* be added, they lose their adverbial form; as, "He died not long before" [that time], &c.

599. There is a peculiar propriety in distinguishing the correct use of the different prepositions. For illustration, we will take the following sentences: "He walks *with* a staff *by* moonlight;" "He was taken *by* stratagem, and killed *with* a sword." Put the one preposition for the other, and say,

---

Will you next parse the remaining exercises?
When should we use adverbs? Note IX.
When adjectives? Note IX.
"William writes good." Wherein is this sentence incorrect?*
Will you now parse and correct the remaining exercises?
LII. What is the meaning of *preposition*? 244.
What are prepositions? 595.
Will you repeat the list? 247.
With what are verbs not unfrequently compounded? 596.
Give an example. 596.
Where is the preposition more frequently placed? 595. Give an example. 596.
Will you name four prepositions which in many instances appear to be adverbs? 598.
How may they be converted into prepositions again? 598.
"He walks by a staff with moonlight."
Will you correct this sentence, and then repeat the phrase?

---

* For the adjective *good*, we should use the adverb *well*, according to Note IX.
† *Reads* agrees with *John* understood, and is, therefore, connected with *writes* by the conjunction *but*, agreeably to Rule XL.

"He walks *by* a staff *with* moonlight;" "He was taken *with* stratagem, and killed *by* a sword;" and it will appear that they differ in signification more than one, at first view, would be apt to imagine.

RULE X.

Prepositions govern the objective case.

EXERCISES IN SYNTAX.

" *John lives within his income.*"

600. *Within* is a PREPOSITION.
Income is a COMMON NOUN, of the THIRD PERSON, SINGULAR NUMBER, NEUTER GENDER, OBJECTIVE CASE, and governed by *within*, according to RULE X.

EXERCISES IN SYNTAX CONTINUED.

"Thomas made his fortune by industry."
"Susan labors with her needle for a livelihood."
"Respecting that affair, there was a controversy."
"In six days God made the world, and all things that are in it

He made the sun to shine by day, and the moon (1.) to give light by night."
"Beneath the oak lie acorns in great abundance."
"John, who is at all times watchful of his own interest, will attend to that concern."

SENTENCES TO BE WRITTEN.

601. Will you fill up the following sentences with suitable prepositions to make sense? "John was — the house when he was seized —— a fit." "The busy bee — summer provides food — the approaching winter — the prudence — a rational being."

Will you supply the objects to the following? "James was catching ——." "He was beating ——." "He supports ——."

Will you supply agents or nominative cases to the following ? —— was running." "—— was dancing."

Will you supply verbs in the following? "A dutiful child —— his parents." "Grammar —— us —— correctly."

Will you compose two or more sentences about *boys*? One, about *whales*? One, about *snakes*? One, about *foxes*? One, about *parents*? One, about *brothers*? One, about *sisters*? One, about *uncles*? One, about *aunts*?

LIII. OF CONJUNCTIONS.

602. A CONJUNCTION is a word that is chiefly used to connect sentences, so as, out of two or more sentences, to make but one.

Will you repeat the rule respecting the government of nouns by prepositions? X. "John lives within his income." Will you parse *within*? 600. *incoms*? 600.
Will you now take the remaining exercises to be parsed; after which, those to be written?

What is a simple sentence? 253. Give an example. A compound sentence? 256. Give an example.
Why called compound? 254.
LIII. Meaning of *conjunction*? 257
What is a conjunction? 602.
Meaning of *copulative*? 204.

(1.) The sense is, " He made the moon." *Moon*, then, is in the objective case, governed by *made* understood, and connected with *sun*, by Rule XI.

503. Relative pronouns, as well as conjunctions, serve to connect sentences; as, "Blessed is the man *who* feareth the Lord."

504. Conjunctions very often unite sentences when they appear to unite only words; as, in the following sentences: "Duty and interest forbid vicious indulgences." "Wisdom or folly governs us." Each of these forms of expression contains two sentences, namely, the first, "Duty forbids vicious indulgences;" "Interest forbids vicious indulgences;" the second, "Wisdom governs us;" "Folly governs us."

RULE XI.

Conjunctions connect verbs of the same mood and tense, and nouns or pronouns of the same case.

EXERCISES IN SYNTAX.

605. "*William writes and ciphers.*"

And is a COPULATIVE CONJUNCTION.

Ciphers is a REGULAR ACTIVE INTRANSITIVE VERB, from the verb to *cipher* — "*Pres.* cipher; *Imperf.* ciphered; *Per. part.* ciphered. 1. I cipher; 2. You cipher; 3. He or *William* ciphers"—made in the INDICATIVE MOOD, PRESENT TENSE, THIRD PERSON SINGULAR, and agrees with *William* understood, and is connected to *writes* by the conjunction *and*, agreeably to RULE XI.

EXERCISES IN SYNTAX CONTINUED.

"John ciphers rapidly, and reads correctly."
"If we contend about trifles, and violently maintain our opinions, we shall gain but few friends."
"Though he is lively, yet he is not too volatile."
"If he has promised, he should act accordingly."
"He denied that he circulated the report."

SENTENCES TO BE WRITTEN.

606. Will you compose a sentence containing the conjunction *if*? One, containing *and*? As many sentences as there are conjunctions which follow; each sentence containing one? *Although. Unless. For. Because. Therefore. Or. Neither. Nor.*

Will you compose a sentence about *Jackson?* One, about *Clay?* One about *Monroe?* One, about *Madison?*

LIV. OF INTERJECTIONS.

607. INTERJECTIONS are words thrown in between the parts of sentences, to express the passions or sudden feelings of the speaker.

What is the use of the copulative conjunction? 265.
Will you repeat the list of copulative conjunctions? 266.
What does *disjunctive* signify? 271.
What does the disjunctive conjunction connect? 274.
Will you repeat the list of them? 275.
What is the rule for connecting words by conjunctions? XI.
What other words, besides conjunctions and prepositions, connect? 603.

Do conjunctions ever connect sentences when they appear to connect words only? 604. Give an example. 604.
"William writes and ciphers." Will you parse *and?* 605. *ciphers?* 605.
Will you, in the next place, take the exercises to be parsed and written, and dispose of them?
LIV. What is the meaning of *interjection?* 283.
What are interjections? 607.

608. We do not say, "Ah, I!" "Oh, I!" but, "Ah, me!" "Oh, me!" using the objective case after the interjection. The pronoun here spoken of, you perceive, is of the first person: hence,

NOTE X. Pronouns of the first person are put in the objective case, after the interjections *Oh! O! ah!* &c.

609. We say, "O thou persecutor!" "Oh, ye hypocrites!" "O thou who dwellest," &c.: hence,

NOTE XI. The interjections *O! oh!* and *ah!* require the nominative case of pronouns in the second person.

EXERCISES IN SYNTAX.

610. "*Ah, me! I must perish.*"

Ah is an INTERJECTION.
Me is a PERSONAL PRONOUN, of the FIRST PERSON, SINGULAR, OBJECTIVE CASE, and governed by *ah*, agreeably to NOTE X.

EXERCISES IN SYNTAX CONTINUED.

"O, thou (1.) who hast murdered thy friend!"
"O, thou who hearest prayer!"
"Ah, me! must I endure all this?"

"Ah! unhappy (2.) thou, who art deaf (3.) to the calls of duty and honor."
"Oh! happy (4.) us, surrounded with so many blessings."

SENTENCES TO BE WRITTEN.

611. Will you compose a sentence containing *alas?* One, containing *oh?* One, about *volcanoes?* One, about *lakes?* One, about *islands?* One, about *Webster* the statesman? One, about a good *scholar?* One, about a poor *scholar?* One, about a good *instructer?*

LV. OF THE AGREEMENT OF NOUNS.

612. APPOSITION, in grammar, signifies the putting of two nouns in the same case.

613. When I say, "John the mechanic has come," I am speaking of only one person; the two nouns, *John* and *mechanic*, both meaning or referring to the same person; consequently they are put, by apposition, in the same case: hence,

RULE XV.

When two or more nouns, in the same sentence, signify the same thing, they are put, by apposition, in the same case.

Will you repeat from the list six interjections? 285.
How may an interjection generally be known? 266.
"Ah, me!" In what case is *me?* 610.
What rule or note applies to *me?* X.
"O thou," &c. What note applies to this? XI.
"Ah, me!" Will you parse *ah? ms?* 210.

Will you now take the remaining exercises to be parsed and written?
LV. Meaning of *apposition?* 612.
"John the mechanic." How many persons are here spoken of? 613. Should then, the two nouns, *John* and *mechanic*, be in the same, or a different case? 613.
What is the rule for this agreement? XV.

(1.) For *thou*, apply Note XI.
(2.) Belongs to *who*, by Rule IV.

(3.) Agrees with *thou*, by Rule IV.
(4.) Apply Rule IV.

EXERCISES.

EXERCISES IN SYNTAX.

614.   " *Webster the statesman has left us.*"
Statesman is a COMMON NOUN, MASCULINE GENDER, THIRD PERSON, SINGULAR NUMBER, NOMINATIVE CASE, and put in apposition with *Webster*, by RULE XV.

EXERCISES IN SYNTAX CONTINUED.

1.

" John the Baptist was beheaded."
" David the thief, was apprehended "
" Johnson, the bookseller, has failed in business."
" I consulted Williams, the lawyer."

" Cicero, the orator, flourished in the time of Catiline, the conspirator."
" I visit Thompson, the professor, often."
" John, the miller, died yesterday."

2.

" If John will not go, I will go myself." (1.)
" You yourself are in fault."
" They themselves were mistaken."

" We will inspect the goods ourselves."
" I, I am the man who committed the deed."

Remark 1.— For the same reason that one noun agrees with another in case, it agrees with it in number and person also.

" I, Alexander, by the grace of God, emperor of all the Russians, promulgate this law."

" We, the representatives of the people of these colonies, do make this declaration."

Remark 2.—When one noun describes or qualifies another, the one so qualifying becomes an adjective in sense, and may be so considered in parsing. Accordingly, *Tremont*, in the phrase, " Tremont House," is an adjective belonging to *House*, by RULE IV.

615.   EXERCISES IN SYNTAX.

" The Marlborough Hotel is situated in Washington-street."
" The firm of Messrs. Williams & Sons, has failed."

" John Dobson was in town yesterday."
" John Johnson, the blacksmith, has broken his leg."

Remark 3.—When the nouns which refer to the same person or thing are separated by verbs ; as, " Webster is a statesman," it is customary to apply one or more of the following rules :
1. *Any verb may have the same case after it as before it, when both words refer to the same thing.*
2. *The verb* TO BE, *through all its variations, has the same case after it as that which next precedes it.*

" Webster the statesman." Will you parse *statesman* ? 614.
Will you now parse the succeeding exercises?
" I will go myself." Will you parse *myself*?
How is the compound personal pronoun formed in the singular ? 386. How in the plural ? 386.
When one noun is put in apposition with another, in what particulars does it agree with it ? Remark 1.
Will you now parse the next exercises?

" Tremont House." What part of speech is *Tremont*? Remark 2. How used here ? Remark 2. Will you parse it in full ?
Will you now parse all the exercises under Remark 2 ?
What is the rule or rules usually given for parsing *statesman*, in the phrase " Webster is a statesman ?" Remark 3. 1, 2, 3, 4.
In the same sentence, do *Webster* and *statesman* both mean or refer to the same person ? In what case, then, ought they to be ? 613. By what rule ? XV.

(1.) *Myself* is a compound personal pronoun, first person, singular, nominative case, and put in apposition with I, by Rule XV

G   9

98   ENGLISH GRAMMAR.

3. *Passive verbs of naming, judging, &c. have the same case after them as before them.*
4. *Neuter verbs have the same case after them as before them.*

616. The foregoing rules, in the opinion of the writer, are wholly unnecessary, tending merely to confuse the mind of the learner by requiring him to make a distinction in form, when there exists none in principle. In corroboration of this fact, Mr. Murray has the following remark : —

617. "By these examples it appears, that the verb *to be* has no government of case, but serves in all its forms as a conductor to the cases; so that the two cases, which, in the construction of the sentence, are the next before and after it, must always be alike. Perhaps this subject will be more intelligible by observing that the words, in the cases preceding and following the verb *to be*, may be said to be in apposition to each other. Thus, in the sentence, 'I understood *it to be him*,' the words *it* and *him* are in apposition; that is, they refer to the same thing, and are in the same case."

618.   EXERCISES IN SYNTAX.

1.

" Webster is a statesman."
" John is a good scholar."
" William will become a distinguished and valuable citizen."
" She walks a queen." (1.)
" He is styled Lord (1.) Mayor (1.) of London."
" He was named John." (1.)

" She moves a queen." (1.)
" Julius Cæsar was that Roman general who conquered the Gauls."
" Tom struts a soldier." (1.)
" Will sneaks a scrivener."
" Claudius Nero, Caligula's uncle, a senseless fellow, obtained the kingdom."

2.

" Susan took her to be Mary." (1.)
" I took him to be John (2.) Ogden."
" We at first took it to be her, but afterwards were convinced that (3.) it was not she."
" He is not the person who (4.) it seemed he was."
" I understood it to be him (1.) who

is the son of Mr. (2.) John Quincy (2.) Adams." (1.)
" She is not now the person whom they represented her (1.) to have been."
" Whom (5.) do you fancy them to be ?"
" The professor was appointed tutor to the prince."

Remark 3.—It not unfrequently happens that the connecting verb is omitted; as, " They made him captain;" that is, *to be* captain.

3.

" They named him John."
" The soldiers made him general."

" They proclaimed him king."
" His countrymen crowned him emperor."

619. SENTENCES TO BE PARSED AND CORRECTED.

" It might have been him, (6.) but there is no proof (7.) of it."
" Though I was blamed, it could not have been me."
" I saw one who I took to be she."

" She is the person who I understood it to have been."
" Who do you think me to be ?"
" Whom do men say that I am ?"
" Whom think ye that I am ?"

What office does the verb *to be* perform between cases ? 617.
Are the cases next before and after it, alike, or different ? 617.
What is the opinion of Mr. Murray respecting the cases before and after *to be* ? 617.
How does he think *it* and *him* should

be parsed in the phrase, " I understood it to be him ?" 617.
Will you now parse lessons 1, 2, and 3 ?
Is the verb *to be* always expressed ? Remark 3. Give an example. Remark 3.
Will you now take the sentences to be parsed and corrected; also, those to be written ?

(1.) Apply Rule XV.   (2.) Remark 2.   (3.) Conjunction.   (4.) *Who* is put in apposition with *he*, Rule XV.   (5.) *Whom* agrees with *them*, by Rule XV   (6.) *Him* should be *he* to agree with it, according to Rule XV.   (7.) Apply Rule VI.

620.   SENTENCES TO BE WRITTEN.

Will you compose a sentence having nouns in apposition? One, having nouns in apposition, but separated by a verb? One, having a noun used as an adjective?

Will you construct a sentence having in it the word *who*? One, having *whose*? One, having *whom*? One, having *what*? One, having *that*? One, having *man*? One, having *woman*? One, having *boy*? One, having *girls*? One, having *parents*?

LVI. OF NOUNS USED INDEPENDENTLY.

621. To *address* signifies to *speak to*; as, "James, your father has come." The name of the person addressed must always be of the second person; and a noun in this situation, when it has no verb to agree with it, and is wholly disconnected with the rest of the sentence, is said to be independent. Hence,

RULE XVI.

When an address is made, the name of the person or thing addressed is in the nominative case independent.

EXERCISES IN SYNTAX.

622.   " *John, will you assist me?*"

John is a PROPER NOUN, of the SECOND PERSON, SINGULAR NUMBER, MASCULINE GENDER, and NOMINATIVE CASE INDEPENDENT, according to RULE XVI.

EXERCISES IN SYNTAX CONTINUED.

1.

" My lords, (1.) the time has come when we must take some decisive measures."
" In making this appeal to you, my fellow-citizens, I rely entirely on your candor."

" Rufus, you must improve your time."
" Gentlemen of the jury."
" James, (1.) study (2.) your book."
" William, do try to get your lesson to-day."

2.

" Boys, attend to your lessons."
" Girls, come into school."
" Did you speak to me, girls?"

" My dear children, let no root of bitterness spring up among you."

LVI. " James, your father has come." Which word here is the name of the person addressed?
What is the meaning of *to address*? 621.
Of what person is a noun when an address is made? 621.

When is a noun independent? 621.
What is the rule for a noun put independently? XVI.
In the sentence, " John, will you assist me?" will you parse *John*? 622.
Will you next parse the rest of the exercises in this rule?

(1.) Rule XVI.   (2.) Imperative mood, and agrees with *thou* or *you* understood, by Rule VII.

LVII. OF NOUNS IN THE CASE ABSOLUTE.

623. In the phrase, "The sun being risen, we set sail," the first clause of the sentence, namely, "The sun being risen," has nothing to do with the remainder: the noun and participle may, therefore, when taken together, be said to be in the nominative case independent; but as we have already one case of this nature, we will, for the sake of making a distinction, call this (the noun joined with a participle) the nominative case absolute. Hence,

RULE XVII.

A noun or pronoun before a participle, and independent of the rest of the sentence, is in the nominative case absolute.

624. EXERCISES IN SYNTAX.

"The sun (1.) being risen, (2.) we departed."
"Egypt being conquered, Alexander returned to Syria."
"Shame being lost, all virtue was lost."
"The soldiers retreating, victory was lost."

"Wellington having returned to England, tranquillity was restored to France."
"Bonaparte being conquered, the king was restored."
"The conditions being observed, the bargain was a mutual benefit."

625. SENTENCES TO BE PARSED AND CORRECTED.

"Him (3.) only excepted, who was a murderer."
"Her being dismissed, the rest of the scholars behaved well."

"Him being destroyed, the remaining robbers made their escape."

LVIII. OF THE INFINITIVE MOOD.

NOTE XII.—A verb in the infinitive mood is sometimes placed independently; as, "To be frank, I own I have injured you."

; 626. EXERCISES IN SYNTAX.

"To confess the truth, I was in fault."
"To display his power, he oppressed his soldiers."

"To tell the plain truth, I persuaded him to stay."
"To convince you, I will continue here till you return."

LVII. "The sun being risen, we set sail." How many words in this sentence, used independently, are taken together? 623.
Why is this case denominated the case absolute? 623.
What is the rule for the case absolute? XVII.
Will you now take the parsing exercises under Rule XVII., and then the sentences to be corrected?

LVIII. "To confess the truth, I was," &c. How is *to confess* used?—Note XII.
What is the rule for it? Note XII.
What is the infinitive mood used for? 479.
How many tenses has it? 528.
What is its usual sign? 517.
Will you now parse the exercises under Note XII.?

(1.) In the nominative case absolute with *being risen*, by Rule XVII. (2.) Rule XII.
(3.) When a noun is in the case absolute, it should be in the nominative case. *Him* should therefore be *he* by Rule XVII.

MOOD. 101

"To play is pleasant." What is pleasant? "To play." The infinitive *to play* is, then, the nominative case to *is*. "Thou shalt not kill, is required of all men." What is required? "Thou shalt not kill." The verb *is required*, then, agrees with "Thou shalt not kill," as its nominative. Hence,

626–1. NOTE XIII.—The infinitive mood, or part of a sentence, is frequently put as the nominative case to a verb of the third person singular.

627. EXERCISES IN SYNTAX.

"To excel requires much exertion."
"To abandon friends will sink a man's character."
"To practise religion is our duty."

"Thou shalt not kill, is the command of God."
"Honor thy father and thy mother, is required of all men."
"To write a fair hand requires practice."

Remark 1.—*To excel* is the nominative case to *requires*, by Note XIII., and *requires* agrees with *to excel*, by Rule VII. In parsing, "Thou shalt not kill," we first apply Rules VI., VII. and IX. The whole phrase is considered the nominative to *is required*, by Note XIII.

2. The infinitive mood, or a part of a sentence, is frequently the object of a transitive verb; as, "Boys love to play." What do boys love? "To play." The object of *love*, then, is *to play*. "Children do not consider how much has been done for them by their parents." Consider what? "*How much has been done for them by their parents;*" including for the object of the verb the whole phrase in italics.

NOTE XIV.—The infinitive mood or part of a sentence, may have an adjective or participle agreeing with it, when there is no noun, either expressed or understood, to which the adjective may belong.

628 EXERCISES IN SYNTAX.

"To see the sun is pleasant."
"To practise virtue will be productive of happiness."
"To be ridiculed is unpleasant."

"Defraud not thy neighbour, is binding on all."
"To do good to our enemies, is not natural to our hearts."

Remarks.—*Pleasant* agrees with, "to see the sun," by Note XIV. *Binding* agrees with, "Defraud not thy neighbour," by the same authority. To *is* apply Rule VII.; to *sun*, Rule VIII.; to the infinitive *to see*, Note XIII.

629. SENTENCES TO BE WRITTEN.

Will you compose one or more sentences having an infinitive governed by a participle? One, using an infinitive after a noun? One, describing the manner of *playing ball*? One, or more, on the manner of *playing tag*? One, on the duty of children to mind their parents? One, or more, on *industry*? One, on *the business* you intend to pursue for life?

"To play is pleasant." What is pleasant? What, then, is the nominative to *is*? 626-1. Rule? Note XIII.
"Thou shalt not kill, is required of all men." What is required? What is the nominative to *is required*? 626-1. Rule? Note XIII.
Will you now parse the remaining exercises under this rule?
"Boys love to play." What is the object of *love*? 627. Remark 2.

Since we have a rule for *to love*, as a verb, there is no necessity for considering it the object in parsing: what rule, then, will you apply to it? XII.
Will you name an example in which there is part of a sentence used as the obje. of a verb? 627. Remark 2.
"To see the sun is pleasant." Will you parse *pleasant? to see? the? sun? is?*
Will you now parse the remaining exercises under Note XIV.

LIX.

630. In the phrase, "John and James are here," the sense is, that "John and James are *both* here;" two persons are therefore spoken of, which renders it necessary to use the plural verb *are*, to agree with two nouns which individually are singular: hence,

RULE XVIII.

Two or more nouns or pronouns, of the singular number, connected together by AND, *either expressed or understood, must have verbs, nouns, and pronouns, agreeing with them in the plural number.*

631.   EXERCISES IN SYNTAX.

"William and James run."
"Mary and Harriet study, and they will therefore excel."
"You and I are in fault."
"John and Thomas say they intend to study Latin."
"John and Joseph can get their lessons."
"Time and tide wait for no man."
"My coat and pantaloons were made by Watson."

Remarks.—*William* is one of the nominatives to the verb *run*. *James* is in the nominative case to the verb *run*, and is connected with the noun *William*, by Rule XI. *Run* agrees with *William* and *James*, by Rule XVIII.

632. SENTENCES TO BE PARSED AND CORRECTED.

"Mary and her cousin has come."
"You and I makes progress in our studies."
"Life and health is both uncertain."
"The farmer and his son is in town."
"Susan and her sister is deceitful."
"William and John both writes a good hand."

Remarks.—For *has come*, we should read *have come*, that the verb may be plural, when it has two nominatives connected by *and*, according to Rule XVIII.
Exception 1.—When *and* connects two or more nouns in the singular, which refer to the same person or thing, the verb must be singular; as, "Pliny the philosopher and naturalist has greatly enriched science."

633. SENTENCES TO BE PARSED AND CORRECTED.

"That superficial scholar and critic have given new evidence of his misguided judgment."
"There go a benevolent man and scholar."
"In that house live a great and distinguished scholar and statesman."
"Mr. Cooper, the sailor and novelist, visit La Fayette, the patriot and philanthropist."

LIX. When I say, "John and James are here," of how many persons do I speak?
Should we, then, use *is* or *are*? 630.
What is the rule for *are*? XVIII.
Will you now parse the exercises under Rule XVIII.?
"William and James run." Will you parse *William* in full? and? *James*? *run*?
Will you parse the next exercises?
"Mary and her cousin has come."—Why is this incorrect? 632.
Will you parse the succeeding exercises?
"Pliny the philosopher and naturalist has greatly enriched science." Why should we use *has*, in this sentence, instead of *have*? Exception 1.
"That superficial scholar and critic have given." Why is *have given* incorrect? Exception 1.
What is the rule for *has come*? Exception 1.
Will you correct and parse the remaining exercises?

Exception 2.—When two or more nouns in the singular, connected by *and*, have *each* or *every* joined with them, the verb must be in the singular number; as, " Every person, every house, and every blade of grass, was destroyed."

634. SENTENCES TO BE PARSED AND CORRECTED.

" Every man, and every woman, and every child, were taken."
" Every tree, stick and twig, were consumed."

" Each man and each woman, were particularly alluded to in the report of the affair."

Remark.—Were, in the first of these examples, should be changed for *was*, because reference is had to each person, individually considered, which, in respect to the verb, is the same in effect as if one person only was spoken of.

NOTE XV. —*Every* is sometimes associated with a plural noun, in which case the verb must be singular; as, " Every hundred years constitutes a century."

635. SENTENCES TO BE PARSED AND CORRECTED.

' Every twenty-four hours afford to us the vicissitudes of day and night."

" Every four years, add another day to the ordinary number of days in a year.

Remark.—Afford, in the example above, is a violation of the rule: it should be *affords*, in the singular number. The reason of this is, that "every twenty-four hours," signifies *a single period of time*, and is, therefore, in reality singular.

NOTE XVI. — A verb in the plural will agree with a collective noun in the singular, when a part only of the individuals are meant; as, " The council were divided in their sentiments." When the noun expresses the idea of unity, the verb should be singular; as, " The council was composed wholly of farmers."

Remarks.—In the foregoing example, we use the plural verb *were divided*, because we refer to the individuals composing the council; but if no allusion of this sort had been made, and we had spoken of it as one entire body, we should have used the singular verb, according to the common rule; as, " The council is composed wholly of farmers."

We apply to *council*, in the first example, NOTE XVI.; to *were divided*, the same note; and to *council*, and *was composed* in the second example, RULES VI. and VII.

636. EXERCISES IN SYNTAX.

" The council were divided in their sentiments."
' A part of the men were murdered."

" My people do not consider."
" The multitude eagerly pursue pleasure as their chief good."

In the first example, under Exception 2, why use *was destroyed*, rather than *were destroyed?* Exception 2.
Will you parse the remaining exercises under this exception, after having corrected them?
" Every twenty-four hours afford to us." What does " every twenty-four hours" signify, one period of time, or more? What is wrong, then? Why?
635. Remark.
What is the rule for this? Note XV.
Will you correct and parse the other example?

" The council were divided." Why not *was?* Note XVI. Remarks. Rule? Note XVI.
When is a noun called *collective?* 306.
In what circumstances would it be proper to use the singular verb? Note XVI. Give an example.
How do you parse *council?* Note XVI.
Remarks. *Were divided?* Note XVI.
Remarks. *Was composed*, in the second example? Note XVI.
Will you now parse and correct the remaining exercises under this note?

637. SENTENCES TO BE PARSED AND CORRECTED.

* "My people doth not consider."
* "The people rejoices in that which should give it sorrow"
* "The multitude rushes to certain destruction."
* "The committee was divided in their sentiments, and has referred the business to a general meeting."

LX.

638. *Negative* means *denying;* and *affirmative, asserting* or *declaring positively.* A sentence in which something is denied is a negative one, and a sentence in which something is affirmed or positively asserted, is an affirmative one. "Vice degrades us," is an affirmative sentence, and "Labor does not injure us," is a negative one. *Not, nothing, none at all, by no means, no, in no wise, neither, no, none, &c.,* are negative terms.

The phrase, "I have nothing," has one negative, and means, "I have not any thing." The phrase, "I have not nothing," cannot mean the same as "I have nothing," but must mean, on the contrary, "I have something." This last, you perceive, is an affirmative sentence, and signifies the same as the foregoing one, "I have not nothing." Two negatives, therefore, are equal to an affirmative. Hence,

RULE XIX.

Two negatives in the same sentence, are equivalent to an affirmative.

639. SENTENCES TO BE PARSED AND CORRECTED.

* "He spends all the day in idleness, and I cannot prevail on him to do nothing."
* "He cannot get no employment in town."
* "I cannot by no means consent."
* "I shall not take no interest in the affair."
* "I never studied no grammar."
* "Be (1.) honest, nor (2.) take (3.) no shape nor semblance of disguise."
* "He is so (4.) indolent, that he will not do nothing."
* "I did not say nothing."
* "He cannot do nothing acceptable to John."

Remarks.—For *nothing*, in the above examples, read *anything*, in accordance with RULE XIX.

LX. What is the meaning of *negative?* 638. *affirmative?* 638.
What is a negative sentence? 638. An affirmative one? 638. Give an example of each.
Will you name a few negative terms? 638.
How many negatives has the phrase "I have nothing," and what does it mean? 638.
Meaning of "I have not nothing"? 638.
How many negatives has it?
What kind of a sentence is "I have something"? 638.

What is "I have not nothing" equal to in expression? 638.
What, then, can we say of two negatives? Rule XIX.
Will you next take the exercises under Rule XIX?
What is a noun? 4. article? 350. adjective? 363. pronoun? 3elt verb? 438. participle? 498. adverb? 589. preposition? 595. conjunction? 602. interjection? 607. common noun? 301. proper noun? 302. definite article? 80. indefinite article? 83.
How many properties in grammar have nouns? 308. How many have verbs?*

(1.) *Be* agrees with *thou* or *you* understood, by Rule VII.
(2.) For *nor,* read *and.*
(3.) *Take* is in the imperative mood and agrees with *thou* or *you* understood, and is therefore connected to *be,* according to Rule XI.
(4.) *Adverb.*
* Mood, tense, number, and person.

640. PROMISCUOUS EXERCISES IN SYNTAX.

"Deep rivers move with silent majesty; but small brooks are noisy."
"Deeds are fruits; words are but leaves."
"It is a bad horse indeed that will not carry his own provender."
"The hog never looks up to him who threshes down the acorns."
"Add not trouble to the grief-worn heart."
"If the counsel be good, it is no matter who gives it."
"By others' faults wise men correct their own."
"When the world says you are wise and good, ask yourself if it be true."
"Sin and misery are constant companions."
"Power discovers the disposition of man."
"Quarrels are easily begun, but with difficulty ended."
"Force without forecast is of little worth."
"Rome was not built in one day."
"In youth and strength think of old age and weakness."
"All are not saints who go to church."
"To say well is good, but to do well is better."
"No fear should deter us from doing good."
"Pride, perceiving Humility honorable, often borrows her cloak."
"Say what is well, but do what is better."

641. SENTENCES TO BE WRITTEN.

Will you compose one sentence describing the business of an *instructer*? One, the business of a *doctor*? One, the business of a *lawyer*? One, of a *dentist*? One, of a *surgeon*? One, of a *farmer*? One, of a *blacksmith*? One, of a *miller*? One, of a *merchant*? One, of a *grocer*? One, of an *apothecary*? One, of a *legislator*? One, of a *judge*? One, of a *colonel*? One, of a *captain*? One, of a *general*? One, of an *agent in a factory*? One, of the *directors of a bank*?

LXI.

642. When I say, "He taught me grammar," I mean, "He taught grammar to me:" *grammar*, then, is the object of the verb, and *me* is governed by the preposition *to*, understood. In the first example, we have two objective cases after the verb *taught*; and since there are many instances like the preceding, in which transitive verbs are followed by two objective cases—hence the following,

---

How many participles are there?*
What are they? 500, 502, 504.
When is a verb active? 439.
When transitive? 440. When intransitive? 441. How may it be known? 154.
Will you decline *I? thou? he? she? it?* 127.
Of what person is *I? my? us? their? you?* 127.
What is mood? 451. the indicative? 452. potential? 453. subjunctive? 456. infinitive? 479. imperative? 472. How many tenses has the indicative? 525. subjunctive? 526. potential? 527. infinitive? 528. imperative? 529. What

are the signs of the present tense? 510. imperfect? 520. perfect? 521. pluperfect? 522. first future? 523. second future? 524.
Will you now parse the promiscuous exercises?
Will you next take the sentences to be written?
LXI. "He taught me grammar." What does this mean? 642. What, then, is the object of the verb, and by what is *grammar* governed? 642. By what is *me* governed? 642.
How many objective cases, then, follow the verb *taught*? 642.

* Three.

RULE XX.

Two objective cases, the one of a person, and the other of a thing, may follow transitive verbs, of asking, teaching, giving, &c.; a preposition being understood.

He taught me grammar."

Remark 1.—In the foregoing example, *me* and *grammar* are both governed by *taught*, according to RULE XX.

643.   EXAMPLES IN SYNTAX.

"He taught me grammar."
"William asked me some questions."
"My mother wrote me a precious letter in the month of May."
"They allowed him his seat in Congress."
"John gave me a detailed account of the whole transaction."

"My instructer gave me a valuable book, for my attention to study."
"She forbade him the presence of the emperor."
"The French denied him the privilege of an American citizen."

LXII.

644. The natural construction of the passive voice requires the object of the active verb to become the nominative to the passive verb; as, "He taught me grammar;" "Grammar was taught me." In some few instances, just the reverse takes place; as, "I was taught grammar;" here the object, *grammar*, is placed after the verb: we therefore derive the following

RULE XXI.

An objective case may follow passive verbs of asking, teaching, and some others; as, "I was taught grammar."

☞ Apply to *I* RULE VI.; to *was taught*, RULE VII.; to *grammar*, RULE XXI.

645.   EXERCISES IN SYNTAX.

"John taught me music."
"Music was taught me by John."
"A question was asked me."
"Theresa was forbidden the presence of the emperor."

"I was taught grammar."
"The presence of the emperor was forbidden Theresa."
"Reading is taught in almost every school."

What rule is given for cases of this description? XX.
By what are *me* and *grammar* governed? 642. Remark 1.
Will you next parse the exercises under Rule XX.?
LXII. What is the natural construction of the passive voice in reference to the object? 644. Give an example. 644. Give an example where the reverse takes place. 644.
Where is the object placed? 644.
"I was taught grammar." Will you parse *I? was taught? grammar?*
Will you next take the exercises under Rule XXI.?

LXIII.

646 When I say, "He came home last May," the sense is, when fully expressed, "He came *to his* home *in* last May." "John continued four years at the university;" that is, "*during* four years." "The horse ran a mile;" that is, "*over* the space of a mile." "John went that way;" that is, "*over* that way." From these facts we derive the following

RULE XXII.

Home, *and nouns signifying* which way, how far, how long, *or* time when, &c., *are in the objective case; a preposition being understood.*

647.   EXERCISES IN SYNTAX.

"He came home last May."
"John continued four years at the university."
"John went home once a month."
"Charles studies six hours every day."
"John rode that way."
"He ran a mile."

"Susan rides out every day."
"William sleeps comfortably all night."
"John was absent from home six years."
"James lived six years at Boston, twelve years at Dedham."

NOTE XVII.—After the words *like* and *unlike*, the preposition *to* or *unto* is frequently understood; as, "He is like his father;" that is, "like *to* his father." "She is unlike her sister;" that is, "unlike *to* her sister."

648.   EXERCISES IN SYNTAX.

"He is like his brother."
"William, unlike his father, falsified his word."

"John behaves like a man in a violent rage."
"He is unlike any other mortal."

NOTE XVIII.—Nouns signifying duration, extension, quantity, quality or valuation, are in the objective case, without any governing word. The following are examples:

"The Atlantic ocean is three thousand miles (1.) wide."
"William's knife is worth eighteen pence, or twenty-five cents."
"For that article, which is richly worth a dollar, (2.) we cannot always get fifty cents."
"The chasm is fifty feet broad."

"The cart weighs fifteen hundred pounds."
"The wall which separates China from Tartary, commonly called the great Chinese wall, is fifteen hundred miles long, and from twenty to thirty feet in height."

Remarks.—(1.) The noun *miles* is governed according to NOTE XVIII. (2.) Apply NOTE XVIII.

LXIII. "He came home last May." What does this mean, when more fully expressed? 646. Will you parse *home? May?*
"John continued four years at the university." "The horse ran a mile." What do these sentences mean, when fully expressed?

Will you parse the exercises under Rule XXII?
What is the note respecting *like* and *unlike?* XVII.
"He is like his father." How is *father* parsed? Note XVII.
Will you next take the remaining exercises under Note XVII?

NOTE XIX.—The conjunction *as*, after *such*, *many* and *same*, is generally considered a relative pronoun; as in the following examples:

"He receives into his school as many scholars as (1.) apply."

"He took such books as pleased him."

"Our instructer, who is scrupulously exact in the execution of justice, punishes severely all such as disobey his commands."

"He exhibited the same course of conduct as was once before exhibited on the same occasion."

Remarks.—(1.) *As* is a conjunction, used here as a relative, according to the NOTE preceding; of the third person plural, masculine gender, agreeing with *scholars*, according to RULE V.; and in the nominative case to *apply*, according to RULE VI.

NOTE XX.—The conjunction *than* seems to have the force of a preposition before the relative *whom*, in a sentence where a comparison is made; as follows:

"Which, when Beelzebub perceived, than whom, (1.) Satan (2.) excepted, (3.) none higher sat."

"Alfred, than whom, Solomon excepted, a wiser king never reigned, was one of the earliest English kings."

Remarks.—(1.) *Whom* is governed by the conjunction *than*, used as a preposition, according to NOTE XX.—(2.) Apply RULE XVII.—(3.) Participle agreeing with *Satan*, by RULE XIII.—It is somewhat remarkable, that if, in the last two examples, the personal pronoun *he* were substituted for *whom*, it would be in the nominative case; as, "A wiser king never reigned than *he*;" that is, "than *he* was."

649. SENTENCES TO BE WRITTEN.

Will you compose a sentence having a proper example under RULE I.? II.? III.? IV.? V.? VI.? VII.? VIII.? IX.? X.? XI.? XII.? XIII.? XIV.? XV.? XVI.? XVII.? XVIII.? XIX.? XX.? XXI.? XXII.?

Will you construct a sentence descriptive of the *calamities arising from fire?* one, on *losses by sea?* one, on the *fatal effects of lightning?* one, on the *character of our forefathers?* one, on *each of the seasons?* one, on the *effects of rain?* one, on the *manner of making hay?* one, on the *appearance of soldiers when training?* one, on the *celebration of the fourth of July?* one, on the *utility of fire?* one, on the *utility of wood?* one, on the *usefulness of the cow?* one, on *fruit?*

When is the conjunction *as* used as a relative pronoun? Note XIX.
Will you parse *as*, in the phrase "He received into his school as many scholars as applied"? Note XIX.
Will you parse the remaining exercises under this Note?
When is *than* considered a preposition? Note XX. Give an example.
What would be the effect of using the personal pronoun instead of the relative? Observation under Note XX. Give an example.
Will you now take the sentences to be parsed and written?
How many articles are there? 351.
Will you name them? 351. When do we use *a*? 87, 357. When *an*? 86.

What does English grammar teach? 288. How many parts of speech are there in English? 289.
What does *orthography* include? 291.
What does it teach us? 291.
What does *etymology* teach? 293.
What are proper nouns? 302.
What are common nouns? 301.
In what manner may proper names be used as common names? 303.
How may common names be used to represent individuals? 304.
What is a collective noun? 306.
What four things belong to nouns? 308.
What is gender? 312. Masculine gender? 314. Feminine gender? 315. Common gender? 316. Neuter gender? 317.

LXIV. OF WORDS USED AS DIFFERENT PARTS OF SPEECH.

650. THAT is a *relative*,

When *who* or *which* may be substituted for it, and make sense; as, "The man that [who] arrived yesterday."

651. THAT is a *demonstrative pronoun*,

When it is joined with a noun to point it out; as, "That man is intelligent."

652. THAT is a *conjunction*,

In all cases when it is neither a relative nor a demonstrative pronoun: as, "He studies that he may learn."

653. BUT is a *preposition*,

When it has the sense of *except*; as, "All but [except] John came."

654. BUT is an *adverb*,

When it has the sense of *only*; as, "This is but [only] doing our duty."

655. BUT is a *conjunction*,

In all cases when it is neither an adverb nor preposition; as, "He called, but I refused to go."

656. As is a *relative*,

When it follows *many*, *such*, or *same*; as, "Let such as hear take heed."

657. As is an *adverb*,

When it is joined to an adverb or adjective in the sense of *so*; as, "He does as well as he can."

658. As is a *conjunction*,

In all cases except when it is an adverb or relative; as, "He did as I directed him."

659. EITHER is a *conjunction*,

When it corresponds to *or*; as, "Either the one or the other."

660. EITHER is a *distributive pronoun*,

When it means, "one of the two;" as, "You can take either road."

661. BOTH is a *conjunction*,

When it is followed by *and*; as, "We assisted him both for his sake and our own."

How may nouns, naturally neuter, be converted into the masculine or feminine gender? 318.

What is the feminine corresponding to *bachelor*? 319. How is the feminine here formed?

Will you spell the feminine corresponding to *lad*? *king*? *benefactor*? 319. How is the feminine here formed?

Will you spell the feminine corresponding to *baron*? *poet*? *priest*? *Jew*? *votary*? *tutor*? *hero*? *duke*? *instructer*? 319.

LXIV. When is *that* a relative? 650. Give an example. A demonstrative pronoun? 651. Give an example. When a conjunction? 652. Give an example.

When is *but* a preposition? 653. Give an example. When an adverb? 654. Give an example. When a conjunction? 655. Give an example.

When is *as* a relative? 656. Give an example. When an adverb? 657. Give an example. When a conjunction? 658. Give an example.

When is *either* a conjunction? 659. Give an example. When a distributive pronoun? 660. Give an example.

When is *both* a conjunction? 661. Give an example. When an adjective pronoun? 662. Give an example.

662. Both is an *adjective pronoun*,
When it means, "the two;" as, "Both the men are guilty."

663. Yet is a *conjunction*,
When it follows *though;* as, "Though he reproves me, yet I esteem him." In all other cases, it is an *adverb;* as, "That event has yet to come."

664. For is a *conjunction*,
When it means the same as *because;* as, "He trusted him, for he knew that he would not deceive him."

665. For is a *preposition*,
In all instances except when it is a conjunction; as, "He works for me."

666. What is a *compound relative*,
When it stands for, "that which;" as, "I will take what [that which] you send me."

667. What is an *interrogative relative pronoun*,
When used in asking questions; as, "What do you want?"

668. What is an *adjective pronoun*,
When joined with a noun; as, "What strange things he said!"

669. What is a *compound adjective pronoun*,
When joined with nouns, and has the sense of two or more words; as, "In what manner he succeeded, is unknown to me;" that is, "The manner *in which* he succeeded, is unknown to me."

670. What is an *interjection*,
When used to express wonder; as, "What! take my money?"

671. Then is a *conjunction*,
When it has the sense of *therefore;* as, "If he has commanded it, then I must obey."

672. Then is an *adverb*,
When it refers to time; as, "Did you hear it thunder then?"

673. Much is a *noun*,
When it stands for quantity; as, "Where much is given, much will be required."

674. Much is an *adjective*,
When it is joined to nouns; as, "Much labour fatigues us."

675. Much is an *adverb*,
When it qualifies the same parts of speech that the adverb does; as, "Thou art much mightier than I."

676. More is a *noun*,
When it implies quantity; as, "The more we have, the more we want."

When is *yet* a conjunction? 663. Give an example. When an adverb? 663. Give an example.
When is *for* a conjunction? 664. Give an example. When a preposition? 665. Give an example.
When is *what* a compound relative? 666. Give an example. When an interrogative relative pronoun? 667. Give an example. When an adjective pronoun? 668. Give an example. When a compound pronoun? 669. Give an example.
When an interjection? 670. Give an example.
When is *then* a conjunction? 671. Give an example. When an adverb? 672. Give an example.
When is *much* a noun? 673. Give an example. When an adjective? 674. Give an example. When an adverb? 675 Give an example.
When is *more* a noun? 676. Give an example.

EXERCISES. 111

677. MORE and MOST are *adjectives*,
When they qualify a noun; as, "The more joy I have, the more sorrow I expect;" "Most men are mistaken in their pursuit of happiness."

678. MORE and MOST are *adverbs*,
When used in comparison; as, "This boy is more obedient than that;" "The soil of Cuba is most fertile."

679. PROMISCUOUS EXERCISES IN SYNTAX.

"They perfume their garments."
"A perfume is a sweet odor."
"They rise early in the morning."
"A rise sometimes signifies the beginning."
"Rufus speaks the language of truth."
"James performed his part well."
"A well is a fountain of water."
"A well man is one who enjoys his health."
"We frequently walk in the garden."
"The Jews fast often."
"He walks very fast."
"The refuse signifies the worthless remains."
"Desert not a friend."
"Joseph's brethren came and bowed down before him."
"William went after his slate."

"His elder brethren came before Benjamin did."
"John left after William came."
"Evil communications corrupt good manners."
"Corrupt conversation is very foolish."
"A walk in the fields in the summer season is delightful."
"A true fast is abstaining from iniquity."
"Sin is a moral evil, and the cause of natural evils."
"Protest not rashly, lest thou have to repent of it."
"A protest is a solemn declaration against a thing."
"Do nothing rashly, lest thou precipitate thyself into inextricable difficulty."
"Hasty promises are seldom kept."

2.

"The man that I saw, was executed."
"That man that you met yesterday in the street, was taken and sent to Boston, that he might have an impartial trial."
"We assisted him both for your sake and our own."

"Did you hear the report of the cannon then?"
"Where much is given, much will be required."
"Future time is yet to come."
"He trusted him, for he knew that he would not deceive him."

When are *more* and *most* adjectives? 677. Give examples of each. When adverbs? 678. Give examples of each.
What is *number*? 5. What does the singular number denote? 8. What the plural? 10.
What nouns have the singular form only? 324. What the plural? 325. What are the same in both numbers? 326.
How is the plural number of nouns generally formed? 327.
When nouns end in *ch, sh*, &c., how do they form the plural? 328.
How do those ending in *f* or *fe*? 329.
How is the plural formed, when the singular ends in *y*, with no other vowel in the same syllable? 330.
What is case? 333. The nominative case? 335. Possessive case? 337. How

formed? 338. How formed when the singular ends in *ss*? 341.
What does the objective case express 343.
Will you decline *man*? *book*? 345. *chair*? 345.
Will you parse the promiscuous exercises?
What is an adjective? 363. What does the positive state express? 365. Comparative? 366. Superlative? 367. How is the comparative formed in monosyllables? 369. How in more syllables than one? 370.
How do you compare the following adjectives? — *good*? *bad*? *wise*? *little*? *small*? *virtuous*? *many*? *old*? 115.
When does an adjective become a noun in parsing? 378.

"Both the men are guilty."
"Although he reproves me, yet I esteem him."
"All but John came."
"This is but doing our duty."
"He called me, but I refused to go."
"Let such as hear take heed."
"He did as I directed him."
"You may take either the one or the other."
"Either road will conduct you to the right place."
"If he has commanded it, then I must obey."

"He works for me."
"He refused what was sent him."
"What strange things he saw!"
"In what manner he succeeded is unknown to me."
"What! will you take my life?"
"The more we have, the more we want."
"The more joy I have, the more sorrow I expect."
"The most dutiful children are the happiest children."
"Much labor fatigues me."
"Thou art much mightier than I am."

3.

"Susan is determined to learn."
"By framing excuses he prolonged his stay."
"The man who is faithfully attached to religion may be relied on with confidence."
"James, do visit me"

"Virtue and vice are opposites."
"When John's father asked him that question, he heard him, but refused to answer him."
"The wall is sixty feet high."
"To meet our friends after a long absence affords us much joy."

LXV. CONTRACTIONS.

680. *Of the Auxiliary* HAVE, *also of* HAD.

"They 've forsaken him."
"I 'd gone when you came."
"They 'd just returned from town."

"I 've satisfied myself."
"They 'd determined to let him go."

681. *Of* WILL *and* WOULD.

"I 'll finish my work first."
"They 'd sing songs till midnight, if they were urged."

"He is still determined that he 'll not forbear."
"He 'll at last mind me."

Will you name a few adjectives which have in themselves a superlative signification? 374.
What is a pronoun? 381. A personal pronoun? 382. Why called personal? 382.
How many persons have pronouns in each number? 383. How many numbers? 384.
To which of the pronouns is gender applied? 382.
How many cases have pronouns? 384.
Will you decline *I*? *thou*? *he*? *she*? *it*? 127
What kind of a pronoun is *myself*? 386. How formed? 386.
What is a relative pronoun? 409. Why called relative? 408.
What is said of the relative *what*? 429.
How ought *who* to be applied? 412.

How *which*? 413. How may *that* be used? 415.
When are pronouns called interrogative? 431
What are adjective pronouns? 390. How many kinds of adjective pronouns are there? 391.
Which are the demonstrative? 392. Why so called? 398. The distributive? 393. Why so called? 393. The indefinite? 402. Why so called? 401.
To what do *this* and *that* refer? 400.
Will you decline *one*? 404. *other*? 403.
What is the rule by which pronouns agree with their antecedents? V.
Which words in sentences are antecedents? V.
What are subsequents? 431.
Will you parse the exercises marked 8?

CONTRACTIONS. 113

682. *Of* AM *and* IS.

"That man's rich."
"'T is true she's dead."
"I'm sorry that you have misspent your time."

"'T is strange that she will not regard the kind assistance of her friend."

683. *Of* CANNOT *and* WILL NOT.

"He can't endure such afflictions."
"You can't be absent at such times."

"He won't disobey me."
"You won't mistake the direction."

684. *Omissions of the Principal Verb after an Interrogative Sentence.*

"Who will assist me?" "John" [will assist me].
"What sent our forefathers to this country?" "The love of liberty."

"What will make me respectable and happy?" "Virtue."
"Who taught him grammar?" "Mr. Williams."

685. *Omissions of the Principal Verb after an Auxiliary.*

"Stephen will go if John will" [go].
"Susan shall walk, but John shall not."
"I have recited; have you?"

"He received me in the same manner that I would you."
"I will do it as soon as I can."
"The work is not completed, but soon will be."

686. *Omissions of the Principal Verb after* THAN *and* AS.

"Thomas is a better scholar than William" [is].
"He was more beloved than Cinthia, but not so much admired."

"Johnson is richer than James."
"Susan is not so beautiful as Mary."
"She is more playful than her brother."

687. *Omissions of the Verb* TO BE.

"Sweet the pleasure, rich the treasure."
"A child of freedom thou."
"Sweet the music of birds."
"Dear the schoolboy's sport."

"Delightful task, to rear the tender thought,
To teach the young idea how to shoot."

What is a verb? 438.
What is an active verb? 439.
When is an active verb transitive? 440. When intransitive? 441.
What is a passive verb? 444. How formed? 510.
How may a transitive verb be known? 154.
How an intransitive? 154.
What is a neuter verb? 450.
Will you next take the exercises marked 3?
What belong to verbs?*.
How many numbers have they? How many persons?†
What is mood? 451. How many are there? 481. Will you name them?
What is the indicative mood used for? 452. The potential? 453. The impera-

tive? 472. Subjunctive? 456. Infinitive? 479.
What are participles? 498. How may the participles in *ing* be distinguished from other words of like termination? 500.
How many, and which are the participles?‡ What does the present express? 500. Perfect? 502. Compound perfect? 504.
LXV. Will you next parse the contractions? 680.
What is tense? 494. What is the present used for? 482. The perfect? Imperfect? 488. Pluperfect? 491. First future? 492. Second future? 493.
Under what circumstances do we use the present tense to denote the relative time of a future action? 484.

---

* Mood, tense, number and person.   † Three.   ‡ Three — the present, perfect, and compound perfect.

H   10*

688. *Omissions of* MAY, MIGHT, COULD, WOULD, *and* SHOULD.

"Live long and be happy."
"Who will entreat the Lord that he spare our lives?"
"I could not think, nor speak, nor hear."

"He might not weep, nor laugh, nor sing."
"Should I forgive you, and allow you to depart, you would not reform."

689. *Omissions of the Conjunction before the Verb in the Subjunctive Mood.*

"If he will repent and reform, I will assist him."
"Unless good order be restored, and the former officers be re-elected, there will be an end to the administration of justice."

"Had I improved my time as I ought to have done, I should have been well qualified for business."
"Were there no alternative, I would not do that."

690. *Omissions of* FOR *after Verb, implying the idea of serving.*

"Make me a pen."
"Order me a carriage."

"Bring me some water."
"Purchase him a knife."

691. *Omissions of the Interjection.*

"Sweet child! lovely child! thy parents are no more."
"Sweet blossom! precious to my heart."

"Thou Preserver and Creator of all mankind."
"My beloved Ulrica! hast thou, too, forgotten me?"

692. *Omissions of the Relative.*

"Several men are there come from Europe."

"I trust that he I desire to see so much, will speedily return."

LXVI. INVERTED SENTENCES.

693. *The Nominative Case placed after the Verb.*

"Smack went the whip, round went the wheels;
Were ever folks so glad?"
"There goes a man alike distinguished for his learning and politeness."
"And in soft ringlets waved her golden hair."

In what sort of descriptions do we use the present for the past tense? 486.
What is the conjugation of a verb? 531.
What is the conjugation of an active verb styled? 532. A passive verb? 532.
How many tenses has the indicative? 525. Potential? 527. Subjunctive? 526. Imperative? 520. Infinitive? 528.
What is the sign of the present indicative? 519. The imperfect? 520. Perfect? 521. Pluperfect? 522. First future? 523. Second future? 524. The potential mood? 515. Infinitive? 517. Subjunctive? 516. How many persons has the imperative? 518. How many tenses? 529. How many forms has the subjunctive mood? 461. In what do they differ? 461.

Will you now parse the omissions? 684, &c.
How is the passive verb formed? 510.
Will you decline *love* in the indicative present, passive? and the verb *to be* in the imperfect? Perfect? Pluperfect? First future? Second future? Present potential? Imperfect? Perfect? Pluperfect? Present subjunctive, common form? Imperfect? Perfect? Pluperfect? First future? Second future?
In what voice, mood, tense, number and person, is, "I love?" "We love?" "They are loved?" "You are?" "I did learn?" "John was instructed?" "He was?" "They have returned?" "Have they gone?" "They have been?" "I had had?" "They had been distinguished?"

SENTENCES TRANSPOSED.

694. *The Objective Case before the Verb.*

"Tyrants no more their savage nature kept,
And foes to virtue wondered how they wept."

"Me glory summons to the martial scene."
"The rolls of fame I will not now explore."

695.   SENTENCES TO BE WRITTEN.

Will you compose a sentence exemplifying Rule VIII.? One, Rule IX.? X.? XI.? XII.? XIII.? XIV.? Will you compose a sentence *on the use of the dog?* One, *on the clouds?* One, *on night?* One, *on wind?* One, *on snow?* One, *on hail?* One, *on ice?* One, *on skating?* One, *on fishing?* One, *on courage?* One, *on cowardice?* One, *on filial duty?* One, *on indolence?* One, *on schools?*

696.   SENTENCES TRANSPOSED.

"Here rests his head upon the lap of earth,
A youth, to fortune and to fame unknown."

Transposed.

"A youth, unknown to fortune and to fame, rests here his head upon the lap of earth."

"When, young, life's journey I began,
The glittering prospect charmed my eyes,
I saw along the extended plain,
Joy after joy successive rise:
But soon I found 't was all a dream,
And learned the fond pursuit to shun,
Where few can reach the purposed aim,
And thousands daily are undone."

Transposed.

"I began life's journey when young, and the glittering prospect charmed my eyes; I saw joy after joy successive rise, along the extended plain: but soon I found it was all a dream; and learned to shun the fond pursuit, where few can reach the purposed aim, and thousands are daily undone."

"Needful austerities our wills restrain,
As thorns fence in the tender plant from harm."

Transposed.

"Needful austerities restrain our wills, as thorns fence in the tender plant from harm."

"Thou hadst been"? "You shall be taught"? "Shall I be punished"? "He shall have been"?
LXVI. Will you parse the inverted sentences? 693, &c.
In what voice, mood, tense, number and person, is "Love thou"? "I may go"? "You may be regarded"? "You might be rejoiced"? "She may have been refused"? "We should have been"? "If I have"? "If thou have"? "If thou hast"? "To have"? "To have been"?
Will you give the synopis of *learn,* through all the moods, tenses, &c., in the first person, including the participle? *Learn,* in like manner, in the passive? The verb *to be* in the same manner?

Will you give the synopis of *desire* in the active voice, with the participles? Of the same in the passive? Of *do* in the active? In the passive?
When is a verb called regular? 533. When irregular? 534.
Will you repeat the present and imperfect tenses, also the perfect participle of *am? see? hear? do? weep? sink? swim?*
Will you next take the sentences to be written?
What are auxiliary verbs? 511.
How many and which are they? 512.
What are defective verbs? 579.
What is an adverb? 598. Why so called? 228.

"On some fond breast the parting soul relies,
Some pious drops the closing eye requires;
E'en from the tomb the voice of nature cries,
E'en in our ashes live their wonted fires."

Transposed.

"The parting soul relies on some fond breast; the closing eye requires some pious drops; the voice of nature cries, even from the tomb; and their wonted fires live even in our ashes."

"From lofty themes, from thoughts that soared on high
And opened wondrous scenes above the sky,
My Muse! descend; indulge my fond desire,
With softer thoughts my melting soul inspire,
And smooth my numbers to a female's praise;
A partial world will listen to my lays,
While Anna reigns, and sets a female name
Unrivalled in the glorious lists of fame."

Transposed.

"O my Muse! descend thou from lofty themes, and from thoughts that soared on high, and opened wondrous scenes above the sky; indulge thou my fond desire; and do thou inspire my melting soul with softer thoughts, and smooth my numbers to a female's praise; a partial world will listen to my lays, while Anna reigns, and sets a female name unrivalled in the glorious lists of fame."

In what manner are adverbs compared? 236, 234.
What are the phrases which do the office of adverbs called? 589.
Will you name a few? 589.
What is a preposition? 595.
Will you repeat the list of prepositions? 247.
What is a conjunction? 602. Conjunction copulative? 265. Why so called? 264. Conjunction disjunctive? 274. Why so called? 271.
Will you repeat the list of copulative conjunctions? 266. Of disjunctive conjunctions? 275.
What is an interjection? 607. Why so called? 283. Mention a few? 285.
What is syntax? 296. What is a sentence? 252. A simple sentence? 253.

What is the rule for the agreement of nouns? XV. Articles? II., III. Adjectives? IV. Pronouns? V. Verbs? VII. Participles? XIII. Agreement of a verb plural with two nouns singular? XVIII. Adjective pronouns and numerals? Note 1.
What is the rule by which a verb agrees with a noun of multitude, or collective noun? Note XVI. Rule for the objective case after a transitive verb? VIII.
What is the rule for the objective case after a preposition? X. After a participle? XIV. Rule for the adverb? IX. Rule respecting the interjections O! ah! ah! &c.? Note X.
Will you parse the sentences marked transposed?

GENERAL OBSERVATIONS.

SYNTAX.

THAT part of Grammar which treats of the formation and sound of the letters, the combination of letters into syllables, and syllables into words, is called Orthography.

That part which treats of the different sorts of words, their various changes and their derivations, is called Etymology.

That part which treats of the union and right order of words in the formation of sentences, is called Syntax.

GRAMMAR may be considered as consisting of two species, *Universal* and *Particular.* Universal Grammar explains the principles which are common to all languages. Particular Grammar applies those principles to a particular language, modifying them according to the genius of that tongue, and the established practice of the best writers and speakers by whom it is used.

LANGUAGE, in the proper sense of the word, signifies the expression of our ideas, and their various relations, by certain articulate sounds, which are used as the signs of those ideas and relations. An articulate sound is the sound of the human voice, formed by the organs of speech.

LETTERS are the representatives of certain articulate sounds, the elements of the language.

The letters of the English Language, called the English Alphabet, are twenty-six in number, each of which constitutes the first principle, or least part of a word.

LETTERS are divided into vowels and consonants.

A vowel is a letter that can be perfectly sounded by itself. The vowels are *a, e, i, o, u,* and sometimes *w* and *y*. *W* and *y* are consonants when they begin a word or syllable; but in every other situation they are vowels.

A consonant is a letter that cannot be perfectly sounded without the aid of a vowel; as, *b, d, f, l*. All letters except the vowels are consonants.

Consonants are divided into mutes and semi-vowels.

The mutes cannot be sounded *at all*, without the aid of a vowel. They are *b, p, t, d, k,* and *c* and *g* hard.

The semi-vowels have an imperfect sound of themselves. They are *f, l, m, n, r, v, s, z, x,* and *c* and *g* soft.

Four of the semi-vowels, namely, *l, m, n, r,* are called liquids, because they readily unite with other consonants, and flow, as it were, into their sounds.

A diphthong is the union of *two* vowels, pronounced by a single impulse of the voice; as, *oi* in *voice, ou* in *ounce.*

A triphthong is the union of *three* vowels, pronounced in like manner; as, *eau* in *beau, iew* in *view.*

A proper diphthong is that in which both the vowels are sounded; as, *oi* in *voice, ou* in *ounce.*

An improper diphthong has but one of the vowels sounded; as, *ea* in *eagle, oa* in *boat.*

A SYLLABLE is a sound, either simple or compounded, uttered by a single impulse of the voice, and constituting a word or part of a word; as, *a, an, ant.*

A word of one syllable is called a Monosyllable; a word of two syllables, a Dissyllable; a word of three syllables, a Trisyllable; a word of four or more syllables, a Polysyllable.

Words are articulate sounds, used by common consent as signs of our ideas.

Words are of two sorts, primitive and derivative.

A *primitive* word is that which cannot be reduced to a simpler word in the language; as, *man, good.*

A *derivative* word is that which may be reduced to a simpler word; as, *manful, goodness.*

The elementary sounds, under their smallest combination, produce a *syllable;* syllables, properly combined, produce a *word;* words, duly combined, produce a *sentence;* and sentences, properly combined, produce an *oration,* or *discourse.*

A sentence is an assemblage of words, forming complete sense.

Sentences are of two kinds, simple and compound.

A simple sentence has in it but one subject, and one finite* verb; as, "Life is short."

A compound sentence consists of two or more simple sentences connected together; as, "Life is short, and art is long."

As sentences themselves are divided into simple and compound, so the members of sentences may be divided likewise into simple and compound members; for whole sentences, whether simple or compound, may become members of other sentences, by means of some additional connection; as in the following example: "The ox knoweth his owner, and the ass his master's crib; but Israel doth not know, my people doth not consider." This sentence consists of two compounded members, each of which is subdivided into two simple members, which are properly called clauses.

A phrase is two or more words rightly put together, making sometimes a part of a sentence, and sometimes a whole sentence.

The principal parts of a simple sentence are the subject, the attribute, and the object.

---

* Finite verbs are those to which number and person appertain. Verbs in the infinitive mood have no respect to number and person.

SYNTAX. 119

The subject is the thing chiefly spoken of, the attribute is the thing or action affirmed or denied of it; and the object is the thing affected by such action.

The nominative case denotes the subject; and usually goes before the verb or attribute; and the word or phrase denoting the object, follows the verb; as, "A wise man governs his passions." Here *a wise man* is the subject; *governs*, the attribute or thing affirmed; and *his passions*, the object.

Syntax principally consists of two parts, Concord and Government. Concord is the agreement which one word has with another in gender, number, case, or person. Government is that power which one part of speech has over another, in directing its mood, tense, or case.

What is Orthography? Etymology? Syntax? How many kinds of grammar are there? What are they? What is universal grammar? Particular grammar? What is language? What is an articulate sound? What are letters? What are the letters of the English language called? What does each constitute? How are letters divided? What is a vowel? Which are they? How many do they make? When are *w* and *y* consonants? when vowels? What is a consonant? Give an example. Which letters are consonants? How are the consonants divided? What is a mute? Which are they? What is a semi-vowel? Which are they? Which of the semi-vowels are called liquids, and why? What is a diphthong? Give an example. What is a triphthong? Give an example. What is a proper diphthong? Give an example. What is an improper diphthong? Give an example. What is a syllable? monosyllable? dissyllable? trisyllable? polysyllable? What are words? Of how many sorts are they? What is a primitive word? Give an example. What is a derivative word? Give an example. What does an elementary sound produce? What do syllables produce? Words? Sentences? What is a sentence? How are sentences divided? What is a simple sentence? Compound sentence? Give an example of each. How are the members of sentences divided? Give an example. What is a phrase? What are the principal parts of a simple sentence? What is the subject? the attribute? the object? What does the nominative case denote? and where is it usually placed in a sentence? Give an example. Of how many parts does Syntax consist? What are they? What is concord? Government?

The right construction of sentences may perhaps be best learned by correcting examples of wrong construction. Exercises in false syntax for the pupil, assisted by rules and notes to parse and correct, will therefore now be given.

The following contain all the notes and observations in Murray's large Grammar, together with all his exercises in false syntax.

RULE VII.
Corresponding with Murray's Grammar.

RULE I.

A verb must agree with its nominative case in number and person.

The following are a few instances of the violation of this rule: "What signifies good opinions, when our practice is bad?" "what signify"

"There's two or three of us, who have seen the work;" "there *are*." "We may suppose there was more impostors than one;" "there *were* more." "I have considered what have been said on both sides in this controversy;" "what *has* been said." "If thou would be healthy, live temperately;" "if thou *wouldst*." "Thou *sees* how little has been done;" "thou *seest*." "Though thou cannot do much for the cause, thou may and should do something;" "*canst not, mayst,* and *shouldst*." "Full many a flower are born to blush unseen;" "*is* born." "A conformity of inclinations and qualities prepare us for friendship;" "*prepares* us.' " "A variety of blessings have been conferred upon us;" "*has* been." "In piety and virtue consist the happiness of man;" "*consists*." "To these precepts are subjoined a copious selection of rules and maxims;" "*is* subjoined."

"If thou would be healthy, live temperately." Which word is wrong in this example? In what particular, wrong? Why? What is the Rule for it? How, then, would you correct the example?—"There was more equivocators." Which word is wrong here? What correction should be made? Why?

☞ *The pupil is first to answer the questions on each Rule or Note, then to correct and parse the subsequent exercises. It is suggested to the teacher, that the pupils should direct their attention first to the Rules and exercises under them, exclusively, omitting the Notes, &c., for a review, when all may be taken in course.*

"Disappointments *sinks* the heart of man; but the renewal of hope *give* consolation."

"The smiles that (1.) encourage severity of judgment *hides* malice and insincerity."

"He *dare* not act (2.) contrary (3.) to his instructions."

"Fifty pounds of wheat *contains* forty pounds of flour."

"The mechanism of clocks and watches *were* totally unknown (4.) a few centuries ago." (5.)

"The number of inhabitants in Great Britain and Ireland, do not exceed sixteen millions."

"Nothing (6.) but vain and foolish pursuits (7.) *delight* some persons."

"A variety of pleasing objects charm the eye."

"So (8.) much (9.) botn (10.) of ability and merit (11.) are seldom (12.) found."

"In the conduct of Parmenio a mixture of wisdom and folly (11.) were very (8.) conspicuous."

"He is an author (13.) of more credit than Plutarch, (14.) or any other (15.) that (11.) writ lives too (12.) hastily."

"The inquisitive (16.) and curious (11.) is generally talkative." (17.)

"Great pains has been taken to reconcile the parties."

"The sincere (16.) is always esteemed."

"Has the goods been sold to advantage? and did thou embrace the proper season?"

"There is many occasions (6.) in life, in which silence and simplicity (11.) is true wisdom."

"The generous (16.) never recounts minutely the actions they have done; nor the prudent, (7.) those (15.) they will do."

"He need not proceed (2.) in such haste."

"The business that (1.) related to ecclesiastical meetings, matters (11.) and persons, (11.) were to be ordered according (18.) to the king's direction."

(1.) See 650. (2.) Apply Rule XII. See 480. (3.) Adjective. (4.) Rule XIII. (5.) *A few centuries ago*—an adverbial phrase, 589; or apply Note XVIII, 645, to *centuries*, and Rule IX. to *ago*. (6.) Rule VI. (7.) Rule XI. (8.) 239. (9.) 673. (10.) 661. (11.) Rule XI. (12.) Adverb. (13.) Rule XV. 613 (14.) "Plutarch is." (15.) Note I. 405, and Rule XI. (16.) 378. (17.) Rule IV. (18.) 247.

SYNTAX. 121

"In him were happily blended true dignity with softness of manners."

"The support of so (1.) many (2.) of his relations, were a heavy tax (3.) upon his industry; but thou knows he paid it cheerfully."

"What (4.) avails the best sentiments (5.) if persons do not live suitably to them?"

"Not one (6.) of them whom thou sees clothed (7.) in purple, are completely happy."

'And the fame of this person, and of his wonderful actions, were diffused (8.) throughout the country."

"The variety of the productions of genius, like (9.) that (10.) of the operations of nature, are without limit."

"In vain (11.) our flocks and fields increase our store,

When our abundance makes us wish (12.) for more."

"Thou shalt love thy neighbour as (13.) sincerely as (14.) thou loves thyself."

"Has thou no better reason for censuring (15.) thy friend and companion?" (16.)

"Thou, who art the Author (17.) and Bestower (16.) of life, can doubtless restore it also; but whether thou will please to restore it, or not, that thou only knows."

"O thou my voice (18.) inspire, Who touched (19.) Isaiah's hallowed lips with fire."

"Accept (20.) these grateful tears for thee they flow;

For thee, that ever felt (21.) another's woe."

"Just to thy word, in every thought sincere;

Who knew (22.) no wish but what the world might hear."

1. The infinitive mood, or part of a sentence, is sometimes put as the nominative case to the verb; as, "To see the sun *is* pleasant;" "To be good *is* to be happy;" "A desire to excel others in learning and virtue *is* commendable;" "That warm climates should accelerate the growth of the human body, and shorten its duration, *is* very reasonable to believe;" "To be temperate in eating and drinking, to use exercise in open air, and to preserve the mind free from tumultuous emotions, *are* the best preservatives of health."

"To see the sun are pleasant." Which word is wrong in this example? In what particular, wrong? What *is pleasant?* What, then, is the nominative case to *is?* Is there one thing, or more than one, here spoken of, as being pleasant? Why, then, should we use *is* in preference to *are?* What is the Rule for *is?* (23.) Rule for, "*To see,*" or, "*To see the sun?*" (24.)

☞ *When examples are referred to without being quoted, the teacher may read them to the pupil.*

"To be temperate in eating," &c. How many things are here spoken of as being the best preservatives? Should we, then, use the singular or plural verb? Rule for it? (25.)

1.

"To do unto all men, as we would that they, in similar circumstances, should do unto us, *constitute* the great principle of virtue."

"From a fear of the world's censure, to be ashamed (24.) of the practice of precepts, which the heart approves and embraces, *mark* a feeble and imperfect character."

(1.) 239. (2.) 378. (3.) Rule XV. 613. (4.) Rule VIII. (5.) Rule VI. (6.) Note I. 405, and Rule VI. (7.) Rule XIII. (8.) 510. (9.) Rule IV (10.) "that *variety*"— Note I. 405, and Rule X. See Note XVII. 647. (11.) Adverbial phrase. (12.) Rule XII. 555. See 480. (13.) Adverb. (14.) Conjunction. (15.) Participial noun. (16.) Rule XI. (17.) Rule XV. 613. (18.) Rule VIII. (19.) "Who *touchedst* or *didst touch.*" (20.) "Accept *thou*'— imp. mood. (21.) "*didst feel.*" (22.) "*Who knewest* or *didst know.*" (23.) Rule VII. (24.) Note XIII. 626. or. Note I. this page. (25.) Rule XVIII.

11

* The erroneous opinions which we form concerning (1.) happiness and misery *gives* rise to all the mistaken (2.) and dangerous passions that *embroils* our life."

To live soberly, righteously, and piously, are required of all men."

That (3.) it is our duty to promote the purity of our minds and bodies, to be just (4.) and kind to our fellow-creatures, and to be pious and faithful to Him that made us, admit not of any doubt in a rational and well (5.) informed mind."

* To be of a pure and humble mind, to exercise benevolence towards others, to cultivate piety towards God, is the sure means (6.) of becoming peaceful and happy."

* It is an important truth, that religion, vital religion, the religion of the heart, are the most powerful auxiliaries of reason, in waging war with the passions, and promoting that sweet composure which constitute the peace of God."

"The possession of our senses entire, of our limbs uninjured, of a sound understanding, of friends and companions, are often overlooked; though it would be the ultimate wish (6.) of many, who, as far as we can judge, deserves it as much as ourselves."

"All (7.) that make a figure on the great theatre of the world, the employments of the busy, the enterprises of the ambitious, and the exploits of the warlike; the virtues which *forms* the happiness, and the crimes which occasions the misery of mankind; originates in that silent and secret recess of thought, which are hidden from every human eye."

2. Every verb, except in the infinitive mood, or the participle, ought to have a nominative case, either expressed or implied; as, "Awake; arise;" that is, "Awake ye; arise ye."

We shall here add some examples of inaccuracy, in the use of the verb without its nominative case. "As it hath pleased him of his goodness to give you safe deliverance, and hath preserved you in the great danger," &c. The verb *hath preserved* has here no nominative case, for it cannot be properly supplied by the preceding word, *him*, which is in the objective case. It ought to be, "and as *he hath preserved* you;" or rather, "and *to preserve* you." "If the calm in which he was born, and lasted so long, had continued;" "and *which* lasted," &c. "These we have extracted from an historian of undoubted credit, and are the same that were practised," &c.; "and *they are* the same." "A man whose inclinations led him to be corrupt, and had great abilities to manage the business;" "and *who* had," &c. "A cloud gathering in the north; which we have helped to raise, and may quickly break in a storm upon our heads;" "and *which* may quickly."

"As it hath pleased," &c. What correction should be made in this example? Why? Recite the Note.

2.

* If the privileges to which he has an undoubted right, and he has long enjoyed, should now be wrested from him, (8.) would be flagrant injustice."

* These curiosities we have imported from China, and are similar to those which were some time ago brought from Africa."

"Will martial flames forever fire thy mind,
And never, never (9.) be to heaven resigned?"

(1.) Preposition. (2.) Rule XIII. (3.) Conjunction. (4.) "just persons." Rule IV. (5.) Adverb. (6.) Rule XV. (7.) Note I. 405. Rule VI. (8.) "it would" (9.) "And wilt thou never be?"

SYNTAX. 123

3. Every nominative case, except the case absolute, and when an address is made to a person, should belong to some verb, either expressed or implied; as, "Who wrote this book?" "James;" that is, "James wrote it." "To whom thus Adam," that is, "spoke."

One or two instances of the improper use of the nominative case, without any verb, expressed or implied, to answer it, may be sufficient to illustrate the usefulness of the preceding observations.

"Which rule, if it had been observed a neighboring prince would have wanted a great deal of that incense which had been offered up to him." The pronoun *it* is here the nominative case to the verb *observed ;* and *which rule* is left by itself, a nominative case without any verb following it. This form of expression, though improper, is very common. It ought to be, "*If this rule* had been observed," &c. "Man, though he has great variety of thoughts, and such from which others as well as himself might receive profit and delight, yet they are all within his own breast." In this sentence, the nominative *man* stands alone, and unconnected with any verb, either expressed or implied. It should be, "*Though man* has great variety," &c.

"Which rule, if it," &c. What is the nominative case to *observed?* Has the noun *rule* any verb following it, to which it may be the nominative case? Is this form of expression much used? Is it not proper? What correction should be made? Why? Recite the Note.

3.

*(1.) Two substantives, *when they come together, and do not signify the same thing, *the former* (2.) must be in the genitive case."

"Virtue, however it may be neglected for a time, men are so constituted as ultimately to acknowledge and respect genuine merit."

4. When a verb comes between two nouns, either of which may be understood as the subject of the affirmation, it may agree with either of them; but some regard must be had to that which is more naturally the subject of it, as also to that which stands next to the verb; as, "His meat *was* locusts and wild honey;" "A great cause of the low state of industry *were* the restraints put upon it;" "The wages of sin *is* death."

"The wages of sin *is* death," or, "Death *is* the wages of sin." What is the nominative case to *is?* Is this nominative, in the first example, before or after *is?* What is the rule for *wages?* (3.) Recite the Note. What do you mean by *the subject of the affirmation?* (4.)

4.

"The crown of virtue is peace and honor."

"His chief occupation and enjoyment were controversy."

5. When the nominative case has no personal tense of a verb, but is put before a participle, independently on the rest of the sentence, it is called the case absolute; as, "Shame being lost, all virtue is lost;" "That having been discussed long ago, there is no occasion to resume it."

As, in the use of the case absolute, the case is, in English, always the nominative, the following example is erroneous, in making it the objective. "Solomon was of this mind; and I have no doubt he made as wise and true proverbs, as any body has done since; *him* only excepted, who was a much greater and wiser man than Solomon." It should be, "*he* only excepted." What is the rule for the case absolute? (5.) "He only excepted." Which word is wrong in this example? In what particular, wrong? What correction should be made?

(1.) "*When two substantives come together.*" (2.) "*the first of them.*"
(3.) Rule XV. 612. (4.) The nominative case. (5.) Rule XVII. 623

5.

————— " Him destroyed,   All this (2.) will soon follow."
Or won to what (1.) may work   ————— " Whose gray top
his utter loss,   Shall tremble, him descending."

The nominative case is commonly placed before the verb; but sometimes it is put after the verb, if it is a simple tense; and between the auxiliary and the verb or participle, if a compound tense; as,

1st. When a question is asked, a command given, or a wish expressed; as, " Confidest thou in me?" " Read thou!" " Mayst thou be happy!" " Long live the king!"

2d. When a supposition is made without the conjunction *if*; as, " Were it not for this;" " Had I been there."

3d. When a verb transitive is used; as, " On a sudden appeared the king."

4th. When the verb is preceded by the adverbs *here, there, then, thence, hence, thus,* &c.; as, " Here am I;" " There was he slain;" " Then cometh the end;" " Thence ariseth his grief;" " Hence proceeds his anger;" " Thus was the affair settled."

5th. When a sentence depends on *neither* or *nor*, so as to be coupled with another sentence; as, " Ye shall not eat of it, neither shall ye touch it, lest ye die."

Some grammarians assert, the phrases *as follows, as appears,* form what are called impersonal verbs; and should, therefore, be confined to the singular number; as, " The arguments advanced were nearly *as follows*;" " The positions were *as appears* incontrovertible;" that is, " as it follows," " as it appears." If we give (say they) the sentence a different turn, and, instead of *as,* say *such as,* the verb is no longer termed impersonal; but properly agrees with its nominative, in the plural number; as, " The arguments advanced were nearly *such as follow*;" " The positions were *such as appear* uncontrovertible."*

They who doubt the accuracy of Horne Tooke's statement, " That *as,* however and whenever used in English, means the same as *it,* or *that,* or *which*;" and who are not satisfied whether the verbs, in the sentence first mentioned, should be in the singular or the plural number, may vary the form of expression. Thus, the sense of the preceding sentences may be conveyed in the following terms:—" The arguments advanced were nearly of the following nature ;" " The following are nearly the arguments which were advanced ;" " The arguments advanced were nearly those which follow ;" " It appears that the positions were incontrovertible;" " That the positions were incontrovertible is apparent;" " The positions were incontrovertible is apparent;" " The positions were apparently incontrovertible."

Where is the nominative case usually placed? Mention a few instances in which the nominative follows the verb. What do some grammarians say of the phrases *as follows, as appears?* What is Dr. Campbell's opinion concerning them?

(1.) *" that which."* 437.   (2.) Note I. 405.

* These grammarians are supported by general usage, and by the authority of an eminent critic on language and composition. " When a verb is used impersonally," says Dr. Campbell, in his Philosophy of Rhetoric, " it ought undoubtedly to be in the singular number, whether the neuter pronoun be expressed or understood." For this reason, analogy and usage, favor this mode of expression; " The conditions of the agreement were *as follows* " and not " *as follow.*" A few late writers have inconsiderately adopted this last form, through a mistake of the construction. For the same reason, we ought to say, " I shall consider his censures so far only *as concerns* my friend's conduct," and not " so far *as concern.*"

RULE XVIII.

Corresponding with Murray's Gramma',

RULE II.

Two or more nouns or pronouns of the singular number, connected together by AND, *either expressed or understood, must have verbs, nouns and pronouns agreeing with them in the plural number.*

This rule is often violated; some instances of which are annexed. "And a) was also James and John, the sons of Zebedee, who were partners with Simon;" "and so *were* also." "All joy, tranquillity and peace, even for ever and ever, doth dwell;" "*dwell* for ever." "By whose power all good and evil is distributed;" "*are* distributed." "Their love, and their hatred, and their envy, is now perished;" "*are* perished." "The thoughtless and intemperate enjoyment of pleasure, the criminal abuse of it, and the forgetfulness of our being accountable creatures, obliterates every serious thought of the proper business of life, and effaces the sense of religion and of God;" it ought to be, "*obliterate*" and "*efface.*"

" All joy, tranquillity, &c., doth dwell." Which word is wrong in this example? In what particular, wrong? What correction, then, should be made? Why? Recite the Rule.

"Idleness and ignorance *is* the *parent* of many vices."

"Wisdom, virtue, happiness, *dwells* with the golden mediocrity."

"In unity *consists* the welfare and security of every society."

"Time and tide *waits* for no man."

"His politeness and good disposition *was*, on failure of their effect, entirely changed."

"Patience and diligence, like (1.) faith, (2.) removes mountains."

"Humility and knowledge, with poor apparel, excels pride and ignorance under costly attire."

"The planetary system, boundless space, and the immense ocean, affects the mind with sensations of astonishment."

"Humility and love, whatever (3.) obscurities may involve religious tenets, constitutes the essence of true religion."

"Religion and virtue, our best support (4.) and highest honour, confers on the mind principles of noble independence."

"What (5.) signifies the counsel and care of preceptors, when youth think they have no (6.) need of assistance?"

1. When the nouns are nearly related, or scarcely distinguishable in sense, and sometimes even when they are very different, some authors have thought it allowable to put the verbs, nouns and pronouns in the singular number; as, "Tranquillity and peace dwells there;" "Ignorance and negligence has produced the effect;" "The discomfiture and slaughter was very great." But it is evidently contrary to the first principles of grammar, to consider two distinct ideas as one, however nice may be their shades of difference; and if there be no difference, one of them must be superfluous, and ought to be rejected.

To support the above construction, it is said, that the verb may be understood as applied to each of the preceding terms; as in the following example: "Sand, and salt, and a mass of iron, *is* easier to bear than a man without understanding." But besides the confusion, and the latitude of

---

(1.) Adverb.   (2.) Rule X. See Note XVII. 647.   (3.) Note I. 485.
(4.) Rule XV.   (5.) Rule VIII.   (6.) can.

11*

application, which such a construction would introduce, it appears to be more proper and analogical, in cases where the verb is intended to be applied to any one of the terms, to make use of the disjunctive conjunction, which grammatically refers the verb to one or other of the preceding terms, in a separate view. To preserve the distinctive uses of the copulative and disjunctive conjunctions, would render the rules precise, consistent and intelligible. Dr. Blair very justly observes, that "two or more substantives, joined by a copulative, must *always* require the verb or pronoun to which they refer, to be placed in the plural number."

"Tranquillity and peace dwells there." What dwells? Is it not, then, a violation of Rule XVIII. to use *dwells* in the singular number? When do some writers think it allowable to put the verbs, nouns and pronouns in the singular number? Is this usage grammatical? In what does the incorrectness consist? If there be no difference in the meaning of terms, are both necessary? What ought to be done with the superfluous one? How do some attempt to support the above construction? How would they read, on this principle, the example beginning with, "Sand, and salt, and a mass of iron, *is* easier," &c. ? (1.) In examples like the last, what conjunction can we substitute in the place of *and*, which will better express the sense? What does Dr. Blair say on this subject?

1.

" Much *does* human pride and self-complacency require correction."
" Luxurious living, and high pleasures, *begets* a languor and satiety that destroys all enjoyment."

" Pride and self-sufficiency stifles sentiments of dependence on our Creator; levity and attachment to worldly pleasures destroys the sense of gratitude to him."

2. In many complex sentences, it is difficult for learners to determine, whether one or more of the clauses are to be considered as the nominative case; and, consequently, whether the verb should be in the singular or the plural number. We shall, therefore, set down a number of varied examples of this nature, which may serve as some government to the scholar with respect to sentences of a similar construction. "Prosperity, with humility, *renders* its possessor truly amiable." "The ship, with all her furniture, *was* destroyed." "Not only his estate, his reputation too *has* suffered by his misconduct." "The general, also, in conjunction with the officers, *has* applied for redress." "He cannot be justified; for it is true, that the prince, as well as the people, *was* blameworthy." "The king, with his life-guard, *has* just passed through the village." "In the mutual influence of body and soul, there *is* a wisdom, a wonderful wisdom, which we cannot fathom." "Virtue, honour, nay, even self-interest, *conspire* to recommend the measure." "Patriotism, morality, every public and private consideration, *demand* our submission to just and lawful government." "Nothing *delights* me so much as the works of nature."

In support of such forms of expression as the following, we see the authority of Hume, Priestley, and other writers; and we annex them for the reader's consideration: "A long course of time, with a variety of accidents and circumstances, *are* requisite to produce those revolutions." "The king, with the lords and commons, *form* an excellent frame of government." "The side A, with the sides B and C, *compose* the triangle." "The fire communicated itself to the bed, which, with the furniture of the room, and a valuable library, *were* all entirely consumed." It is, however, proper to observe, that these modes of expression do not appear to be warranted by the just principles of construction. The words, "A long course of time," "The king," "The side A," and "which," are the true nominatives to the respective verbs. In the last example, the word *all* should be expunged. As the preposition *with* governs the *objective* case in English, and, if translated into Latin, would govern

---

,1.) " Cand *is* easier, and salt *is* easier, and a mass of iron *is* easier," &c.

SYNTAX. 127

the *ablative* case, it is manifest, that the clauses following *with*, in the preceding sentences, cannot form any part of the *nominative* case. They cannot be at the same time in the objective and the nominative cases. The following sentence appears to be unexceptionable, and may serve to explain the others: " The lords and commons are essential branches of the British constitution: the king, with them, *forms* an excellent frame of government."

" The side A, with the sides B and C, compose the triangle.". In this sentence, what is the nominative case to *compose?* Should the verb, then, be singular or plural? What difficulty is mentioned in the beginning of this Note?

2.

Good order in our affairs, not mean savings, *produce* great profits."

" The following treatise, together with those that accompany it, *were* written many years ago, for my own private satisfaction."

" That great senator, in concert with several other eminent persons, *were* the *projectors* (1.) of the revolution."

" The religion of these people, as well as their customs and manners, *were* strangely misrepresented."

" Virtue, joined to knowledge and wealth, confer great influence and respectability. But knowledge, with wealth united, if virtue is wanting, have a very limited influence, and are often despised."

" That superficial scholar and critic, like some renowed critics of our own, have (2.) furnished most decisive proofs that they (3.) knew not the characters of the Hebrew language."

" The buildings of the institution have been enlarged; the expense of which, added (4.) to the increased price of provisions, render it necessary to advance the terms of admission."

" One, added to nineteen, make twenty."

" What (5.) black despair, what horror, fills the mind!"

3. If the singular nouns and pronouns, which are joined together by a copulative conjunction, be of several persons, in making the plural pronouns agree with them in person, the second person takes place of the third, and the first of both; as, " James, and thou, and I, *are* attached to *our* country;" " Thou and he shared it between *you.*"

" James, and thou, and I, am attached to our country." What is wrong in this example? In what particular, wrong? What correction should be made? Why? " Thou and he shared it between him." Will you correct this example? Why use *you* instead of *him?* Will you repeat the Note?

3.

" Thou, and the gardener, and the huntsman, must share the blame of this business amongst *them.*"

" My sister and I, as well as my brother, are daily employed in their respective occupations."

---

* Though the construction will not admit of a plural verb, the sentence would certainly stand better thus: " The king, the lords, and the commons, *form* an excellent constitution."
(1.) Rule XV. 613.   (2.) 602. Exception 1.   (3.) " As been."
(4.) Rule XIII. 557.   (5.) 434.

RULE XXIII.
Corresponding with Murray's Grammar,
RULE III.

The conjunction disjunctive has an effect contrary to that of the conjunction copulative; for as the verb, noun or pronoun, is referred to the preceding terms taken separately, it must be in the singular number; as, "Ignorance or negligence *has* caused this mistake;" "John, James, or Joseph, *intends* to accompany me;" "There *is*, in many minds, neither knowledge nor understanding.

The following sentences are variations from this rule: "A man may see a metaphor or an allegory in a picture, as well as read them in a description;" "read *it*." "Neither character nor dialogue were yet understood;" "*was* yet." "It must indeed be confessed, that a lampoon or a satire do not carry in them robbery or murder;" "*does* not carry in *it*." "Death, or some worse misfortune, soon divide them;" it ought to be, "*divides*."

"Neither character nor dialogue were yet understood." What is wrong in this example? Why? Will you correct it? What is the Rule for this correction?

"Man's happiness or misery *are*, in a great measure, put into his own hands."

' Man is not such a machine as a clock or a watch, which *move* merely as *they are* moved?"

"Despise no infirmity of mind or body, nor any condition of life; for they are, perhaps, to be your own lot."

"Speaking impatiently to servants, or anything that betrays inattention or ill-humour, are certainly criminal."

"There are many faults in spelling, which neither analogy nor pronunciation justify."

"When sickness, infirmity, or reverse of fortune affect us, the sincerity of friendship is proved."

"Let (1.) it be remembered, (2.) that (3.) it is not the uttering, or the hearing of certain words, that constitute the worship of the Almighty."

"A tart reply, a proneness to rebuke, or a captious and contradictious spirit, are capable of imbittering (4.) domestic life, (5.) and of setting friends at variance."

1. When singular pronouns, or a noun and pronoun of different persons, are disjunctively connected, the verb must agree with that person which is placed nearest to it; as, "I or thou *art* to blame;" "Thou or I *am* in fault;" "I, thou, or he, *is* the author of it;" "George or I *am* the person." But it would be better to say, "Either I am to blame, or thou art," &c.

"I or thou am to blame." How should this be altered? What is the Rule for it?

1.

"Either (6.) thou or I art greatly mistaken, in our judgment on the subject."

"I or thou am the person (7.) who must undertake the business proposed."

(1.) Imperative mood, agreeing with *thou* or *you* understood, by Rule VI.
(2.) Infinitive, 489. (3.) Conjunction. (4.) Rule X. (5.) Rule XIV. 580.
(6.) 659. (7.) Rule XV. 613.

SYNTAX. 129

2. When a disjunctive occurs between a singular noun, or pronoun, and a plural one, the verb is made to agree with the plural noun and pronoun, as "Neither poverty nor riches *were* injurious to him;" "I or they *were* offended by it." But in this case, the plural noun or pronoun, when it can conveniently be done, should be placed next to the verb.

"I or they was offended." What is wrong in this example? What is the Rule for the correction?

2.

'Both (1.) of the scholars, or one of them at least, was present at the transaction."
'Some parts of the ship and cargo were recovered; but neither (2.) the sailors nor the captain was saved."

"Whether one person or more was concerned in the business, does not appear."
"The cares of this life, or the deceitfulness of riches, has choked the seeds of virtue in many a promising (3.) mind."

NOTE XVI.
Corresponding with Murray's Grammar.

RULE IV.

A verb in the plural will agree with a collective noun in the singular, when a part only of the individuals ar meant; as, "The council were divided in their sentiments." *When the noun expresses the idea of unity the verb should be singular; as,* "The council was composed wholly of farmers."

We ought to consider whether the term will immediately suggest the idea of the number it represents, or whether it exhibits to the mind the idea of the whole, as one thing. In the former case, the verb ought to be plural; in the latter, it ought to be singular. Thus, it seems improper to say, "The peasantry *goes* barefoot, and the middle sort *makes* use of wooden shoes." It would be better to say, "The peasantry *go* barefoot, and the middle sort *make* use," &c., because the idea, in both these cases, is that of a number. On the contrary, there is a harshness in the following sentences, in which nouns of number have verbs plural, because the ideas they represent seem not to be sufficiently divided in the mind: "The court of Rome *were* not without solicitude." "The house of commons *were* of small weight." "The house of lords *were* so much influenced by these reasons." "Stephen's party *were* entirely broken up by the captivity of their leader." "An army of twenty-four thousand *were* assembled." "What reason *have* the church of Rome for proceeding in this manner?"—"There is indeed no constitution so tame and careless of *their* own defence."—"All the virtues of mankind are to be counted upon a few fingers, but *his* follies and vices are innumerable." Is not *mankind*, in this place, a noun of multitude, and such as requires the pronoun referring to be in the plural number, *their?*

"The peasantry goes barefoot," &c. What correction is necessary in this example? Why?

*The people *rejoices* in that which should give *it* sorrow."
'The flock, and not the fleece, *are*, or ought to be, the objects of the shepherd's care."

"The court *have* just ended, after having sat through the trial of a very long cause."
"The crowd *were* so great, that the judges with difficulty made their way through them."

130 ENGLISH GRAMMAR.

"The corporation of York *consist* of a mayor, aldermen, and a common council."

"The British parliament are composed of king, lords and commons."

"When the nation complain, the rulers should listen to their voice."

"In the days of youth, the multitude eagerly pursues pleasure as *its* chief good."

"The church have no power to inflict corporal punishment."

"The fleet were seen sailing (1.) up the channel."

"The regiment consist of a thousand (2.) men."

"The meeting have established several salutary regulations."

"The council was not unanimous, and it separated without coming (3.) to any determination."

"The fleet is all arrived and moored (4.) in safety."

"This people *draweth* near to me with their mouth, and *honoreth* me with their lips, but their heart is far from me."

"The committee *was* divided in *its* sentiments, and *it has* referred the business to the general meeting."

"The committee were very full when this point was decided; and their judgment has not been called in question."

"Why (6.) do this generation wish for greater evidence, when so much (5.) is already given?"

"The remnant of the people were persecuted with great severity."

"Never were any people so (6.) much (6.) infatuated (7.) as the Jewish nation."

"The shoal of herrings were of an immense extent."

"No society are chargeable with the disapproved (8.) misconduct of particular members."

RULE V.

Corresponding with Murray's Grammar,

RULE V.

Pronouns must agree with the nouns for which they stand, in gender, number and person.

Of this rule there are many violations to be met with; a few of which may be sufficient to put the learner on his guard. "*Each* of the sexes should keep within *its* particular bounds, and content *themselves* with the advantages of *their* particular districts;" better thus; "The sexes should keep within *their* particular bounds," &c. "Can any one, on their entrance into the world, be fully secure that they shall not be deceived?" "on *his* entrance," and "that *he* shall." "One should not think too favorably of ourselves;" "of *one's self*." "He had one acquaintance which poisoned his principles;" "*who* poisoned."

Every relative must have an antecedent to which it refers, either expressed or implied; as, "Who is fatal to others, is so to himself;" that is, "*the man who* is fatal to others."

Who, which, what, and the relative *that*, though in the objective case, are always placed before the verb; as are also their compounds, *whoever, whosoever*, &c.; as, "He whom ye seek;" "This is what, or the thing which, or that you want;" "Whomsoever you please to appoint."

What is sometimes applied in a manner which appears to be exceptionable; as, "All fevers, except what are called nervous," &c. It would at least be better to say, "except *those which* are called nervous."

"One should not think too favorably of ourselves." How should this sentence be altered? What is the Rule for it? Are the relatives placed before or after the verb?

(1.) Rule XIII.   (2.) Note I. 405.   (3.) 561.   (4.) Rule XI.   (5.) 672.
(6.) Adverb   (7.) " *were infatuated* "   (8.) Rule XIII

SYNTAX 131

* The exercise of reason appears as (1.) little (2.) in these sportsmen, as in the beasts *whom* they sometimes hunt, and by *whom* they are sometimes hunted."
"They *which* seek Wisdom will certainly find *her*."
"The male amongst birds seems to discover no beauty, but in the color of its species."
"Take handfuls of ashes of the furnace, and let Moses sprinkle *it* towards heaven, in the sight of Pharaoh; and *it* shall become small dust."
"Rebecca took goodly raiment, which *were* with her in the house, and put *them* upon Jacob."
"The wheel killed another man, which is the sixth *which have* lost *their lives* by this means."
"The fair sex, whose task is not to mingle in the labors of public life, has its own part assigned it to act."
"The Hercules man-of-war foundered at sea; she overset, and lost most (3.) of her men."
"The mind of man cannot be long without some food to nourish the activity of his thoughts."

"What is the reason that our language is less refined than those of Italy, Spain, or France?"
"I do not think any one should incur censure for being (4.) tender (5.) of their reputation."
"Thou who hast been a witness (6.) of the fact, can give an account of it."
"In religious concerns, or what (7.) is conceived to be such, (8.) every man must stand or fall by the decision of the great Judge."
"Something like (9.) what (10.) have been here premised, are the conjectures of Dryden."
"Thou great First Cause, (11.) least understood! (12.)
Who all my sense confined, (13.) To know but this, that thou art good,
And that myself (11.) am blind; Yet gave (14.) me in this dark estate," &c.
"What (6.) art thou, (11.) speak, that, (15.) on designs unknown, (16.)
While others sleep, thus range (17.) the camp alone?"

1. Personal pronouns, being used to supply the place of the noun, are not employed in the same part of a sentence as the noun which they represent; for it would be improper to say, " The king *he* is just;" " I saw *her* the queen ;" " The men *they* were there ;" " Many words *they* darken speech ;" " My banks *they* are furnished with bees." These personals are superfluous, as there is not the least occasion for a substitute in the same part where the principal word is present. The nominative case *they*, in the following sentence, is also superfluous: " Who, instead of going about doing good, *they* are perpetually intent upon doing mischief."
" The king he is just." Will you correct this sentence, and tell why it is wrong ?

1.

"Whoever (18.) entertains such an opinion, *he* judges erroneously."
"The cares of this world, *they* often choke the growth of virtue."
" Disappointments and afflictions, however disagreeable, *they* often improve us."

2. The pronoun *that* is frequently applied to persons as well as to things; but after an adjective in the superlative degree, and after the pronominal

(1.) Rule IX.   (2.) Adverb.   (3.) 676.   (4.) 561.   (5.) Rule IV.
(6.) Rule XV.   (7.) "*those which*." 437.   (8.) "such *concerns*," Rule IV.
(9.) Rule IV.   (10.) Rule VI. and X. Note XVII.   (11.) Rule XV.   (12.) Rule XIII.   (13.) "*confinedst*."   (14.) "*gavest*."   (15) Conjunction.
(16.) Rule XIII.   (17.) " *dost* range."   (18.) " *He who*."

adjective *same*, it is generally used in preference to *who* or *which;* as, "Charles XII. king of Sweden, was one of the greatest madmen *that* the world ever saw ;" " Catiline's followers were the most profligate *that* could be found in any city ." " He is the same man *that* we saw before." There are cases wherein we cannot conveniently dispense with this relative as applied to persons: as, first, after *who*, the interrogative ; " Who, *that* has any sense of religion, would have argued thus ?" Secondly, when persons make but a part of the antecedent; " The woman, and the estate, *that* became his portion, were too much for his moderation." In neither of these examples could any other relative have been used.

To what is the pronoun *that* applied? and when is it used in preference to *who* or *which*? (416. 1, 2, 3. 4, 5.) Give an example.

2.

" Moses was the meekest man whom we read of in the Old Testament."
" Humility is one of the most amiable virtues *which* we can possess."

" They are the same persons *who* assisted us yesterday."
" The men and things *which* he has studied, have not improved his morals."

3. The pronouns *whichsoever, whosoever*, and the like, are elegantly divided by the interposition of the corresponding substantives : thus, " On whichsoever side the king cast his eyes," would have sounded better, if written, " On which side soever," &c.

Will you give an example in which the compound pronoun *whichsoever* may be divided with propriety?

3.

" Howsoever beautiful they appear, they have no real merit."
" In whatsoever light we view him, his conduct will bear inspection."
" On whichsoever side they are

contemplated, they appear to advantage."
" However much he might despise the maxims of the king's administration, he kept a total silence on that subject."

4. Many persons are apt, in conversation, to put the objective case of the personal pronouns, in the place of *these* and *those ;* as, " Give me them books," instead of "*those* books." We may sometimes find this fault even in writing; as, " Observe *them* three there." We also frequently meet with *those* instead of *they*, at the beginning of a sentence, and where there is no particular reference to an antecedent; as, " *Those* that sow in tears, sometimes reap in joy;" " *They* that, or *they* who sow in tears."

It is not, however, always easy to say, whether a personal pronoun or a demonstrative is preferable, in certain constructions. " We are not unacquainted with the calumny of *them* [or those] who openly make use of the warmest professions."

Give me them books." Why is this sentence incorrect?

4.

" Which of *them* two persons has most distinguished himself?"
" None (1.) more impatiently suffer

injuries, than those (2.) that are most (3.) forward in doing (4.) them. (5.)

5. In some dialects, the word *what* is improperly used for *that*, and sometimes we find it in this sense in writing ; " They will never believe but *what* I have been entirely to blame." " I am not satisfied but what," &c., instead of " but *that*." The word *somewhat*, in the following sentence, seems to be used improperly : " These punishments seem to have been exercised in somewhat

SYNTAX. 133

an arbitrary manner." Sometimes we read, "In somewhat of." The meaning is, "in a manner which is, in some respects, arbitrary."
Will you give an example of the improper use of *what* instead of *that* ?

5.

"He would not be persuaded but *what* (1.) I was greatly in fault.

"These commendations of his children appear to have been made in *somewhat* (2.) *an injudicious manner*.

6. The pronoun relative *who* is so much appropriated to persons, that there is generally harshness in the application of it, except to the proper names of persons, or the general terms *man, woman*, &c. A term which only implies the idea of persons, and expresses them by some circumstance or epithet, will hardly authorize the use of it; as, "That the faction in England *who* most powerfully opposed his arbitrary pretensions." "That faction *which*," would have been better; and the same remark will serve for the following examples: " France, *who* was in alliance with Sweden." "The court *who*," &c. "The cavalry *who*," &c. "The cities *who* aspired at liberty." "That party among us *who*," &c. "The family *whom* they consider as usurpers."
In some cases, it may be doubtful, whether this pronoun is properly applied or not; as, "The number of substantial inhabitants with *whom* some cities abound." For when a term directly and necessarily implies persons, it may in many cases claim the personal relative. "None of the company *whom* he most affected could cure him of the melancholy under which he labored." The word *acquaintance* may have the same construction.

How is the relative *who* used ?

6.

"He instructed and fed the crowds *who* (3.) surrounded him."

"Sidney was one of the wisest and most active governors, *which* Ireland had enjoyed for several years."

"He was the ablest minister which James ever possessed."

"The court, who gives currency to manners, ought to be exemplary." (4.)

"I am happy in the friend which I have long proved."

7. We hardly consider little children as persons, because that term gives us the idea of reason and reflection; and, therefore, the application of the personal relative *who*. in this case, seems to be harsh: "A child *who*." It is still more improperly applied to animals: "A lake frequented by that fowl *whom* nature has taught to dip the wing in water."

Do we say, "A child who," or "A child which" ? Will you repeat the Note for this ?

7.

"The child *whom* we have just seen, is wholesomely fed, and not injured by bandages or clothing."

"He is *like* (4.) a beast (5.) of prey, who destroys without pity."

8. When the name of a person is used merely as a name, and it does not refer to the person, the pronoun *who* ought not to be applied. "It is no wonder if such a man did not shine at the court of queen Elizabeth, *who* was but another name for prudence and economy." Better thus: "whose name was but another word for prudence," &c. The word *whose* begins likewise to be restricted to persons; yet it is not done so generally, but that good writers, even in prose, use it when speaking of things. The construction is not, however, generally pleasing, as we may see in the following instances: "Pleasure, *whose* nature," &c. "Call every production, *whose* parts and *whose* nature," &c.

(1.) "*that*." Conjunction. (2.) "*in a manner which is, in some respects, injudicious*." (3.) "*that*." (4.) Rule IV (5.) Rule X. Note XVII.

12

In one case, however, custom authorizes us to use *which*, with respect to persons; and that is, when we want to distinguish one person of two, or a particular person among a number of others. We should then say, '*Which* of the two," or " *Which* of them is he or she ?"

"The court of queen Elizabeth, who," &c. Will you correct this sentence, and give the Note for it?

8.

'Having once disgusted (1.) him, he could never regain the favor of Nero, *who was indeed another name* for cruelty."

"Flattery, *whose nature* (2.) is to deceive and betray, should be avoided as the poisonous adder."

"Who of those men came to his assistance?"

9. As the pronoun relative has no distinction of number, we sometimes find an ambiguity in the use of it; as, when we say, "The disciples of Christ, *whom* we imitate," we may mean the imitation either of Christ, or of his disciples. The accuracy and clearness of the sentence depend very much upon the proper and determinate use of the relative, so that it may readily present its antecedent to the mind of the hearer or reader, without any obscurity or ambiguity

What is remarked in this Note on the use of the relative pronoun?

9.

"The king (3.) dismissed his minister without any inquiry; who had never before committed so unjust an action."

"There are millions of people in the empire (4.) of China whose support is derived almost entirely from rice."

10. *It is* and *it was* are often, after the manner of the French, used in a plural construction, and by some of our best writers; as, "*It is* either a few great men who decide for the whole, or *it is* the rabble that follow a seditious ring-leader;" "*It is* they that are the real authors, though the soldiers are the actors of the revolution;" " *It was* the heretics that first began to rail," &c.; "'*T is these* that early taint the female mind." This license in the construction of *it is*, (if it be proper to admit it at all,) has, however, been certainly abused in the following sentence, which is thereby made a very awkward one: "*It is* wonderful the very few accidents, which, in several years, happen from this practice."

How are *it is* and *it was* often used? Give an example in which they are used incorrectly in this sense.

10.

"It is remarkable his continual endeavors to serve us, notwithstanding our ingratitude." (5.)

"It is indisputably true his assertion, though *it is a paradox.*" (6.)

11. The interjections *O! oh!* and *ah!* require the objective case of a pronoun in the first person after them; as, "O me! Oh me! Ah me!" but the nominative case in the second person; as, "O thou persecutor!" " O ye hypocrites!" " O thou who dwellest," &c.

The neuter pronoun, by an idiom peculiar to the English language, is frequently joined, in explanatory sentences, with a noun or pronoun of the masculine or feminine gender; as, "It was I;" "It was the man or woman that did it."

The neuter pronoun *it* is sometimes omitted and understood: thus we say, "As appears, as follows," for "As it appears, as it follows;" and "May be," for "It may be."

(1.) "*Having disgusted.*" Rule XIII. (2.) "*the nature of which.*" (3.) " *The ting, who had never,*" &c. (4.) " *There are in the empire,*" &c. (5.) " *His continual,*" &c.; ending the sentence with, " *are remarkable.*" (3.) "*His assertion, though paradoxical.*" &c.

SYNTAX.

The neuter pronoun *it* is sometimes employed to express,

1st. The subject of any discourse or inquiry; as, "*It* happened on a summer's day;" "Who is *it* that calls on me?"

2d. The state or condition of any person or thing; as, "How is *it* with you?"

3d. The thing, whatever it be, that is the cause of any effect or event; or any person considered merely as a cause; as, "We heard her say *it* was not he;" "The truth is, *it* was I that helped her."

Why is it incorrect to say, "Oh I"? Why incorrect to say, "Oh thee"

11.

Ah! unhappy thee, who art deaf to the calls of duty and of honor." "Oh! happy we, surrounded with so many blessings."

RULE XXIV.

Corresponding with Murray's Grammar.

RULE VI.

The relative is the nominative case to the verb, when no nominative case comes between it and the verb; as, "The master *who* taught us;" "The trees *which* are planted."

When a nominative case comes between the relative and the verb, the relative is governed by some word in its own member of the sentence; as, "He *who* preserves me, to *whom* I owe my being, *whose* I am, and *whom* I serve, is eternal."

In the several members of the last sentence, the relative performs a different office. In the first member, it marks the agent; in the second, it submits to the government of the preposition; in the third, it represents the possessor; and in the fourth, the object of an action: and therefore it must be in the three different cases, correspondent to those offices.

When both the antecedent and relative become nominatives, each to different verbs, the relative is the nominative to the former, and the antecedent to the latter verb; as, "*True philosophy, which is* the ornament of our nature, *consists* more in the love of our duty, and the practice of virtue, than in great talents and extensive knowledge."

A few instances of erroneous construction will illustrate both branches of the sixth rule. The three following refer to the first part: "How can we avoid being grateful to those whom, by repeated kind offices, have proved themselves our real friends?" "These are the men whom, you might suppose, were the authors of the work." "If you were here, you would find three or four, whom you would say passed their time agreeably." In all these places, it should be *who*, instead of *whom*. The two latter sentences contain a nominative between the relative and the verb; and, therefore, seem to contravene the rule; but the student will reflect, that it is not the nominative of the verb with which the relative is connected.—The remaining examples refer to the second part of the rule: "Men of fine talents are not always the persons who we should esteem." "The persons who you dispute with are precisely of your opinion." "Our tutors are our benefactors, who we owe obedience to, and who we ought to love." In these sentences, *whom* should be used instead of *who*.

"These are the men whom, you might suppose, were." &c. Will you correct this example, and give the rule for it?

"We are dependent on each others' assistance: *whom* is there that can subsist by himself?"

"If he will not hear his best friend, *whom* shall be sent to admonish him?"

"They *who* (1.) much is given *to*, will have much (2.) to answer for." (3.)

"It is not to be expected that they, *whom* in early life have been dark and deceitful, should afterwards become fair and ingenuous."

"They who have labored to make us wise and good, are the persons who we ought to love and respect, and who we ought to be grateful to."

"The persons, who conscience and virtue support, may smile at the caprices of fortune."

"From the character of those who you associate with, your own will be estimated."

"That (4.) is the student who I gave the book to, and whom, I am persuaded, deserves it."

1. When the relative pronoun is of the interrogative kind, the noun or pronoun containing the answer, must be in the same case as that which contains the question; as, "*Whose* books are these?" "They are *John's*." "*Who* gave them to him?" "*We*." "Of *whom* did you buy them?" "Of a bookseller; *him* who lives at the Bible and Crown." "*Whom* did you see there?" "Both *him* and the shopman." The learner will readily comprehend this rule, by supplying the words which are understood in the answers. Thus, to express the answers at large, we should say, "They are John's books;" "We gave them to him;" "We bought them of him who lives," &c.; "We saw both him and the shopman." As the relative pronoun, when used interrogatively, refers to the subsequent word or phrase containing the answer to the question, that word or phrase may properly be termed the *subsequent* to the interrogative.

"Of whom did you buy them?" "Of a bookseller; he who lives," &c. What is wrong in this sentence, and how may it be corrected? What is the Note for it?

1.

"Of whom were the articles bought?" "Of a mercer; he (5.) who resides near (6.) the mansion-house."

"Was any person besides (6.) the mercer present?" "Yes, both him and his clerk."

"Who was the money paid to?" "To the mercer and his clerk."

"Who counted it?" "Both the clerk and him."

RULE XXV.

Corresponding with Murray's Grammar.

RULE VII.

When the relative is preceded by two nominatives of different persons, the relative and verb may agree in person with either, according to the sense; as, "I am the man *who* command you;" *or,* "I am the man *who* commands you."

The form of the first of the two preceding sentences expresses the meaning rather obscurely. It would be more perspicuous to say, "I, who command you, am the man." Perhaps the difference of meaning produced by referring the relative to different antecedents, will be more evident to the learner in the

---

(1.) "*to whom.*" (2.) 673. (3.) 596. (4.) Note I. 405.
(5.) Rule XV. (6.) 247.

SYNTAX. 137

following sentences: "I am the general who *gives* the orders to-day;" "I am the general, who *give* the orders to-day;" that is, "I, who give the orders to-day, am the general."

When the relative and the verb have been determined to agree with either of the preceding nominatives, that agreement must be preserved throughout the sentence; as in the following instance: "I am the Lord, that *maketh* all things; that *stretcheth* forth the heavens alone." *Isa.* xliv. 24. Thus far is consistent: the *Lord*, in the third person, is the antecedent, and the verb agrees with the relative in the third person: "I am *the Lord*, which Lord, or he, that *maketh* all things." If *I* were made the antecedent, the relative and verb should agree with it in the first person; as, "*I* am the Lord, *that make* all things; *that stretch* forth the heavens alone." But should it follow, "*that spreadeth* abroad the earth by myself," there would arise a confusion of persons, and a manifest solecism.

"I am the man who command you." "I am the man who commands you." What is the nominative to *command* in the first sentence? What to *commands* in the second? Rule for each? Why is the verb of a different person in different sentences?

"I acknowledge that (1.) I am the teacher, (5.) who adopt that sentiment, and *maintains* the propriety of such measures." (2.)

"Thou art a friend (5.) that hast often relieved me, and that has not deserted me now, in the time of peculiar need."

"I am the man who approves of wholesome discipline, and who *recommend* it to others; but I am not a person who promotes useless severity, or who *object* to mild and generous treatment."

"I perceive that thou art a pupil who possesses bright parts, but who hast cultivated them but (3.) little." (4.)

"Thou art he (5.) who breathest on the earth with the breath of spring, and who covereth it with verdure and beauty."

"I am the Lord (5.) thy God, (5.) who teacheth thee to profit, and who lead thee by the way thou shouldst go."

"Thou art the Lord who did choose Abraham, and broughtest him forth (4.) out of (6.) Ur of the Chaldees."

RULE IV.
Corresponding with Murray's Grammar,
RULE VIII.

Adjectives belong to the nouns which they describe.

NOTE I. Adjective pronouns and numerals must agree in number with the nouns to which they belong.

1. ADJECTIVE PRONOUNS.

A few instances of the breach of this rule are here exhibited: "I have not travelled this twenty years;" "*these* twenty." "I am not recommending these kind of sufferings;" "*this* kind." "Those set of books was a valuable present;" "*that* set."

"I have not travelled this twenty years." How should this be altered? Why?

"*These* kind of indulgences soften and injure the mind."

"Instead (7.) of improving (8.) yourselves, you have been

playing (9.) *this* two hours." (10.)

"Those sort of favors did real injury, under the appearance of kindness."

(1.) 652.   (2.) "*adopts* and *maintains*," or "*adopt* and *maintain*."   (3.) 654.
(4.) Adverb.   (5.) Rule XV.   (6.) 247.   (7.) 247.   (8.) 561.   (9.) Rule XIII.   (10.) Rule XXII. 646.

12*

* The chasm made (1.) by the earthquake was twenty foot (2.) broad, (3.) and one hundred fathom (4.) in depth."

" How many a sorrow (5) should we avoid, if we were not industrious to make them:"
" He saw one or more persons (6.) enter (7.) the garden."

1. The word *means*, in the singular number, and the phrase "*by this means*," "*by that means*," are used by our best and most correct writers; namely, Bacon, Tillotson, Atterbury, Addison, Steele, Pope, &c.* They are indeed, in so general and approved use, that it would appear awkward, if not affected, to apply the old singular form, and say, "by this *mean* ;" "by that *mean* ;" "it was by a *mean* ;" although it is more agreeable to the general analogy of the language. "The word *means* (says Priestley) belongs to the class of words, which do not change their termination on account of number; for it is used alike in both numbers."

The word *amends* is used in this manner, in the following sentences: "Though he did not succeed, he gained the approbation of his country; and with *this amends* he was content." "Peace of mind is *an* honorable *amends* for the sacrifices of interest." "In return, he received the thanks of his employers, and the present of a large estate: these were ample *amends* for all his labors." "We have described the rewards of vice, the good man's *amends* are of a different nature."

It can scarcely be doubted, that this word *amends* (like the word *means*) had formerly its correspondent form in the singular number, as it is derived from the French *amende*, though now it is exclusively established in the plural form. If, therefore, it be alleged, that *mean* should be applied in the singular, because it is derived from the French *moyen*, the same kind of argument may be advanced in favor of the singular *amende*; and the general analogy of the language may also be pleaded in support of it.

Campbell, in his Philosophy of Rhetoric, has the following remark on the subject before us: "No persons of taste will, I presume, venture so far to violate the present usage, and consequently to shock the ears of the generality of readers, as to say, 'By this *mean*, by that *mean*.'"

(1.) Rule XIII.   (2.) Note XVIII. C48.   (3.) "*chasm—broad*." Rule IV
(4.) Rule IX.   (5.) "*many sorrows*."   (6.) "*one person, or more than one*."
(7.) Rule XII.

* " *By this means* he had them the more at vantage, being tired and harassed with a long march." BACON.
" *By this means* one great restraint from doing evil would be taken away." " And *this is an* admirable *means* to improve men in virtue." " *By that means* they have rendered their duty more difficult." TILLOTSON.
" It renders us careless of approving ourselves to God, and by *that means* securing the continuance of his goodness." " A good character, when established, should not be rested in as an end, but employed as *a means* of doing still further good."
ATTERBURY.
" *By this means* they are happy in each other." " He *by that means* preserves his superiority." ADDISON.
" Your vanity *by this means* will want its food." STEELE.
" *By this means* alone, their greatest obstacles will vanish." POPE.
" Which *custom* has proved the most effectual *means* to ruin the nobles."
DEAN SWIFT.
" There *is* no *means* of escaping the persecution." " Faith is not only a *means* of obeying, but a principal act of obedience." DR. YOUNG.
" He looked on money as a necessary *means* of maintaining and increasing power."
LORD LYTTLETON'S HENRY II.
" John was too much intimidated not to embrace *every means* afforded for his safety." GOLDSMITH.
" Lest *this means* should fail." " By *means* of *ship-money*, the late king," &c.
" The *only means* of securing a durable peace." HUME
" *By this means* there was nothing left to the parliament of Ireland," &c.
BLACKSTONE.
" *By this means* so many slaves escaped out of the hands of their masters."
DR. ROBERTSON.
" *By this means* they bear witness to each other." BURKE.
" *By this means* the wrath of man was made to turn against itself." DR. BLAIR.
* " A magazine, which has, by *this means*, contained," &c. " Birds, in general, pro cure their food by *means* of their *beak*." DR PALEY

Lowth and Johnson seem to be against the use of *means* in the singular number. They do not, however, speak decisively on the point; but rather dubiously, as if they knew that they were questioning eminent authorities as well as general practice. That they were not decidedly against the application of this word to the singular number, appears from their own language: "Whole sentences, whether simple or compound, may become members of other sentences by means of some additional connection."— Dr. Lowth's *Introduction to English Grammar.*

"There is no other method of teaching that of which any one is ignorant, but by *means* of *something* already known."—Dr. Johnson. *Idler.*

It is remarkable that our present version of the Scriptures makes no use, as far as the compiler can discover, of the word *mean*; though there are several instances to be found in it of the use of *means*, in the sense and connection contended for. "By *this means* thou shalt have no portion on this side the river." Ezra iv. 16. "That by *means* of *death*," &c. Heb. ix. 15. It will scarcely be pretended, that the translators of the sacred volumes did not accurately understand the English language; or that they would have admitted one form of this word, and rejected the other, had not their determination been conformable to the best usage. An attempt, therefore, to recover an old word, so long since disused by the most correct writers, seems not likely to be successful: especially as the rejection of it is not attended with any inconvenience.

The practice of the best and most correct writers, or a great majority of them, corroborated by general usage, forms, during its continuance, the standard of language; especially if, in particular instances, this practice continue after objection and due consideration. Every connection and application of words and phrases, thus supported, must therefore be proper and entitled to respect, if not exceptionable in a moral point of view.

"*Si volet usus*
"*Quem penes arbitrium est, et jus, et norma loquendi.*" Hor.

On this principle, many forms of expression, not less deviating from the general analogy of the language than those before mentioned, are to be considered as strictly proper and justifiable. Of this kind are the following: "*None* of them *are* varied to express the gender;" and yet *none* originally signified *no one*. "He *himself* shall do the work:" here, what was at first appropriated to the objective, is now properly used as the nominative case. "*You* have behaved yourselves well:" in this example, the word *you* is put in the nominative case plural, with strict propriety; though formerly it was confined to the objective case, and *ye* exclusively used for the nominative.

With respect to anomalies and variations of language, thus established, it is the grammarian's business to submit, not to remonstrate. In pertinaciously opposing the decision of proper authority, and contending for obsolete modes of expression, he may, indeed, display learning and critical sagacity; and, in some degree, obscure points that are sufficiently clear and decided; but he cannot reasonably hope either to succeed in his aims, or to assist the learner, in discovering and respecting the true standard and principles of language.

Cases which custom has left dubious, are certainly within the grammarian's province. Here, he may reason and remonstrate on the ground of derivation, analogy, and propriety: and his reasonings may refine and improve the language: but when authority speaks out, and decides the point, it were perpetually to unsettle the language, to admit of cavil and debate. Anomalies, then, under the limitation mentioned, become the law, as clearly as the plainest analogies.

The reader will perceive that, in the following sentences, the use of the word *mean* in the old form has a very uncouth appearance: "By the *mean* of adversity we are often instructed." "He preserved his health by *mean* of exercise." "Frugality is one *mean* of acquiring a competency." They should be, "By *means* of adversity," &c.; "By *means* of exercise," &c.; "Frugality is one *means*," &c.

Good writers do indeed make use of the substantive (1.) *mean* in the singu-

---

(1.) *Nouns* are sometimes called *substantives*

lar number, and in that number only, to signify mediocrity, middle rate &c., as, "This is *a mean* between the two extremes." But in the sense of instrumentality, it has long been disused by the best authors, and by almost every writer.

This means and *that means* should be used only when they refer to what is singular; *these means* and *those means*, when they respect plurals; as, "He lived temperately, and by *this means* preserved his health;" "The scholars were attentive, industrious, and obedient to their tutors; and by *these means* acquired knowledge."

We have enlarged on this article, that the young student may be led to reflect on a point so important as that of ascertaining the standard of propriety in the use of language.

In what number is the word *means* used? What does Dr. Priestley remark concerning the use of this word? What other word is used in this manner? What does Dr. Campbell remark in regard to the use of the phrase, "By this mean?" Do Dr. Lowth and Dr. Johnson approve of the use of *means* in the singular number? Do good writers make use of the substantive (1.) *mean* in the singular number? Give an example. When should "This means" and "That means" be used? When "These means" and "Those means?"

1.

"Charles was extravagant, and by *this mean* became poor and despicable."

"It was by that ungenerous *mean* that (2.) he obtained his end."

"Industry is the *mean* of obtaining competency."

"Though a promising measure, it is a *mean* which I cannot adopt."

"This person embraced every opportunity to display his talents; and by *these* means rendered himself ridiculous."

"Joseph was industrious, frugal and discreet; and by this means obtained property and reputation."

2. When two persons or things are spoken of in a sentence, and there is occasion to mention them again for the sake of distinction, *that* is used in reference to the former, and *this*, in reference to the latter: as, "Self-love, which is the spring of action in the soul, is ruled by reason: but for *that*, man would be inactive; and but for *this*, he would be active to no end."

How are the pronouns *that* and *this* used?

2.

"Religion raises men above themselves; irreligion sinks them beneath the brutes: *that* (3.) binds them down (4.) to a poor, pitiable speck of perishable earth; *this* opens for them a prospect to the skies."

"More rain falls in the first two summer months, than in the first two winter ones; but it makes a much greater show upon the earth in *those* than in *these*; because there is a much slower evaporation."

Rex and Tyrannus are of very different characters. The one (3.) rules his people by laws to which they consent; the other (5.) by his absolute will and power: *this* is called freedom *that* (5.) tyranny."

3. The distributive adjective pronouns *each, every, either,* agree with the nouns, pronouns and verbs, of the singular number only; as, "The king of Israel, and Jehoshaphat, the king of Judah, sat *each* on *his* throne;" "*Every* tree *is* known by *its* fruit;" unless the plural noun convey a collective idea; as, "*Every* six months;" "*Every* hundred years." The following phrases are exceptionable: "Let *each* esteem others better than themselves;" it ought to be, "*himself*." "The language should be both perspicuous and correct: in proportion as *either* of these two qualities are wanting, the language is imperfect;" it should be, "*is* wanting." "*Every*

(1.) Note 1, p. 139 (2.) 652. (3.) 407. Rule VI. (4.) Adverb.
(5.) Rule XI.

SYNTAX.

one of the letters bear regular dates, and contain proofs of attachment;" "*bears* a regular *date*, and *contains*." "*Every* town and village were burned; *every* grove and *every* tree were cut down;" "*was* burned, and *was* cut down."

Either is often used improperly, instead of *each*; as, "The king of Israel, and Jehoshaphat the king of Judah, sat *either* of them on his throne;" "Nadab and Abihu, the sons of Aaron, took *either* of them his censer." *Each* signifies both of them taken distinctly or separately; *either* properly signifies only the one or the other of them, taken disjunctively.

"The king of Israel, and Jehoshaphat the king of Judah, sat either of them on their throne." Will you correct this, and give the rule for it?

3.

"Each of them, in *their* (1.) turn, receive the benefits to which they are entitled."

"My counsel to each of you is, that *you* (2.) should make it *your* endeavor to come to a friendly agreement."

"By discussing what (3.) relates to each particular, in *their* order, we shall better understand the subject."

"Every person, whatever (4.) be *their* station, (5.) *are* bound by the duties of morality and religion."

"Every leaf, every twig, (6.) every drop of water, *teem* with life."

"Every man's heart and temper is productive of much (7.) inward joy or bitterness."

"Whatever (8.) he undertakes, either (9.) his pride or his folly disgust us."

"Every man and every woman were numbered."

"Neither of those men *seem* to have any idea that *their* opinions may be ill founded."

"When benignity and gentleness reign within, (7.) we are always (7.) least (7.) in hazard from without: (10.) every person and every occurrence are beheld in the most favorable light."

"On either side of the river was there the tree of life."

4. Adjectives are sometimes improperly applied as adverbs; as, "Indifferent honest; excellent well; miserable poor;" instead of "Indifferently honest; excellently well; miserably poor." "He behaved himself conformable to that great example;" "*conformably.*" "Endeavor to live hereafter suitable to a person in thy station;" "*suitably.*" "I can never think so very mean of him;" "*meanly.*" "He describes this river agreeable to the common reading;" "*agreeably.*" "Agreeable to my promise, I now write;" "*agreeably.*" "Thy exceeding great reward;" when united to an adjective, or adverb not ending in *ly*, the word *exceeding* has *ly* added to it; as, "exceedingly dreadful, exceedingly great;" "exceedingly well, exceedingly more active:" but when its joined to an adverb or adjective, having that termination, the *ly* is omitted; as, "Some men think exceeding clearly, and reason exceeding forcibly;" "She appeared on this occasion, exceeding lovely."—"He acted in this business *bolder* than was expected." "They behaved the *noblest*, because they were disinterested." They should have been, "*more boldly, most nobly.*" The adjective pronoun *such* is often misapplied; as, "He was such an extravagant young man, that he spent his whole patrimony in a few years;" it should be, "*so extravagant a young man.*" "I never before saw such large trees;" "*saw trees so large.*" When we refer to the species or nature of a thing, the word *such* is properly applied; as, "Such a temper is seldom found:" but when degree is signified, we use the word *so;* as, "So bad a temper is seldom found."

Adverbs are likewise improperly used as adjectives; as, "The tutor ad dressed him in terms rather warm, but suitably to his offence;" "*suitable.*"

(1.) "*his.*"   (2.) "*he.*"   (3.) 437.   (4.) Rule XV.   (5.) Rule VI
(6.) Rule XI.   (7.) Adverb.   (8. Rule VIII.   (9.) 652.   (10.) "*from without.*" i. e. "*externally.*" 589

"They were seen wandering about solitarily and distressed," "*solitary.*" "He lived in a manner agreeably to the dictates of reason and religion;" "*agreeable.*" "The study of syntax should be previously to that of punctuation;" "*previous.*"

Young persons who study grammar, find it difficult to decide, in particular constructions, whether an adjective, or an adverb, ought to be used. A few observations on this point, may serve to inform their judgment, and direct their determination. They should carefully attend to the definitions of the adjective and the adverb; and consider whether, in the case in question, *quality* or *manner* is indicated. In the former case, an adjective is proper; in the latter, an adverb. A number of examples will illustrate this direction and prove useful on other occasions.

"She looks cold—She looks coldly on him."
"He feels warm—He feels warmly the insult offered to him."
"He became sincere and virtuous—He became sincerely virtuous."
"She lives free from care—He lives freely at another's expense."
"Harriet always appears neat—She dresses neatly."
"Charles has grown great by his wisdom—He has grown greatly in reputation."
"They now appear happy—They now appear happily in earnest."
"The statement seems exact—The statement seems exactly in point."

The verb *to be*, in all its moods and tenses, generally requires the word immediately connected with it to be an adjective, not an adverb; and consequently, when this verb can be substituted for any other, without varying the sense or the construction, that other verb must also be connected with an adjective. The following sentences elucidate these observations: "This is agreeable to our interest." "That behaviour was not suitable to his station." "Rules should be conformable to sense." "The rose smells [is] sweet." "How sweet the hay smells [is]!" "How delightful the country appears [is]!" "How pleasant the fields look [are]!" "The clouds look [are] dark." "How black the sky looked [was]!" "The apple tastes [is] sour!" "How bitter the plums tasted [were]!" "He feels [is] happy." In all these sentences, we can, with perfect propriety, substitute some tenses of the verb *to be*, for the other verbs. But in the following sentences we cannot do this: "The dog smells disagreeably." "George feels exquisitely." "How pleasantly she looks at us!"

The directions contained in this Note are offered as useful, not as complete and unexceptionable. Anomalies in language every where encounter us; but we must not reject rules, because they are attended with exceptions.

Why is "indifferent honest" an incorrect expression? Do we say, "exceeding dreadful," and "exceeding great"? What, then, do we use in the place of *exceeding*? When, then, do we use *exceedingly*? When *exceeding*? "The tutor addressed him in terms rather warm, but suitably to his offence." Why is this sentence wrong? Correct it. How can we tell whether an adjective or an adverb ought to be used? Which do we use, when quality is indicated? Which, when manner is indicated? Which does the verb *to be* generally require to be connected with it, the adjective or adverb? To illustrate the distinct and proper use of both the adverb and adjective, I will give you some examples. Would you then say, "He is diligently and attentively," or "diligent and attentive"? "She will be happy," or "happily"? "He looks cold," or "coldly"? "She looks cold on him." Can we use *is* for *looks*, and make sense? Would you, then, say, "She looks cold on him," or "coldly on him"? "She lives freely [is] from care"? Why? "He lives free at another's expense"? "He feels warmly"? "He feels warm the insult offered him'"? "He became sincerely and virtuously"? "He became sincere virtuous"? Why? "Harriet always appears neatly—She dresses neat"? "Charles has grown great by his wisdom—He is grown great in his reputation"? "They now appear happily—They now appear happy in earnest"? "The statement seems exactly—The statement seems exact in point?" "How sweetly the hay smells!"? "How delightful the country appears!"? "How pleasant the fields look!"? "The clouds look darkly"? "The apples taste sourly"?

4.

"She reads *proper*, writes very *neat*, and composes *accurate*."

"He was *extreme* prodigal, and his property is now *near* exhausted."

"They generally succeeded; for they lived *conformable* to the rules of prudence."

"We may reason very *clear* and exceeding *strong*, without knowing that there is such a thing as a syllogism."

"He had many virtues, and was *exceeding beloved*."

"The amputation was exceeding well performed, and saved the patient's life."

"He came agreeable to his promise, and conducted himself suitable to the occasion."

"He speaks very fluent, reads excellent, but does not think very coherent."

"He behaved himself submissive, and was exceeding careful not to give (1.) offence."

"They rejected the advice, and conducted themselves exceedingly indiscreetly."

"He is a person of great abilities, and *exceeding* upright; and is *like* to be a very useful member (2.) of the community."

"The conspiracy was the easier (3.) discovered, from its (4.) being known (5.) to many."

"Not being fully acquainted with the subject, he could *affirm no stronger* (6.) than he did."

"He was so deeply impressed with the subject, that few could speak nobler upon it."

"We may credit his testimony, for he says express, that he saw the transaction."

"Use a little wine for thy stomach's sake, and thine often (7.) infirmities."

"From these favorable beginnings, we may hope for a soon (8.) and prosperous issue."

"He addressed several exhortations to them suitably to their circumstances."

"Conformably to their vehemence of thought, was their vehemence of gesture."

"We should implant in the minds of youth such seeds and principles of piety and virtue, as (9.) are likely to take soonest and deepest root."

"Such (10.) an amiable disposition will secure universal regard."

"Such distinguished virtues seldom occur."

5. Double comparatives and superlatives should be avoided; such as, "a worser conduct;" "on lesser hopes;" "a more serener temper;" "the most straitest sect;" "a more superior work." They should be, "worse conduct;" "less hopes;" "a more serene temper;" "the straitest sect;" "a superior work."

"A worser conduct." Will you correct this sentence, and give the Rule for it?

5.

"'T is *more* easier to build two chimneys than to maintain one."

"The tongue is like (11.) a racehorse, (12.) which runs the faster (13.) the *lesser* weight it carries."

"The pleasures of the understanding are *more preferable than* (14.) those of the imagination, or of sense."

"The nightingale sings: hers is the most sweetest voice in the grove."

(1.) Rule XII. (2.) Rule XV. (3.) "*more easily.*" (4.) Rule I.
(5.) "*being known*"— participial noun. (6.) "*not affirm more strongly.*"
(7.) "*thy frequent.*" (8.) "*speedy.*" (9.) 656. (10.) "A disposition *so amiable,*" &c. See the Note, a few lines before the close. (11.) Rule IV.
(12.) Rule X.—Note XVII. 647. (13.) 590. (14.) "*preferable to.*"

"The Most Highest hath created us for his glory, and for our own happiness." "The Supreme Being is the most wisest, and most powerfullest, and the most best of beings."

6. Adjectives that have in themselves a superlative signification, do not properly admit of the superlative or comparative form superadded; such as *chief, extreme, perfect, right, universal, supreme,* &c.; which are sometimes improperly written *chiefest, extremest, perfectest, rightest, most universal, most supreme,* &c. The following expressions are, therefore, improper: "He sometimes claims admission to the *chiefest* offices." "The quarrel became *so universal* and national." "A method of attaining the *rightest* and greatest happiness." The phrases, "so perfect," "so right," "so extreme," "so universal," &c., are incorrect; because they imply that one thing is less perfect, less extreme, &c., than another, which is not possible.

Is it proper to say, "The most perfect work?" Why not?

6.

"Virtue confers *the supremest* (1.) dignity on man; and should be his chiefest desire."

"His assertion was *more true* (2.) than that of his opponent; nay, the words of the latter were most untrue." (3.)

"His work is perfect; (4.) his brother's, more perfect; and his father's, the most perfect of all."

"He gave the fullest and most sincere proof of the truest friendship."

7. Inaccuracies are often found in the way in which the degrees of comparison are applied and construed. The following are examples of wrong construction in this respect: "This noble nation hath, of all others, admitted fewer corruptions." The word *fewer* is here construed precisely as if it were the superlative. It should be, "This noble nation hath admitted fewer corruptions than any other." We commonly say, "This is the weaker of the two," or, "the weakest of the two;" but the former is the regular mode of expression, because there are only two things compared. "The vice of covetousness is what enters deepest into the soul of any other." "He celebrates the church of England as the most perfect of all others." Both these modes of expression are faulty: we should not say, "the best of any man," or, "the best of any other man," for, "the best of men." The sentences may be corrected by substituting the comparative in the room of the superlative: "The vice, &c., is what enters deeper into the soul than any other." "He celebrates, &c., as more perfect than any other." It is also possible to retain the superlative, and render the expression grammatical: "Covetousness, of all vices, enters the deepest into the soul." "He celebrates, &c., as the most perfect of all churches." These sentences contain other errors, against which it is proper to caution the learner. The words *deeper* and *deepest*, being intended for adverbs, should have been *more deeply, most deeply.* The phrases *more perfect* and *most perfect* are improper; because perfection admits of no degrees of comparison. We may say, *nearer* or *nearest* to perfection, or more or less imperfect.

In speaking of two persons, should we say, "The weaker of the two," or, "The weakest of the two?" Why?

7.

"A talent of this kind would, perhaps, prove the likeliest of *any other* (5.) to succeed."

"He is the *strongest* of the two, but not the *wisest.*"

"He spoke with so much propriety, that I understood him the best of all *the others* (6.) *who* spoke on the subject."

"Eve was the fairest of all her daughters."

(1.) "*the supremest—supreme.*"
(4.) "*well executed—still better—best.*"
(2.) "*better founded.*"
(5.) "*all.*"
(3.) "*not true.*"
(6.) "*of all who.*"

SYNTAX. 145

8. In some cases, adjectives should not be separated from their substantives, even by words which modify their meaning, and make but one sense with them; as, "A large enough number, surely." It should be, "A number large enough." "The lower sort of people are good enough judges of one not very distant from them."

The adjective is usually placed before its substantive; as, "A *generous* man;" "How *amiable* a woman!" The instances in which it comes after the substantive, are the following:
1st. When something depends upon the adjective; and when it gives a better sound, especially in poetry; as, "A man *generous* to his enemies;" "Feed me with food *convenient* for me;" "A tree three feet *thick;*" "A body of troops fifty thousand *strong;*" "The torrent tumbling through rocks *abrupt.*"
2d. When the adjective is emphatical; as, "Alexander the *Great;*" "Lewis the *Bold;*" "Goodness *infinite;*" "Wisdom *unsearchable.*"
3d. When several adjectives belong to one substantive; as, "A man just, wise, and charitable;" "A woman modest, sensible, and virtuous."
4th. When the adjective is preceded by an adverb; as, "A boy regularly studious;" "A girl unaffectedly modest."
5th. When the verb *to be*, in any of its variations, comes between a substantive and an adjective, the adjective may frequently either precede or follow it; as, "The man is *happy*," or, "*Happy* is the man, who makes virtue his choice:" "The interview was *delightful;*" or, "*Delightful* was the interview."
6th. When the adjective expresses some circumstance of a substantive placed after an active verb; as, "Vanity often renders its possessors *despicable.*" In an exclamatory sentence, the adjective generally precedes the substantive; as, "How *despicable* does vanity often render its possessor!"
There is sometimes great beauty, as well as force, in placing the adjective before the verb, and the substantive immediately after it; as, "Great is the Lord! just and true are thy ways, thou King of saints!"
Sometimes the word *all* is emphatically put after a number of particulars comprehended under it. "Ambition, interest, honor, *all* concurred." Sometimes a substantive, which likewise comprehends the preceding particulars, is used in conjunction with this adjective; as, "Royalists, republicans, churchmen, sectaries, courtiers, *all parties*, concurred in the illusion."
An adjective pronoun, in the plural number, will sometimes properly associate with a singular noun; as, "Our desire, your intention, their resignation." This association applies rather to things of an intellectual nature, than to those which are corporeal. It forms an exception to the general rule.
A substantive with its adjective is reckoned as one compounded word; whence they often take another adjective, and sometimes a third, and so on; as, "An old man; a good old man; a very learned, judicious, good old man."
"Though the adjective always relates to a substantive, it is, in many instances, put as if it were absolute; especially where the noun has been mentioned before, or easily understood, though not expressed; as, "I often survey it."

Is it correct to say, "A large enough number"? How should it be altered? What is the Note for it? Should the adjective be placed usually before or after the noun?

8.

*He spoke in a distinct enough manner to be heard by the whole assembly."
*Thomas is equipped with a new (1.) pair of shoes, and a new pair of gloves: he is the servant of an old rich (2.) man."
"The *two first* (3.) in the row are cherry-trees, the *two others* are pear-trees."

(1.) "*a pair of new shoes.*" (2.) "*rich old.*" (3.) Note I.—Rule VI.
K 13

RULE II

Corresponding with Murray's Grammar.

RULE IX.

The indefinite article, A *or* AN, *belongs to nouns of the singular number.*

RULE III.

The definite article, THE, *belongs to nouns of the singular or plural numbers.*

The articles are often properly omitted: when used, they should be justly applied, according to their distinct nature; as, "Gold is corrupting; the sea is green; a lion is bold."

It is the nature of both the articles to determine or limit the thing spoken of. *A* determines it to be one single thing of the kind, leaving it still uncertain which; *the* determines which it is, or, if many, which they are.

The following passage will serve as an example of the different uses of a and *the*, and of the force of the substantive without any article: "*Man* was made for society, and ought to extend his good will to all men; but *a man* will naturally entertain a more particular kindness for *the men* with whom he has the most frequent intercourse; and enter into a still closer union with *the man* whose temper and disposition suit best with his own."

As the articles are sometimes misapplied, it may be of some use to exhibit a few instances: "And I persecuted this way unto *the* death." The apostle does not mean any particular sort of death, but death in general: the definite article, therefore, is improperly used: it ought to be, "unto death," without any article.

"When he, the Spirit of truth, is come, he will guide you into all truth;' that is, according to this translation, "into all truth whatsoever, into truth of all kinds;"—very different from the meaning of the evangelist, and from the original, "into all *the* truth;" that is, "into all evangelical truth, all truth necessary for you to know."

"Who breaks a butterfly upon *a* wheel?" it ought to be "*the* wheel," used as an instrument for the particular purpose of torturing criminals. "The Almighty hath given reason to *a* man to be a light unto him:" it should rather be, "to *man*," in general. "This day is salvation come to this house, forasmuch as he also is *the* son of Abraham:" it ought to be, "*a* son of Abraham."

These remarks may serve to show the great importance of the proper use of the article, and the excellence of the English language in this respect; which, by means of its two articles, does most precisely determine the extent of signification of common names.

What is the nature of the articles? What does the article *a* determine?
What the article *the*?

" *The* fire, *the* air, *the* earth, and *the* water, are four elements (1.) of the philosophers."

" (4.) Wisest and best men sometimes commit errors."

" Reason was given to *a* man to control his passions."

" Beware of drunkenness; it impairs understanding; wastes an estate; destroys a reputation; consumes the body; and renders the (5.) man of the brightest parts the (5.) common jest (6.) of the meanest clown."

" We have within us an intelligent principle, distinct from (2.) body and from matter."

" *A* man is the noblest work of (3.) creation."

(1.) " Fire, air," &c.——" the four ;" &c.   (2.) " *the* body."   (3.) · *the* creation."   (4.) " *The* wisest."   (5.) " a."   (6.) RULE IV

"He is a much better writer than a reader."
"The king has conferred on him the title of a duke."
"There are some evils of life which equally affect prince and people."
"We must act our part with a constancy, though reward of our constancy be (1.) distant."
We are placed here under a trial of our virtue."
"The virtues like his are not easily acquired. Such qualities honor the nature of a man."

"Purity has its seat in the heart, but extends its influence over so much of outward conduct, as to form the great and material part of a character."
"The profligate man is seldom or never found to be *the* good husband, *the* good father, or *the* beneficent neighbor."
"True charity is not the meteor which occasionally glares, but the luminary which, in its orderly and regular course, dispenses benignant influence."

1. A nice distinction of the sense is sometimes made by the use or omission of the article *a*. If I say, "He behaved with *a* little reverence," my meaning is positive. If I say, "He behaved with little reverence," my meaning is negative. And these two are by no means the same, or to be used in the same cases. By the former, I rather praise a person; by the latter, I dispraise him. For the sake of this distinction, which is a very useful one, we may better bear the seeming impropriety of the article *a* before nouns of number. When I say, "There were few men with him," I speak diminutively, and mean to represent them as inconsiderable: whereas, when I say, "There were *a* few men with him," I evidently intend to make the most of them.

What is the difference in meaning between the expressions, "We behaved with a little reverence," and, "We behaved with little reverence?"

1.

"He has been much censured for conducting himself with *a* little attention to his business."
"So bold a breach of order called for (2.) little severity in punishing the offender."
"His error was accompanied with so little contrition and candid acknowledgment, that he found *a* few persons to intercede for him."

"There were so many mitigating (3.) circumstances attending his misconduct, particularly that (4.) of his open confession, that he found (5.) few friends who were disposed to interest themselves in his favor."
"As his misfortunes were the fruit of his own obstinacy, a few persons pitied him."

2. In general, it may be sufficient to prefix the article to the former of two words in the same construction; though the French never fail to repeat it in this case. "There were many hours, both of the night and day, which he could spend, without suspicion, in solitary thought." It might have been, "of *the* night and *of the* day." And, for the sake of emphasis, we often repeat the article in a series of epithets. "He hoped that this title would secure him *an* ample and *an* independent authority."
Is the article to be repeated before two words in the same construction?

2.

"The fear of shame, (6.) the desire of approbation, prevent many bad actions."
"In this business he was influenced by a just and (7.) generous principle."

"He was fired with desire of doing something, though he knew not yet, with distinctness, either end or means."

(1.) 464. (2.) "*a* little." (3.) 559. (4.) "that circumstance" Note 1.—
Rule XIV (5.) "a few." 359. (6.) "and the." (7.) "a generous."

3. In common conversation, and in familiar style, we frequently omit the articles, which might be inserted with propriety in writing, especially in a grave style. "At worst, time might be gained by this expedient." "At *the* worst" would have been better in this place. "Give me here John Baptist's head." There would have been more dignity in saying, "John *the* Baptist's head;" or, "The head of John the Baptist."

The article *the* has sometimes a good effect in distinguishing a person by an epithet. "In the history of Henry the Fourth, by Father Daniel, we are surprised at not finding him *the* great man." "I own I am often surprised that he should have treated so coldly a man so much *the* gentleman."

This article is often elegantly put, after the manner of the French, for the pronoun possessive; as, "He looks him full in *the* face;" that is, "in *his* face." "In his presence they were to strike *the* forehead on the ground;" that is, "*their foreheads.*"

We sometimes, according to the French manner, repeat the same article, when the adjective, on account of any clause depending upon it, is put after the substantive. "Of all the considerable governments among the Alps, a commonwealth is a constitution *the* most adapted of any to the poverty of those countries." "With such a specious title as that of blood, which, with the multitude, is always a claim *the* strongest, and *the* most easily comprehended." "They are not the men in the nation *the* most difficult to be replaced."

"At worst, time might be gained," &c. What word may properly be inserted in the beginning of this sentence? What is the Note for it?

3.

" At worst, I could but incur a gentle reprimand."

"At best, his gift was but a poor offering, when we consider his estate."

RULE I.

Corresponding with Murray's Grammar,

RULE X.

The possessive case is governed by the following noun.

When the annexed substantive signifies the same thing as the first, there is no variation of case; as, "George, king of Great Britain, elector of Hanover," &c.; "Pompey contended with Cæsar, the greatest general of his time;" "Religion, the support of adversity, adorns prosperity." Nouns thus circumstanced are said to be in *apposition* to each other. The interposition of a relative and verb will sometimes break the construction; as, "Pompey contended with Cæsar, *who was* the greatest general of his time." Here the word *general* is in the nominative case, according to Rule XV., or Note 4, under Rule VIII.

The preposition *of*, joined to a substantive, is not always equivalent to the possessive case. It is only so, when the expression can be converted into the regular form of the possessive case. We can say, "the reward of virtue," and, "virtue's reward;" but though it is proper to say, "a crown of gold," we cannot convert the expression into the possessive case, and say, "gold's crown."

Substantives govern pronouns as well as nouns, in the possessive case; as, "Every tree is known by *its* fruit;" "Goodness brings *its* reward;" "That desk is *mine*."

The genitive (1.) *its* is often improperly used for *'t is* or *it is;* as, "Its my book;" instead of, "It is my book."

The pronoun *his*, when detached from the noun to which it relates, is to be considered, not as a possessive pronoun, but as the genitive case of the personal pronoun; as, "This composition is *his*." "Whose book is that?" "*His*." If we used the noun itself, we should say, "This composition is

(1.) Or possessive.

SYNTAX. 149

John's." "Whose book is that?" "Eliza's." The position will be still more evident, when we consider that both the pronouns in the following sentences must have a similar construction: "Is it her or his honor that is tarnished?" "It is not hers, but his."

Sometimes a substantive in the genitive or possessive case stands alone, the latter one by which it is governed being understood; as, "I called at the bookseller's," that is, "at the bookseller's shop."

"Religion, the support of adversity, adorns prosperity." What is said of the nouns religion, and support, in respect to each other? When is the preposition of joined to a substantive equivalent to the possessive case? Give an example.

"My ancestors virtue is not mine." (1.)
"His brothers offence will not condemn him."
"I will not destroy the city for ten sake."
"Nevertheless, Asa his heart (2.) was perfect with the Lord."

"A mothers tenderness, and a fathers care are natures gifts for mans advantage."
"A mans manners' frequently influence his fortune."
"Wisdoms precepts' form the good mans interest and happiness."

"They slew Varus, he that was mentioned before."
"They slew Varus, who was him that I mentioned before."

1. If several nouns come together in the genitive (3.) case, the apostrophe with *s* is annexed to the last, and understood to the rest; as, "John and Eliza's books;" "This was my father, mother and uncle's advice." But when any words intervene, perhaps on account of the increased pause, the sign of the possessive should be annexed to each; as, "They are John's as well as Eliza's books;" "I had the physician's, the surgeon's and the apothecary's assistance."

"John's and Eliza's books." Will you correct this sentence, and give the Rule for it?

1.

"It was the men's, (4.) women's (5.) and children's lot to suffer great calamities."
"Peter's, John's and Andrew's occupation, was that of fishermen."

"This measure gained the king, as well as the people's approbation."
"Not only the counsel's and attorney's but the judge's opinion also, favored his cause."

2. In poetry, the additional *s* is frequently omitted, but the apostrophe retained, in the same manner as in substantives of the plural number ending in *s*; as, "The wrath of Peleus' son." This seems not so allowable in prose, which the following erroneous example will demonstrate: "Moses' minister;" "Phinehas' wife;" "Festus came into Felix' room;" "These answers were made to the witness' questions." But in cases which would give too much of the hissing sound, or increase the difficulty of pronunciation, the omission takes place even in prose; as, "For righteousness' sake;" "For conscience' sake."

Is the additional *s* ever omitted? Give an example.

2.

And he cast himself down at Jesus feet."
"Moses rod was turned into a serpent."
"For Herodias sake, his brother Philips wife."

"If ye suffer for righteousness' sake, happy are ye."
"Ye should be subject for conscience's sake."

(1) Rule I. (2.) "Asa's heart." (3.) Or possessive. (4.) "Men" is here in the possessive case, the apostrophe being understood; therefore apply Rule I. (5.) "Men women;" or "it was the lot of" &c

12*

3. Little explanatory circumstances are particularly awkward between a genitive case and the word which usually follows it; as, "She began to extol the farmer's, as she called him, excellent understanding." It ought to be, "the excellent understanding of the farmer, as she called him."

"She began to extol the farmer's, as she called him, excellent understanding." Will you correct this sentence, and give the Rule for it?

3.

"They very justly condemned the prodigal's, as he was called, senseless and extravagant conduct." (1.)

"They implicitly obeyed the protector's, as they called him, imperious mandates."

4. When a sentence consists of terms signifying a name and an office, or of any expressions by which one part is descriptive or explanatory of the other, it may occasion some doubt to which of them the sign of the genitive case should be annexed; or whether it should be subjoined to them both. Thus, some would say, "I left the parcel at Smith's the bookseller;" others, "at Smith the bookseller's;" and perhaps others, "at Smith's the bookseller's." The first of these forms is most agreeable to the English idiom; and if the addition consists of two or more words, the case seems to be less dubious; as, "I left the parcel at Smith's, the bookseller and stationer." But as this subject requires a little further explanation, to make it intelligible to the learners, we shall add a few observations tending to unfold its principles.

A phrase in which the words are so connected and dependent, as to admit of no pause before the conclusion, necessarily requires the genitive sign at or near the end of the phrase; as, "Whose prerogative is it?" "It is the king of Great Britain's;" "That is the duke of Bridgewater's canal;" "The bishop of Landaff's excellent book;" "The Lord Mayor of London's authority;" "The captain of the guard's house."

When words in apposition follow each other in quick succession, it seems also most agreeable to our idiom, to give the sign of the genitive a similar situation; especially if the noun which governs the genitive be expressed; as, "The emperor Leopold's;" "Dionysius the tyrant's;" "For David my *servant's* sake;" "Give me John the *Baptist's* head;" "Paul the *apostle's* advice." But when a pause is proper, and the governing noun not expressed; and when the latter part of the sentence is extended; it appears to be requisite that the sign should be applied to the first genitive, and understood to the other; as, "I reside at lord Stormont's, my old patron and benefactor;" "Whose glory did he emulate? He emulated Cæsar's, the greatest general of antiquity." In the following sentences, it would be very awkward to place the sign either at the end of each of the clauses, or at the end of the latter one alone: "These psalms are David's, the king, priest, and prophet of the Jewish people;" "We staid a month at lord Lyttleton's, the ornament of his country, and the friend of every virtue." The sign of the genitive case may very properly be understood at the end of these members, an ellipsis at the latter part of sentences being a common construction in our language; as the learner will see by one or two examples: "They wished to submit, but he did not;" that is, "he did not *wish to submit*." "He said it was their concern, but not his;" that is, *not his concern*."

If we annex the sign of the genitive to the end of the last clause only, we shall perceive that a resting-place is wanted, and that the connecting circumstance is placed too remotely, to be either perspicuous or agreeable; as, "Whose glory did he emulate? He emulated Cæsar, the greatest general of *antiquity's*;" "These psalms are David, the king, priest, and prophet of the Jewish *people's*." It is much better to say, "This is *Paul's* advice, the Christian hero, and great apostle of the gentiles," than "This is Paul the Christian hero, and great apostle of the *gentiles*' advice." On the other hand, the application of the genitive sign to both or all of the nouns in apposition, would be generally harsh and displeasing, and perhaps in some cases incorrect; as, "The emperor's Leopold's;" "King's George's;" "Charles's the

---

(1.) "*the senseless,*" &c. ——"*of the prodigal, as he was called.*"

SYNTAX.   151

second's;" "The parcel was left at Smith's the bookseller's and stationer's." The rules which we have endeavored to elucidate will prevent the inconvenience of both these modes of expression; and they appear to be simple, perspicuous, and consistent with the idiom of the language.

Which is most agreeable to the English idiom, to say, "Smith's the bookseller," or, "Smith the bookseller's?" When the words are connected and dependent, where is the genitive (1.) sign to be placed?

When words in apposition follow each other in quick succession, where should the sign of the genitive be placed? What effect is perceived if we annex the sign of the genitive to the end of the last clause only of the sentence? Give an example. What is the effect of applying the genitive sign to both or all the nouns in apposition? Give an example.

4.

"I bought the knives at Johnson's (2.) the *cutler's*." (3.)
"The silk was purchased at Brown's the *mercer's* and *haberdasher's*."
"Lord Feversham the general's tent." (4.)
"This palace *had been* the grand *sultan's* Mahomet's."

"I will not for *David's* thy father's sake."
"He took refuge at the governor, the king's representative's."
"Whose (5.) works are these? They are Cicero, the most eloquent of men's."

5. The English genitive has often an unpleasant sound; so that we daily make more use of the particle *of*, to express the same relation. There is something awkward in the following sentences, in which this method has not been taken: "The general, in the army's name, published a declaration;" "The commons' vote;" "The lords' house;" "Unless he is very ignorant of the kingdom's condition." It were certainly better to say, "In the name of the army;" "The votes of the commons;" "The house of lords;" "The condition of the kingdom." It is also rather harsh to use two English genitives with the same substantive; as, "Whom he acquainted with the pope's and the king's pleasure." "The pleasure of the pope and the king," would have been better.

We sometimes meet with three substantives dependent on one another, and connected by the preposition *of* applied to each of them; as, "The severity of the distress of the son of the king, touched the nation;" but this mode of expression is not to be recommended. It would be better to say, "The severe distress of the king's son touched the nation." We have a striking instance of this laborious mode of expression, in the following sentence: "*Of* some *of* the books *of* each *of* these classes *of* literature, a catalogue will be given at the end *of* the work."

"In the army's name." How may this expression be altered for the better?

5.

"The world's government is not left to chance." (6.)
"She married my son's wife's brother." (7.)
"This is my wife's brother's partner's house." (8.)

"It was necessary to have both the physician's and the surgeon's advice." (9.)
"The extent of the prerogative of the king of England is sufficiently ascertained."

6. In some cases, we use both the genitive termination and the preposition *of*; as, "It is a discovery of Sir Isaac Newton's." Sometimes, indeed, unless we throw the sentence into another form, this method is absolutely necessary, in order to distinguish the sense, and to give the idea of property, strict-

---

(1.) Or possessive.   (2.) "Johnson's *shop*." Rule I.   (3.) "*cutler*." See Note I. under this Rule.   (4.) "*The tent of lord*," &c.   (5.) 431.   (6.) "*The government of the world*."   (7.) "*the brother of my son's wife*."   (8.) "*The house belongs to the partner of my wife's brother*."   (9.) '*the advice both of*"

ly so called, which is the most important of the relations expressed by the genitive case; for the expressions, "This picture of my friend," and, "This picture of my friend's," suggest very different ideas. The latter only is that of property, in the strictest sense. The idea would, doubtless, be conveyed in a better manner, by saying, "This picture, belonging to my friend."

When this double genitive, as some grammarians term it, is not necessary to distinguish the sense, and especially in a grave style, it is generally omitted. Except to prevent ambiguity, it seems to be allowable only in cases which suppose the existence of a plurality of subjects of the same kind. In the expressions, "A subject of the emperor's;" "A sentiment of my brother's;" more than one subject, and one sentiment, are supposed to belong to the possessor. But when this plurality is neither intimated, nor necessarily supposed, the double genitive, except as before mentioned, should not be used; as, "This house of the governor is very commodious;" "The crown of the king was stolen;" "That privilege of the scholar was never abused." But, after all that can be said for this double genitive, as it is termed, some grammarians think that it would be better to avoid the use of it altogether, and to give the sentiment another form of expression.

Are there any cases in which we use both the genitive termination and the preposition *of*? Give an example. Is this double genitive ever omitted?

6.

"That picture of the *king's* does not much resemble (1.) him."

"These pictures of the *king* (2.) were sent to him from Italy."

"This estate of the corporation's is much encumbered."

"That is the eldest son of the king of England's."

7. When an entire clause of a sentence, beginning with a participle of the present tense, is used as one name, or to express one idea or circumstance, the noun on which it depends may be put in the genitive case: thus, instead of saying, "What is the reason of this person dismissing his servant so hastily?" that is, "What is the reason of this person in dismissing his servant so hastily?" we may say, and perhaps ought to say, "What is the reason of this person's dismissing of his servant so hastily?" just as we say, "What is the reason of this person's hasty dismission of his servant?" So also. we say, "I remember it being reckoned a great exploit;" or, more properly, "I remember its being reckoned," &c. The following sentence is correct and proper: "Much will depend on the *pupil's composing*, but more on *his reading* frequently." It would not be accurate to say, "Much will depend on the *pupil composing*," &c. We also properly say, "This will be the effect *of the pupil's composing* frequently;" instead of, "*of the pupil composing* frequently."

"What is the reason of this person dismissing his servant so hastily?" Will you correct this sentence, and give the rule for it?

7

"What (3.) *can* be the cause of the *parliament* neglecting so important a business."

"Much depends on this *rule* being observed."

"The time of *William* making the experiment, at length arrived."

"It is very probable that this assembly was called, to clear some doubt which the king had about the lawfulness of the Hollanders their throwing off the monarchy of Spain, and *their* withdrawing entirely their allegiance to that crown."

"If we alter the situation of any of the words, we shall presently be sensible of the melody suffering."

"Such will ever be the effect of youth associating with vicious companions."

(1.) 386.   (2.) Or. "*These pictures belonging to the king*," &c.   (3.) Rule XV

RULE VIII.

Corresponding with Murray's Grammar,
RULE XI.

Active transitive verbs govern the objective case.

In English, the nominative case, denoting the subject, usually goes before the verb; and the objective case, denoting the object, follows the verb active; and it is the order that determines the case in *nouns* ; as, "Alexander conquered the Persians." But the *pronoun*, having a proper form for each of those cases, is sometimes, when it is in the objective case, placed before the verb; and, when it is in the nominative case, follows the object and verb; as " *Whom* ye ignorantly worship, *him* declare I unto you."

This position of the pronoun sometimes occasions its proper case and government to be neglected; as in the following instances: " Who should I esteem more than the wise and good?" " By the character of those who you choose for your friends, your own is likely to be formed." Those are the persons who he thought true to his interests." " Who should I see the other day but my old friend?" " Whosoever the court favors." In all these places, it ought to be *whom*, the relative being governed in the objective case by the verbs *esteem, choose, thought*, &c. " He, who, under all proper circumstances, has the boldness to speak truth, choose for thy friend;" it should be "*him* who,"

Verbs neuter and intransitive do not act upon, or govern, nouns and pronouns. " He *sleeps*," " they *muse*," &c., are not transitive. They are, therefore, not followed by an objective case, specifying the object of an action. But when this case, or an object of action, comes after such verbs, though it may carry the appearance of being governed by them, it is affected by a preposition or some other word understood; as, " He resided many years [that is, *for* or *during* many years] in that street;" " He rode several miles [that is, *for* or *through* the space of several miles] on that day;" " He lay an hour [that is, *during* an hour] in great torture." In the phrases, " To dream a dream," " To live a virtuous life," " To run a race," " To walk the horse," " To dance the child," the verbs certainly assume a transitive form, and may not, in these cases, be improperly denominated transitive verbs.

How is the nominative case usually known in English? How the objective? Do neuter verbs govern nouns and pronouns? In the phrase, " He resided many years in that street," how do you parse *years* ? When verbs naturally neuter assume a transitive form, what may they then be called?

" They *who* opulence has made proud, and *who* luxury has corrupted, cannot relish the simple pleasures of nature."

" You have reason to dread his wrath, which one day (1.) will destroy ye both."

" *Who* have I reason to love so (2.) much (2.) as this friend (3.) of my youth?"

" *Ye*, who were dead, hath he quickened."

" *Who* did they entertain so freely?"

" The man *who he* raised from obscurity, is dead."

" Ye only have I known of all the families of the earth."

" He and they we know, but who (4.) are you?"

" *She* that is idle and mischievous, reprove sharply."

" Who did they send to him on so important an errand?"

" That is the friend (4.) who you must receive cordially, and who you cannot esteem too highly."

" He invited my brother and I to see and examine (3.) his library."

" He who committed the offence, you should correct, not I, who am innocent."

" We should fear and obey the Author of our being, even He who has power to reward or punish us forever."

" They who he had most (5.) injured, he had the greatest reason to love."

(1.) Rule XXII (2.) Adverb (3.) Rule VI (4.) Rule XV. (5.) 67k

1. Some writers, however, use certain neuter or intransitive verbs as if they were transitive, putting after them the objective case, agreeably to the French construction of reciprocal verbs; but this custom is so foreign to the idiom of the English tongue, that it ought not to be adopted or imitated. The following are some instances of this practice: "*Repenting* him of his design." "The king soon found reason *to repent* him of his provoking such dangerous enemies." "The popular lords did not fail to *enlarge* themselves on the subject." "The nearer his successes *approached* him to the throne." "Go, *flee* thee away into the land of Judah." "I think it by no means a fit and decent thing to *vie* charities," &c. "They have spent their whole time and pains to *agree* the sacred with the profane chronology."

"Repenting him of his design." Will you repeat the note which shows this sentence to be incorrect?

1.

* Though he now takes pleasure in them, he will one day (1.) repent *him* (2.) of indulgences so unwarrantable."

"The nearer his virtues approached him to the great example before him, the humbler he grew."

"It will be very difficult to agree his conduct with (3.) the principles he professes."

2. Active-transitive verbs are sometimes as improperly made neuter or intransitive; as, "I must *premise* with three circumstances;" "Those who think to *ingratiate with* him by calumniating me."

"I must premise with three circumstances." Will you correct this sentence, and give the rule for it?

2.

"To ingratiate (4.) with some by traducing others, makes a base and despicable mind."

"I shall premise *with* two or three general observations."

3. The neuter verb (5.) is varied like the active; but, having, in some degree, the nature of the passive, it admits, in many instances, of the passive form, retaining still the neuter signification, chiefly in such verbs as signify some sort of motion, or change of place or condition; as, "I am come;" "I was gone;" "I am grown;" "I was fallen." The following examples, however, appear to be erroneous, in giving the neuter verbs a passive form, instead of an active one: "The rule of our holy religion, from which we *are* infinitely *swerved*." "The whole obligation of that law and covenant *was* also *ceased*." "Whose number *was* now *amounted* to three hundred." "This mareschal, upon some discontent, *was entered* into a conspiracy against his master." "At the end of a compaign, when half the men *are deserted* or killed.' It should be, "*have* swerved," "*had* ceased," &c.

"I am come." Why should not this be "I have come"?

3.

* If such maxims and such practices (6.) prevail, what *has* (7.) *become* of decency and virtue?"

* "I *have* come, according to the time proposed; but I *have* fallen upon an evil hour."

"The mighty rivals *are now* at length agreed."

"The influence of his corrupt example was (8.) then entirely ceased."

"He was entered into the connection before the consequences were considered."

(1.) Rule XXII. (2.) "*repent of.*" (3.) "*to make——agree with,*" &c.
(4.) "ingratiate *ourselves.*" (5.) By *neuter* and *active*, Mr. Murray here means what in this work are styled *intransitive* and *transitive* verbs. - (6.) Rule XL
(7.) "*is* become." (8.) "*had*"

SYNTAX.

RULE XV. When two or more nouns, or nouns and pronouns, signifying the same thing, come together, they are put by apposition in the same case

☞ *The examples which follow may be corrected by this Rule or the following Note.*

4. The verb *to be*, through all its variations, has the same case after it as that which next precedes it. "*I* am *he* whom they invited." "*It* may he (*or*, it might have been) *he*, but *it* cannot be, (*or*, could not have been) *I*." "*It* is impossible to be *they*." "*It* seems to have been *he* who conducted himself so wisely." "*It* appeared to be *she* that transacted the business." "I understood *it* to be *him*." "I believe it to have been *them*." "We at first took it to be *her* ; but were afterwards convinced that *it* was not *she*." "He is not the person *who* it seemed he was." "He is really the person *who* he appeared to be." "She is not now the woman *whom* they represented *her* to have been." "*Whom* do you fancy *him* to be ?" By these examples, it appears that this substantive verb has no government of case ; but serves, in all its forms, as a conductor to the cases ; so that the two cases which, in the construction of the sentence, are the *next* before and after it, must always be alike. Perhaps this subject will be more intelligible to the learner, by observing, that the words in the cases preceding and following the verb *to be*, may be said to be in *apposition* to each other. Thus, in the sentence, "I understood it to be him," the words *it* and *him* are in apposition ; that is, "they refer to the same thing, and are in the same case."
The following sentences contain deviations from the rule, and exhibit the pronoun in a wrong case. "It might have been *him*, but there is no proof of it." "Though I was blamed, it could not have been *me*." "I saw one whom I took to be *she*." "She is the person, *who* I understood it to have been." "*Who* do you think me to be ?" "*Whom* do men say that I am ?" "And *whom* think ye that I am ?"

Passive verbs, which signify naming, &c., have the same case before and after them ; as, "He was called Cæsar ;" "She was named Penelope ;" "Homer is styled the prince of poets ;" "James was created a duke ;" "The general was saluted emperor ;" "The professor was appointed tutor to the prince."

"I am him whom they invited." Will you correct this sentence, and give the rule for it ?

4.

1 "Well may you be afraid ; it is *him* indeed."

2 "I would act the same part, if I were *him*, (1.) or in his situation."

3 "Search the Scriptures, for in them ye think ye have eternal life ; and they are *them* which testify of me."

4 "Be composed : it is me : you have no cause for fear."

5 "I cannot tell who has befriended me, unless it is him from whom I have received many benefits."

6 "I know not whether *it* were *them*

(2.) who conducted the business ; but I am certain it was not him."

"He so much resembled my brother, that, at first sight, I took it to be he."

"After all their professions, is it possible to be them ?"

"It could not have been her, for she always behaves discreetly."

"If it was not him, who do you imagine it to have been ?"

"Who do you think him to be ?"

"Whom do the people say that we are ?"

---

* When the verb *to be* is *understood*, it has the same case, before and after it, as when it is *expressed*; as, "He seems the leader of the party ;" "He shall continue steward ;" "They appointed me executor ;" "I supposed him a man of learning ;" — that is, "He seems *to be* the leader of the party," &c. Nouns in apposition are in the same case ; as, "We named the man Pompey ;" "They may term Charles a visionary, but they cannot call him a deceiver ;" "Hortensius died a martyr ;" "The gentle Sidney lived the shepherd's friend."

(1.) Rule XV. (2.) "*they were the persons.*"

5. The auxiliary *let* governs the objective case; as, "Let *him* beware; "Let *us* judge candidly;" "Let *them* not presume;" "Let *George* study his lesson."

"Let us judge candidly." In what case is *us?* What is the rule?

5.
" Whatever (1.) others do, let (2.) "Let them and we unite to oppose *thou* and *I* act wisely." this growing (3.) evil."

RULE XII.
Corresponding with Murray's Grammar,
RULE XII.

The infinitive mood may be governed by verbs, participles, adjectives, nouns and pronouns.

The preposition *to*, though generally used before the latter verb, is sometimes properly omitted; as, "I heard him say it;" instead of, "*to* say it."

The verbs which have commonly other verbs following them, in the infinitive mood, without the sign *to*, are, *bid, dare, need, make, see, hear, feel*, and also *let*, not used as an auxiliary; and perhaps a few others; as, "I bade him do it;" "Ye dare not do it;" "I saw him do it;" "I heard him say it;" "Thou lettest him go."

Will you name the verbs which have commonly other verbs in the infinitive mood after them, without the sign *to?*

"It is better (4.) *live* on a little, (5.) than *outlive* a good deal."
"You ought not walk too hastily."
"I wish him not wrestle with his happiness."

"I need not *to* solicit him to do a kind action."
"I dare not to proceed so hastily, lest I should give offence."
"I have seen some young persons to conduct themselves very discreetly."

1. In the following passages, the word *to*, the sign of the infinitive mood, where it is distinguished by Italic characters, is superfluous and improper: "I have observed some satirists *to* use," &c. "To see so many *to* make so little conscience of so great a sin." "It cannot but be a delightful spectacle to God and angels, to see a young person, besieged by powerful temptations on every side, *to* acquit himself gloriously, and resolutely *to* hold out against the most violent assaults; to behold one in the prime and flower of his age, that is courted by pleasures and honors, by the devil, and all the bewitching vanities of the world, to reject all these, and *to* cleave steadfastly unto God."

This mood has also been improperly used in the following places: "I am not like other men, *to* envy the talents I cannot reach." "Grammarians have denied, or at least doubted, them *to be* genuine." "That all our doings may be ordered by thy governance, *to do* always what is righteous in thy sight."

The infinitive is frequently governed by adjectives, substantives, and participles; as, "He is eager to learn;" "She is worthy to be loved;" "They have a desire to improve;" "Endeavoring to persuade."

The infinitive mood has much of the nature of a substantive, expressing the action itself which the verb signifies, as the participle has the nature of an adjective. Thus the infinitive mood does the office of a substantive in different cases:—in the nominative; as, "To *play* is pleasant;"—in the objective; as, "Boys love to *play;*" "For *to will* is present with me, but *to perform* that which is good, I find not."

The infinitive mood is often made absolute, or used independently on the rest of the sentence, supplying the place of the conjunction *that* with the potential mood; as, "To confess the truth, I was in fault;" "To begin with the first;" "To proceed;" "To conclude;"—that is, "That I may confess," &c.

(1.) Rule VIII. (2.) Imp. Rule VI. (3.) 559. (4.) "*to live.*" Rule XII
(5.) Noun

SYNTAX. 157

"I have observed some satirists to use," &c. What is incorrect in this sentence?
In the expression, "He is eager to learn," will you parse *to learn?* What is the rule? (1.) "To play is pleasant." Will you parse *to play*, and give a rule for it? (1.) "To confess the truth, I was in fault." How is *to confess* parsed? What is the rule for it? (2.)

1.

'It is a great support to virtue, when we see a good mind *to* maintain (3.) its patience and tranquillity, under injuries and affliction, and *to* cordially forgive its oppressors."
"It is the difference of their conduct, which makes us *to* approve the one, and *to* reject the other."
"We should not be like many persons, *to* (4.) depreciate the virtues *we* (5.) do not possess."

"To see (6.) young persons who are courted by health and pleasure, to resist all the allurements of vice, and to steadily pursue virtue and knowledge, is cheering and delightful to every good mind."
"They acted with so much reserve, that some persons doubted *them to be sincere.*" (7.)
"And the multitude wondered, when they saw the lame to walk, and the blind to see." (8.)

RULE XXVI.
Corresponding with Murray's Grammar,
RULE XIII.

In the use of words and phrases which, in point of time, relate to each other, a due regard to that relation should be observed. Instead of saying, "The Lord hath given, and the Lord hath taken away," *we should say,* "The Lord gave, and the Lord hath taken away." *Instead of,* "I remember the family more than twenty years," *it should be,* "I have remembered the family more than twenty years."

It is not easy to give particular rules for the management of the moods and tenses of verbs with respect to one another, so that they may be proper and consistent. The best rule that can be given, is this very general one—"To observe what the sense necessarily requires." It may, however, be of use to give a few examples of irregular construction. "The last week I intended *to have written*," is a very common phrase; the infinitive being in the past time, as well as the verb which it follows. But it is certainly wrong; for how long soever it now is since I thought of writing, *to write* was then present to me, and must still be considered as present, when I bring back that time, and the thoughts of it. It ought, therefore, to be, "The last week I intended *to write.*" The following sentences are also erroneous: "I cannot excuse the remissness of those whose business it should have been, as it certainly was their interest, to *have interposed* their good offices." "There were two circumstances which made it necessary for them to *have lost* no time." "History painters would have found it difficult to *have invented* such a species of beings." They ought to be, *to interpose, to lose, to invent.* "On the morrow, because he would have known the certainty wherefore he was accused of the Jews, he loosed him." It ought to be, "because he *would know*," or, rather, "*being willing to know.*" "The

---
(1.) Rule XII.   (2.) Note XII. LVIII.   (3.) For *to maintain* read *maintain*. (4.) "*who.*"   (5.) "*they*"   (6.) Note XIII.   (7.) "*their sincerity.*" (8.) "*persons who had been lame, walking: and those who had been blind, seeing.*"

14

blind man said unto him, Lord, that I *might* receive my sight." "If by any means I *might* attain unto the resurrection of the dead." *May*, in both places, would have been better. "From this biblical knowledge, he appears to study the Scriptures with great attention;" "*to have studied*," &c. "I feared that I should have lost it, before I arrived at the city;" "*should lose it.*" "I had rather walk;" it should be, "I *would* rather walk." "It would have afforded me no satisfaction, if I could perform it;" it should be, "if I *could have* performed it;" or, "It *would afford* me no satisfaction, if I *could perform* it."

To preserve consistency in the time of verbs, we must recollect that, in the subjunctive mood, the present and imperfect tenses often carry with them a future sense; and that the auxiliaries *should* and *would*, in the imperfect times, are used to express the present or future, as well as the past.

"I intended to have written." Will you point out the incorrectness of this sentence, and give a rule for it?

" The next new year's day I shall be (1.) at school three years."

" And he that *was* dead (2.) sat up, and began to speak."

" I should be obliged to him, if he *will* gratify me in that particular."

" And the multitude wondered, when they saw the dumb to speak, the maimed to be whole, the lame walk, and the blind seeing." (3.)

" I have compassion on the multitude, because they *continue* with me now three days."

" In the treasury belonging to the cathedral in this city *is* preserved (4.) with the greatest veneration, for upwards of six hundred years, a dish which they pretend to be made of emerald."

" The court of Rome gladly laid hold on all the opportunities, which the imprudence, weakness, or necessities of princes afford it, to extend its authority."

" Fierce as he *moved*, his silver shafts resound."

" They maintained that scripture conclusion, that all mankind rise from one head."

" John will earn his wages when his service is completed."

" Ye will not come unto me that ye might have life."

" Be that as it *will*, he cannot justify his conduct."

" I have been at London a year, and seen the king last summer."

" After we visited London, we returned, content and thankful, to our retired and peaceful habitation."

1. It is proper further to observe, that verbs of the infinitive mood in the following form — *to write, to be writing*, and *to be written* — always denote something *contemporary with* the time of the governing verb, or *subsequent to it*; but when verbs of that mood are expressed as follows — *to have been writing, to have written*, and *to have been written* — they always denote something *antecedent* to the time of the governing verb. This remark is thought to be of importance; for, if duly attended to, it will, in most cases, be sufficient to direct us in the relative application of these tenses.

The following sentence is properly and analogically expressed: "I found him better than I expected to find him." " Expected *to have found* him," is irreconcilable alike to grammar and to sense. Indeed, all verbs expressive of hope, desire intention, or command, must invariably be followed by the present, and not the perfect of the infinitive. Every person would perceive an error in this expression—" It is long since I commanded him *to have done* it;" yet "expected to *have found*," is no better. It is as clear that the *finding* must be posterior to the expectation, as that the *obedience* must be posterior to the command.

In the sentence which follows, the verb is with propriety put in the perfect tense of the infinitive mood: " It would have afforded me great pleasure, as

---

(1.) "shall *have been*." (2.) "*had been* dead." (3.) See the last example under the preceding Rule. (4.) "a dish *has been* preserved."

often as I reflected upon it, *to have been* the messenger of such intelligence.' As the message, in this instance, was antecedent to the pleasure, and not contemporary with it, the verb expressive of the message must denote that antecedence, by being in the perfect of the infinitive. If the message and the pleasure had been referred to as contemporary, the subsequent verb would, with equal propriety, have been put in the present of the infinitive; as, "It would have afforded me great pleasure, *to be* the messenger of such intelligence." In the former instance, the phrase in question is equivalent to these words—"*If I had been* the messenger;" in the latter instance, to this expression—"*Being* the messenger."

It is proper to inform the learner, that, in order to express the past time with the defective verb *ought*, the perfect of the infinitive must always be used; as, "He ought *to have done* it." When we use this verb, this is the only possible way to distinguish the past from the present.

In support of the positions advanced under this rule, we can produce the sentiments of eminent grammarians; amongst whom are Lowth and Campbell. But there are some writers on grammar who strenuously maintain, that the governed verb in the infinitive ought to be in the past tense, when the verb which governs it is in the past time. Though this cannot be admitted, in the instances which are controverted under this rule, or in any instances of a similar nature; yet there can be no doubt that, in many cases, in which the thing referred to preceded the governing verb, it would be proper and allowable. We may say, "From a conversation I once had with him, he *appeared to have studied* Homer with great care and judgment." It would be proper also to say, "From his conversation, he *appears to have studied* Homer with great care and judgment;" "That unhappy man *is supposed to have died* by violence." These examples are not only consistent with our rule, but they confirm and illustrate it. It is the tense of the governing verb, only, that marks what is called the absolute time; the tense of the verb governed marks solely its relative time with respect to the other.

To assert, as some writers do, that verbs in the infinitive mood have no tenses, no relative distinctions of present, past and future, is inconsistent with just grammatical views of the subject. That these verbs associate with verbs in all the tenses, is no proof of their having no peculiar time of their own. Whatever period the governing verb assumes, whether present, past, or future, the governed verb in the infinitive always respects that period, and its time is calculated from it. Thus, the time of the infinitive may be before, after, or the same as, the time of the governing verb, according as the thing signified by the infinitive is supposed to be before, after, or present with the thing denoted by the governing verb. It is, therefore, with great propriety, that tenses are assigned to verbs of the infinitive mood. The point of time from which they are computed, is of no consequence; since present, past, and future, are completely applicable to them.

We shall conclude our observations under this rule, by remarking, that, though it is often proper to use the perfect of the infinitive after the governing verb, yet there are particular cases in which it would be better to give the expression a different form. Thus, instead of saying, "I wish to have written to him sooner," "I then wished to have written to him sooner," "He will one day wish to have written sooner;" it would be more perspicuous and forcible, as well as more agreeable to the practice of good writers, to say, "I wish that I had written to him sooner," "I then wished that I had written to him sooner," "He will one day wish that he had written sooner." Should the justness of these strictures be admitted, there would still be numerous occasions for the use of the past infinitive; as we may perceive by a few examples: "It would ever afterwards have been a source of pleasure, to have found him wise and virtuous." "To have deferred his repentance longer, would have disqualified him for repenting at all." "They will then see, that to have faithfully performed their duty, would have been their greatest consolation."

"I expected to have found him." Will you correct this sentence, and give a rule for it? What tense of the infinitive must be used to express past time with the defective verb *ought*? Give an example. Is it proper ever to use the perfect of the infinitive after the governing verb? Give an example.

1.

"I purpose to go to London in a few months, and after I *shall finish* (1.) my business there, to proceed (2.) to America."

"These prosecutions of William seem *to be* the most iniquitous measures pursued by the court during the time that the use of parliaments was suspended."

"From the little conversation I had with him, he appeared to *have been* a man of letters."

"I always intended to *have rewarded* my son according to his merit."

"It would, on reflection, have given me great satisfaction, to *relieve* him from that distressed situation."

"It required so much care, that I thought I should *have lost* it before I reached home."

"We have done no more than it was our duty to *have* done."

"He would have assisted one of his friends, if he could *do* it without injuring the other; but as that could not *have been* done, he avoided all interference."

"Must it not be expected that he would *have defended* an authority, which had been so long exercised without controversy?" (3.)

"These enemies of Christianity were confounded, whilst they were expecting to have found an opportunity to have betrayed its author."

"His sea-sickness was so great, that I often feared he would have died before our arrival."

"If these persons had intended to deceive, they would have taken care to *have avoided* what would *expose* them to the objections of their opponents."

"It was a pleasure to have received his approbation of my labors, for which I cordially thanked him."

"It would have afforded me still greater pleasure, *to receive* his approbation at an earlier period; but to receive (4.) it at all, reflected credit upon me."

"To be censured by him, would soon have proved an insuperable discouragement."

"Him portioned maids, apprenticed orphans blest,
The young who *labor*, and the old who *rest*."

"The doctor, in his lecture, said, that fever always produced thirst."

RULE XIV.

Corresponding with Murray's Grammar.

RULE XIV.

Active participles from active transitive verbs govern the objective case.

• Esteeming (5.) *theirselves* wise, they became fools."

• Suspecting not only *ye*, but *they* also, I was studious to avoid all intercourse."

• I could not avoid considering, (6.) in some degree, they as enemies to me; and he as a suspicious friend."

"From having exposed (7.) hisself too freely, in different climates, he entirely lost his health."

1. Participles are sometimes governed by the article; for the present participle, with the definite article *the* before it, becomes a substantive, and must have the preposition *of* after it; as, "These are the rules of grammar, by the observing of which, you may avoid mistakes." It would not be proper to

---

(1.) "*shall have finished.*" (2.) Rule IX. (3.) "*Might* it not *have been,*" &c. (4.) "*to have* received." Note XIII. (5.) Rule XIII. (6.) Rule VIII. (7.) 561

say, 'by the observing which," nor, "by observing of which;" but the phrase, without either article or preposition, would be right; as, "by observing which." The article a or an has the same effect; as, "This was a betraying of the trust reposed in him."

This rule arises from the nature and idiom of our language, and from as plain a principle as any on which it is founded: namely, that a word which has the article before it, and the possessive preposition *of* after it, must be a noun; and, if a noun, it ought to follow the construction of a noun, and not to have the regimen of a verb. It is the participial termination of this sort of words, that is apt to deceive us, and make us treat them as if they were of an amphibious species, partly nouns and partly verbs.

The following are a few examples of the violation of this rule: "He was sent to prepare the way by preaching of repentance;" it ought to be, "by the preaching of repentance," or, "by preaching repentance." "By the continual mortifying our corrupt affections;" it should be, "by the continual mortifying *of*," or, "by continually mortifying our corrupt affections." "They laid out themselves towards *the* advancing and promoting the good of it;" "towards advancing and promoting the good." "It is *an* overvaluing ourselves, to reduce every thing to the narrow measure of our capacities;" "it is overvaluing ourselves," or, "*an* overvaluing *of* ourselves." "Keeping of one day in seven," &c.; it ought to be, "*the* keeping *of* one day," or, "keeping one day."

A phrase in which the article precedes the present participle, and the possessive preposition follows it, will not, in every instance, convey the same meaning as would be conveyed by the participle without the article and preposition. "He expressed the pleasure he had in the hearing of the philosopher," is capable of a different sense from, "He expressed the pleasure he had in hearing the philosopher." When, therefore, we wish, for the sake of harmony or variety, to substitute one of these phraseologies for the other, we should previously consider whether they are perfectly similar in the sentiments they convey.

"By the observing of which." Will you parse *observing ?* Rule for it ? What words in this sentence may be omitted with propriety ? Would it be proper to omit one of them only ?

1

By observing *of* truth, you will command esteem, as well as secure peace."

"He prepared them for this event, by *the* sending to them proper information."

"A person may be great or rich by chance; but cannot be wise or good without *the* taking pains for it."

"Nothing could have made her so unhappy, as *the* marrying a man who possessed such principles."

"The changing times and seasons, the removing and setting up kings, belong to Providence alone."

"The middle station of life seems to be the most advantageous situated for gaining of wisdom Poverty turns our thoughts too much upon the supplying our wants; and riches upon the enjoying our superfluities."

"Pliny, speaking of Cato the Censor's disapproving the Grecian orators, expressed himself thus."

"Propriety of pronunciation is the giving to every word that sound, which the most polite usages of the language appropriates to it."

"*The* not attending (1.) to this rule, is the cause (2.) of a very common error."

"This was in fact *a* converting the deposite to his own use."

2. The same observations which have been made respecting the effect of the article and participle, appear to be applicable to the pronoun and participle, when they are similarly associated; as, "Much depends on *their* observ-

(1.) Rule VI. (2.) Rule XV

ing of the rule, and error will be the consequence of *their neglecting of* it;" instead of "*their observing* the rule, and *their neglecting* it." We shall perceive this more clearly, if we substitute a noun for the pronoun; as, "Much depends upon *Tyro's observing of* the rule," &c. But, as this construction sounds rather harshly, it would, in general, be better to express the sentiment in the following, or some other form : " Much depends on the *rule's being observed ;* and error will be the consequence on *its being neglected ;*" or, " on observing the rule ;" and, "of neglecting it." This remark may be applied to several other modes of expression to be found in this work ; which, though they are contended for as strictly correct, are not always the most eligible, on account of their unpleasant sound.

We sometimes meet with expressions like the following : " *In forming of* his sentences, he was very exact;" " *From calling of* names, he proceeded to blows." But this is incorrect language ; for prepositions do not, like articles and pronouns, convert the participle itself into the nature of a substantive; as we have shown above in the phrase, "by observing which." And yet the participle, with its adjuncts, may be considered as a substantive phrase in the objective case, governed by the preposition or verb, expressed or understood ; as, " By *promising much, and performing but little,* we become despicable ;" " He studied to avoid *expressing himself too severely.*"

" Much depends on their observing of the rule." Would this sentence be correct if the preposition *of* were omitted? Will you repeat the note ?

2.

" There will be no danger of *their* (1.) spoiling their faces, or of *their* gaining converts."

" For *his* avoiding that precipice, he is indebted to his friend's care."

" It was from *our* misunderstanding the directions, that we lost our way."

" In tracing *of* his history, we discover little that is worthy of imitation."

" By reading of books written by the best authors, his mind became highly improved."

3. As the perfect participle and the imperfect tense are sometimes different in their form, care must be taken that they be not indiscriminately used. It is frequently said, " He begun," for " he began ;" " He run," for " he ran ;" " He drunk," for " he drank ;" the participle being here used instead of the imperfect tense : and much more frequently the imperfect tense instead of the participle ; as, " I had wrote," for " I had written ;" " I was chose," for " I was chosen ;" " I have eat," for " I have eaten." " His words were interwove with sighs ;" " were *interwoven.*" " He would have spoke ;" " *spoken.*" " He hath bore witness to his faithful servants ;" " *borne.*" " By this means he overrun his guide ;" " *overran.*" " The sun has rose ;" " *risen.*" " His constitution has been greatly shook, but his mind is too strong to be shook by such causes ;" " *shaken,*" in both places. "They were verses wrote on glass ;" " *written.*" " Philosophers have often mistook the source of true happiness ;" it ought to be, " *mistaken.*"

The participle ending in *ed* is often improperly contracted by changing *ed* into *t ;* as, " In good behavior he is not surpast by any pupil of the school ;" " She was much distrest ;" they ought to be, "*surpassed,*" " *distressed.*"

Is it correct to say, " He begun" ? What is wrong in the expression? Will you repeat Note 3 ? Can the participle ending in *ed* be contracted to *t*, with propriety ?

3.

" By too eager pursuit, he *run* a great risk of being disappointed." (2.)

" he had not long enjoyed repose, before he begun to be weary of having nothing to do."

" He was greatly heated, and drunk with avidity."

" Though his conduct was, in some respects, exceptionable, yet he dared not commit so great an offence as that which was proposed to him."

(1.) Omit "*their.*"   (2.) *Pres. pass. part.* used as a noun.—P.4le X.

SYNTAX. 163

"A second deluge learning thus o'errun,
And the monks finished what the Goths begun."
"If some events had not fell out very unexpectedly, I should have been present."
"He would have went with us, had he been invited."
He returned the goods which he had stole, and made all the reparation in his power."
"They have chose the part of honor and virtue."
"His vices have weakened his mind, and broke his health."
"He had mistook his true interest, and found himself forsook by his former adherents."
"The bread that has been eat is soon forgot."
"No contentions have arose amongst them since their reconciliation."
"The cloth had no seam, but was wove throughout."
"The French language is spoke in every state in Europe.

"His resolution was too strong to be shook by slight opposition."
"He was not much restrained afterwards, having took improper liberties at first."
"He has not yet wore off the rough manners which he brought with him."
"You who have forsook your friends, are entitled to no confidence."
"They who have bore a part in the labor, shall share the rewards."
"When the rules have been wantonly broke, there can be no plea for favor."
"He writes as the best authors would have wrote, had they writ on the same subject."
"He heapt up great riches, but past his time miserably."
"He talkt and stampt with such vehemence, that he was suspected to be insane."

RULE XXVII.

Corresponding with Murray's Grammar,

RULE XV.

Adverbs, though they have no government of case, tense &c., require an appropriate situation in the sentence viz. for the most part, before adjectives, after verbs active or neuter, and frequently between the auxiliary and the verb; as, "He made a *very sensible* discourse; he *spoke unaffectedly* and *forcibly,* and *was attentively heard* by the whole assembly."

A few instances of erroneous positions of adverbs may serve to illustrate the rule. "He must not expect to find study agreeable always;" "*always* agreeable." "We always find them ready when we want them;" "we find them *always* ready," &c. "Dissertations on the prophecies which have remarkably been fulfilled;" "which have been *remarkably*." "Instead of looking contemptuously down on the crooked in mind or in body, we should look up thankfully to God, who hath made us better;" "Instead of looking down *contemptuously,* &c., we should *thankfully look up,*" &c. "If thou art blessed naturally with a good memory, continually exercise it;" "*naturally blessed,*" &c. "exercise it *continually.*"
Sometimes the adverb is placed with propriety before the verb, or at some distance after it; sometimes between the two auxiliaries; and sometimes after them both; as in the following examples: "Vice *always* creeps by degrees, and *insensibly* twines around us those concealed fetters, by which we are at last *completely* bound." "He encouraged the English barons to carry their opposition *farther;*" "They compelled him to declare that he would abjure the realm *forever;*" instead of, "to carry farther their opposition;"

and "to abjure forever the realm." "He has *generally* been reckoned an honest man;" "The book may *always* be had at such a place;" in preference to "has been generally," and "may be always." "These rules will be *clearly* understood, after the have been *diligently* studied," is preferable to, "These rules will *clearly* be understood, after they have *diligently* been studied."

From the preceding remarks and examples, it appears that no exact and determinate rule can be given for the placing of adverbs, on all occasions. The general rule may be of considerable use; but the easy flow and perspicuity of the phrase, are the things which ought to be chiefly regarded.

The adverb *there* is often used as an expletive, or as a word that adds nothing to the sense; in which case it precedes the verb and the nominative noun; as, "There is a person at the door;" "There are some thieves in the house;" which would be as well, or better, expressed by saying, "A person is at the door;" "Some thieves are in the house." Sometimes, it is made use of to give a small degree of emphasis to the sentence; as, "*There* was a man sent from God, whose name was John." When it is applied in its strict sense, it principally follows the verb and the nominative case; as, "The man stands *there*."

What word is misplaced in the sentence, "He must not expect to find study agreeable always"? Will you correct the sentence, and give the Rule for the position of adverbs? How is the adverb sometimes placed with respect to the verb? With respect to the auxiliary?

"He was *pleasing not often,* (1.) because he was vain."
"William *nobly acted,* though he was unsuccessful."
"We may *happily live,* though our possessions are small."
"From whence (2.) we may date likewise the period of this event."
"It cannot be impertinent or ridiculous, therefore, to remonstrate."
"He offered an apology, which not being admitted, he became submissive."
"These things should be never separated."
"Unless he have more government of himself, he will be always discontented."
"*Never* (3.) sovereign was (4.) so much beloved by the people."
"He was determined to invite back the king, and to call together his friends."

"So well educated a boy gives great hopes to his friends."
"Not only he found her employed, but pleased and tranquil also."
"We always should prefer our duty to our pleasure."
"It is impossible continually to be at work."
"The heavenly bodies are in motion perpetually."
"Having not known, or having not considered, the measures proposed, he failed of success."
"My opinion was given on *rather a* (5.) cursory perusal of the book."
"It is too common with mankind, to be engrossed and overcome totally, by present events."
"When the Romans were pressed with a foreign enemy, the women contributed all their rings and jewels voluntarily, to assist the government."

1. The adverb *never* generally precedes the verb; as, "I never was there;" "He never comes at a proper time." When an auxiliary is used, it is placed indifferently, either before or after this adverb; as, "He was never seen (or never was seen) to laugh from that time." *Never* seems to be improperly used in the following passages: "Ask me never so much dowry and gift." "If I make my hands never so clean." "Charm he never so wisely." The word *ever* would be more suitable to the sense.

(1.) "*not often pleasing.*" (2.) 589. (3.) · *No.*" (4.) "*ever so*"
(5.) "*a rather.*"- Rule IX.

SYNTAX.

How is the adverb *never* generally placed with respect to the verb? Give an example. Give an example where the word *never* is improperly used instead of *ever*.

1.

"They could not persuade him, though they were *never* so eloquent."	"If some persons' opportunities were never so favorable, they would be indolent to improve them."

2. In imitation of the French idiom, the adverb of place *where* is often used instead of the pronouns relative and a preposition. "They framed a protestation, *where* they repeated all their former claims;" i. e. "*in which* they repeated." "The king was still determined to run forwards, in the same course *where* he was already, by his precipitate career, too fatally advanced;" i. e. "*in which* he was." But it would be better to avoid this mode of expression.

The adverbs *hence, thence,* and *whence,* imply a preposition; for they signify, "from this place," "from that place," "from what place." It seems, therefore, strictly speaking, to be improper to join a preposition with them, because it is superfluous; as, "This is the leviathan, from whence the wits of our age are said to borrow their weapons;" "An ancient author prophesies from hence." But the origin of these words is little attended to, and the preposition *from* so often used in construction with them, that the omission of it, in many cases, would seem stiff, and be disagreeable.

The adverbs *here, there, where,* are often improperly applied to verbs signifying motion, instead of the adverbs *hither, thither, whither ;* as, "He came *here* hastily;" "They rode *there* with speed." They should be, He came *hither ;*" "They rode *thither,*" &c.

"They framed a protestation where they repeated all their former claims." Will you correct this sentence, and repeat Note 2?

2.

"He drew up a petition, *where* he too freely represented his own merits."	"George is active; he walked there in less than an hour." (1.)
"His follies had reduced him to a situation *where* he had much to fear, and nothing to hope."	"Where are you all going in such haste?"
"It is reported that the prince will come *here* to-morrow."	"Whither have they been since they left the city?"

3. We have some examples of adverbs being used for substantives: "In 1687, he erected it into a community of regulars, since *when* it has begun to increase in those countries as a religious order;" i. e. "since *which time.*" "A little while, and I shall not see you;" i. e. *a short time.*" "It is worth their while;" i. e. "it deserves their time and pains." But this use of the word rather suits familiar than grave style. The same may be said of the phrase, "To do a thing *anyhow ;*" i. e. "in any manner;" or, "*somehow ;*" i. e. "in some manner." "Somehow, worthy as these people are, they are under the influence of prejudice."

Will you repeat this note, and give an example under it?

3.

"Charles left the seminary too early, since when he has made very little improvement." (2.)	"Nothing is better worth the while (3.) of young persons, than the acquisition of knowledge and virtue."

(1.) Rule XXII.   (2.) " *and from that time* he," &c.; or, " *and has since made,*" &c.   (3.) " *the time and attention of,*" &c.

RULE XIX.
Corresponding with Murray's Grammar.
RULE XVI.

Two negatives, in the same simple sentence, are equivalent to an affirmative; as, "Nor did they not perceive him;" *i. e.* "They did perceive him."

It is better to express an affirmation by a regular affirmative, than by two separate negatives, as in the former sentence; but when one of the negatives is joined to another word, as in the latter sentence, the two negatives form a pleasing and delicate variety of expression.

Some writers have improperly employed two negatives instead of one; as, in the following instances: "I never did repent of doing good, nor shall not now;" "*nor shall I now.*" "Never no imitator grew up to his author;" "*never did any,*" &c. "I cannot by no means allow him what his argument must prove;" "I cannot by *any* means," &c.; or, "*I can by no means.*" "Nor let no comforter approach me;" "nor let *any* comforter," &c. "Nor is danger ever apprehended in such a government, no more than we commonly apprehend danger from thunder or earthquakes;" it should be, "*any more.*" "Ariosto, Tasso, Galileo, *no more* than Raphael, were *not* born in republics;" "Neither Ariosto, Tasso, nor Galileo, any more than Raphael, was born in a republic."

Should we express an affirmation by an affirmative, or by two separate negatives? Will you give an example of the improper use of two negatives?

"Neither riches nor honors, nor *no* such perishing goods, can satisfy the desires of an immortal spirit."

"Be honest, nor take *no* shape *nor* semblance of disguise."

"We need not, nor (I.) do not, confine his operations to narrow limits."

"I am resolved not to comply with the proposal, *neither* at present, *nor* at any other time."

"There cannot be nothing more insignificant than vanity."

"Nothing never affected her so much, as this misconduct of her child."

"Do not interrupt me yourselves, nor let no one disturb my retirement."

"These people do not judge wisely, nor take no proper measure to effect their purpose."

"The measure is so exceptionable, that we cannot by no means permit it."

"I have received no information on the subject, *neither* from him nor from his friend."

"Precept nor discipline is not so forcible as example."

"The king nor the queen was not all deceived in the business."

RULE X.
Corresponding with Murray's Grammar.
RULE XVII.

Prepositions govern the objective case.

The following are examples of the nominative case being used instead of the objective: "Who servest thou under?" "Who do you speak to?" "We are still much at a loss who civil power belongs to." "Who dost thou ask for?" "Associate not with those who none can speak well of." In all these places, it ought to be, "*whom.*"

The prepositions *to* and *for* are often understood, chiefly before the pronouns: as, "Give me the book;" "Get me some paper;" that is, '*to me,*"

SYNTAX. 167

"*for* me." "Wo is me;" i. e. "*to* me." "He was banished England;" i. e. "*from* England."
"Who do you speak to?" Will you correct this sentence, and explain why it is wrong? "Give me the book." What is understood in this sentence?

"We are all accountable creatures, each for *hisself*."
"They willingly, and of *theirselves*, endeavored to make up the difference."
"He laid the suspicion upon somebody, I know not *who* in the company."
"I hope it is not I *who* (1.) he is displeased with."
"To poor we, there is not much hope remaining."
"Does that boy know who he speaks to? Who does he offer such language to?"
"It was not he that they were so angry with."
"What concord can subsist between those who commit crimes, and *they* (2.) who abhor them?"
"The person who I travelled with, has sold the horse which he rode on during our journey."
"It is not I he is engaged with."
"Who did he receive that intelligence from?"

1. The preposition is often separated from the relative which it governs; as, "Whom wilt thou give it to?" instead of, "To whom wilt thou give it?" "He is an author whom I am much delighted with;" "The world is too polite to shock authors with a truth, which generally their booksellers are the first that inform them of." This is an idiom to which our language is strongly inclined; it prevails in common conversation, and suits very well with the familiar style in writing: but the placing of the preposition before the relative is more graceful, as well as more perspicuous, and agrees much better with the solemn and elevated style.

Will you repeat this Note, and give an example under it?

1.
"To have no one whom we heartily wish well to, and whom we are warmly concerned for, is a deplorable state."
"He is a friend whom I am highly indebted to."

2. Some writers separate the preposition from its noun, in order to connect different prepositions with the same noun; as, "To suppose the zodiac and planets to be efficient *of*, and antecedent *to*, themselves." This, whether in the familiar or the solemn style, is always inelegant, and should generally be avoided. In forms of law, and the like, where fulness and exactness of expression must take place of every other consideration, it may be admitted.

Is it correct to separate the preposition from the noun which it governs? When may it be admitted?

2
"On these occasions, the pronoun is governed by (3.) and consequently agrees with, the preceding word."
"They were refused entrance into, and forcibly driven from, the house."

3. Different relations, and different senses, must be expressed by different prepositions, though in conjunction with the same verb or adjective. Thus we say, "To converse *with* a person, *upon* a subject, *in* a house," &c. We also say, "We are disappointed *of* a thing," when we cannot get it, "and disappointed *in* it," when we have it, and find it does not answer our expectations. But two different prepositions must be improper in the same constructions, and in the same sentence; as, "The combat *between* thirty French *against* twenty English."

In some cases, it is difficult to say, to which of two prepositions the preference is to be given, as both are used promiscuously, and custom has not decided in favor of either of them. We say, "Expert at," and "Expert in a thing;" "Expert at finding a remedy for his mistakes;" "Expert in deception."

(L.) "*with whom.*" (2.) "*those.*" (3.) "by the preceding word, and consequently agrees with it."

When prepositions are subjoined to nouns, they are generally the same that are subjoined to the verbs from which the nouns are derived; as, "A compliance with," "to comply with;" "A disposition to tyranny," "disposed to tyrannize."

Do we express different relations and different sense by the same, or a different preposition?

3.

"We are often disappointed of things, which, before possession, promised much enjoyment."

"I have frequently desired their company, but have always hitherto been disappointed in that pleasure."

4. As an accurate and appropriate use of the preposition is of great importance, we shall select a considerable number of examples of impropriety in the application of this part of speech.

1st, With respect to the preposition *of*. "He is resolved of going to the Persian court;" "*on* going," &c. "He was totally dependent of the Papal crown;" "*on* the Papal," &c. "To call of a person," and "to wait of him;" "*on* a person," &c. "He was eager of recommending it to his fellow-citizens;" "*in* recommending," &c. *Of* is sometimes omitted, and sometimes inserted, after *worthy*; as, "It is worthy observation," or, "of observation." But it would have been better omitted in the following sentences: "The emulation, who should serve their country best, no longer subsists among them, but *of* who should obtain the most lucrative command." "The rain hath been falling *of* a long time;" "falling a long time." "It is situation chiefly which decides of the fortune and characters of men;" "decides the fortune," or, "*concerning* the fortune." "He found the greatest difficulty of writing;" "*in* writing." "It might have given me a greater taste of its antiquities." A taste *of* a thing implies actual enjoyment of it; but a taste *for* it, implies only a capacity for enjoyment. "This had a much greater share of inciting him, than any regard after his father's commands;" "share *in* inciting," and "regard *to* his father's," &c.

2d. With respect to the prepositions *to* and *for*. "You have bestowed your favors to the most deserving persons;" "*upon* the most deserving," &c. "He accused the ministers for betraying the Dutch;" "*of* having betrayed." "His abhorrence to that superstitious figure;" "*of* that," &c. "A great change to the better;" "*for* the better." "Your prejudice to my cause;" "*against*." "The English were very different people then to what they are at present;" "*from* what," &c. "In compliance to the declaration;" "*with*," &c. "It is more than they thought for;" "thought *of*." "There is no need for it;" "*of* it." *For* is superfluous in the phrase, "More than he knows *for*." "No discouragement for the authors to proceed;" "*to* the authors," &c. "It was perfectly in compliance to some persons;" "*with*." "The wisest princes need not think it any diminution to their greatness, or derogation to their sufficiency, to rely upon counsel;" "diminution *of*," and "derogation *from*."

3d, With respect to the prepositions *with* and *upon*. "Reconciling himself with the king." "Those things which have the greatest resemblance with each other, frequently differ the most." "That such rejection should be consonant with our common nature." "Conformable with," &c. "The history of Peter is agreeable with the sacred texts." In all the above instances, it should be "*to*," instead of "*with*." "It is a use that, perhaps, I should not have thought on;" "thought *of*." "A greater quantity may be taken from the heap, without making any sensible alteration upon it;" "*in* it." "Intrusted to persons on whom the parliament could confide;" "*in* whom." "He was made much on at Argos;" "much *of*." "If policy can prevail upon force;" "*over* force." "I do likewise dissent with the examiner;" "*from*."

4th, With respect to the prepositions *in*, *from*, &c. "They should be informed in some parts of his character;" "*about*," or "*concerning*." "Upon such occasions as fell into their cognizance;" "*under*." "That variety of factions into which we are still engaged;" "*in* which." "To restore myself into the favor;" "*to* the favor." "Could he have profited from his repeated experiences;" "*by*." *From* seems to be superfluous after *forbear*; as, "He could not forbear from appointing the pope. &c. "A strict observance after times and fashions;" "*of* times." "The character which we may now value ourselves by drawing;" "*upon* drawing." "Neither of them shall make me swerve out of the path;" "*from* the path." "Ye blind guides, which strain *at* a gnat, and swallow a camel;" it ought to be, "which strain *out* a gnat, or, take a gnat out of the liquor by straining it." The impropriety of the preposition has wholly destroyed the meaning of the phrase.

The preposition *among* generally implies a number of things. It cannot be properly used in conjunction with the word *every*, which is in the singular number; as, "Which is found among every species of liberty," "The opinion seems to gain ground among every body."

"He is resolved of going to the Persian court." Will you correct this sentence? "You have bestowed your favors to the most deserving persons." How should this sentence be altered? "Reconciling himself with the king." What inaccuracy is there in this sentence? "They should be informed in some parts of his character." Will you correct this sentence?

4.

"She finds a difficulty *of* fixing her mind."
"Her sobriety is no derogation *to* her understanding."
"There was no water, and he died for (1.) thirst."
"We can fully confide on (2.) none but the truly good."
"I have no occasion of his services."
"Many have profited from good advice."
"Many ridiculous practices have been brought in vogue."
"The error was occasioned by compliance to earnest entreaty."
"This is a principle in unison to our nature."
'We should entertain no prejudices to simple and rustic persons."
"They are at present resolved of doing their duty."
"That boy is known under the name of the idler."
"Though conformable with custom, it is not warrantable."
"This remark is founded in truth."
"His parents think on him and his improvements, with pleasure and hope."
"His excuse was admitted *of by* (3.) his master."
"What went ye out for to see?"
"There appears to have been a million men brought into the field."
'His present was accepted of by his friends."
"More than a thousand of men were destroyed."
"It is my request that he will be particular in speaking to the following points."
"The Saxons reduced the greater part of Britain to their own power."
"He lives opposite the royal exchange."
"Their house is situated to the northeast side of the road."
"The performance was approved of by all who understood it."
"He was accused with having acted unfairly."
"She has an abhorrence to all deceitful conduct."
"They were some distance (4.) from home, when the accident happened."
"His deportment was adapted for conciliating regard."
"My father writes me very frequently."
"Their conduct was agreeable with their profession."
"We went leisurely above stairs, and came hastily below. We shall write up stairs this forenoon, and down stairs in the afternoon."
"The politeness of the world has the same resemblance with benevolence, that the shadow has with its substance."
"He had a taste of such studies, and pursued them earnestly."
"When we have had a true taste for the pleasures of virtue, we can have no relish for those of vice."
"How happy it is to know how we live at times by one's self, to leave one's self in regret, to find one's self again with pleasure! The world is then less necessary for us."
"Civility makes its way among every kind of persons."

5. The preposition *to* is made use of before nouns of place, when they follow verbs and participles of motion; as, "I went *to* London;" "I am going *to* town." But the preposition *at* is generally used after the neuter verb *to be;* as, "I have been *at* London;" "I was *at* the place appointed;" "I shall be *at* Paris." We likewise say, "He touched, arrived *at* any place." The preposition *in* is set before countries, cities, and large towns; as, "He lives in France, in London, or in Birmingham." But before villages, single houses, and cities which are in distant countries, *at* is used; as, "He lives at Hackney;" "He resides at Montpellier."

It is a matter of indifference, with respect to the pronoun *one another*, whether the preposition *of* be placed between the two parts of it, or before them both. We may say, "They were jealous of one another;" or, "They were jealous one of another;" but perhaps the former is better.

Participles are frequently used as prepositions; as, *excepting, respecting, touching, concerning, according.* "They were all in fault *except* or *excepting* him."

How is the preposition *to* used with nouns of place? Give an example. Are participles ever used as prepositions? Give an example.

5.

"I have been to London, after having resided a year at France; and I now live at Islington."
"They have just landed in Hull, and are going for Liverpool. They intend to reside some time in Ireland."

RULE XI.
Corresponding with Murray's Grammar,
RULE XVIII.

Conjunctions usually connect verbs of the same mood and tense, and nouns or pronouns of the same case.

A few examples of inaccuracy respecting this rule may further display its utility. "If he prefer a virtuous life, and is sincere in his professions, he will succeed;" "if he *prefers*." "To deride the miseries of the unhappy, is inhuman; and wanting compassion towards them, is unchristian;" "and *to want* compassion." "The parliament addressed the king, and has been prorogued the same day;" "and *was* prorogued." "His wealth and him bid adieu to each other;" "and *he*." "He entreated us, my comrade and I, to live harmoniously;" "comrade and *me*." "My sister and her were on good terms;" "and *she*." "We often overlook the blessings which are in our possession, and are searching after those which are out of our reach;" it ought to be "and *search* after."

"His wealth and him bid adieu to each other." Will you correct this sentence, and give the rule for Conjunctions?

"Professing regard, and *to act* (1.) differently, discover a base mind."
"Did he not tell me his fault, and *entreated* me to forgive him?"
"My brother and *him* are tolerable grammarians."
"If he understand the subject, and *attends* to it industriously, he can scarcely fail of success."
"You and us enjoy many privileges."
"She and him are very unhappily connected."

"To be moderate in our views, and proceeding temperately in the pursuit of them, is the best way to ensure success."
"Between him and I there is some disparity of years; but none between him and she."
"By forming themselves on fantastic models, and ready to vie with one another in the reigning follies, the young begin with being ridiculous, and end with being vicious and immoral."

1. Conjunctions are, indeed, frequently made to connect different moods and tenses of verbs; but in these instances, the nominative must generally, if

(1. "acting," or "To profess regard, and to act," &c.

SYNTAX. 171

not always, be repeated, which is not necessary, though it may be done, under the construction to which the rule refers. We may say, "He *lives* temperately, *and* he should live temperately;" "He *may return*, but he *will not continue;*" "She *was* proud, though she *is* now humble:" but it is obvious, that, in such cases, the nominative ought to be repeated; and that, by this means, the latter members of these sentences are rendered not so strictly dependent on the preceding, as those are which come under this rule. When, in the progress of a sentence, we pass from the affirmative to the negative form, or from the negative to the affirmative, the subject or nominative is always resumed; as, "He is rich, but he is not respectable." There appears to be, in general, equal reason for repeating the nominative, and resuming the subject, when the course of the sentence is diverted by a change of the mood or tense. The following sentences may therefore be improved: "Anger glances into the breast of a wise man, but will rest only in the bosom of fools;" "but *rests* only;" or, "but *it will* rest only." "Virtue is praised by many, and would be desired also, if her worth were really known;" "and *she* would." "The world begins to recede, and will soon disappear;" "and *it* will."

Do conjunctions ever connect different moods and tenses of verbs? What case must generally be repeated in such instances? Give an example.

1.

"We have met with many disappointments; and, if life continue, shall (1.) probably meet with many more."

"Rank may confer influence, but will (2.) not necessarily produce virtue."

"He does not want courage, but is defective in sensibility."

"These people have indeed acquired great riches, but do not command esteem."

"Our seasons of improvement are short, and, whether used or not, will soon pass away."

"He might have been happy, and is now (3.) fully convinced of it."

"Learning strengthens the mind, and if properly applied, will improve our morals too."

RULE XXVIII.
Corresponding with Murray's Grammar.

RULE XIX.

Some conjunctions require the indicative, some the subjunctive, mood after them. It is a general rule, that when something contingent or doubtful is implied, the subjunctive ought to be used; as, "If I were to write, he would not regard it;" "He will not be pardoned, unless he repent."

Conjunctions that are of a positive and absolute nature require the indicative mood. "As virtue advances, so vice recedes;" "He is healthy, because he is temperate."

The conjunctions *if, though, unless, except, whether*, &c., generally require the subjunctive mood after them; as, "*If* thou *be* afflicted, repine not;" "*Though* he *slay* me, yet will I trust in him;" "He cannot be clean, *unless* he *wash* himself;" "No power, *except* it *were* given from above;" "*Whether* it *were* I or they, so we preach." But even these conjunctions, when the sentence does not imply doubt, admit of the indicative; as, "*Though* he *is* poor, he is contented."

The following example may, in some measure, serve to illustrate the distinction between the subjunctive and the indicative moods: "*Though* he *were* divinely inspired, and spoke therefore as the oracles of God, with supreme authority; *though* he *were* endued with supernatural powers, and could, therefore, have confirmed the truth of what he uttered, by miracles; yet, in compliance with the way in which human nature and reasonable creatures are usually wrought upon, he reasoned." That our Saviour was divinely inspired, and endued with supernatural powers, are positions that are here taken for granted, as not admitting the least doubt; they would therefore have been better expressed in the indicative mood: "*Though* he *was* divinely inspired; *though* he *was* endued with supernatural powers." The subjunctive is used in the like improper manner, in the following example: "*Though* he *were* a son, yet learned he obedience, by the things which he suffered." But, in a similar passage, the indicative, with great propriety, is employed to the same purpose; "*Though* he *was* rich, yet for your sakes he became poor."

What conjunctions generally require the subjunctive mood after them?

"If he *acquires* (1.) riches, they will corrupt his mind, and be useless to others."

"Though he *urges* me yet more earnestly, I shall not comply, unless he advances more forcible reasons."

"I shall walk in the fields to-day, unless it *rains*."

"As the governess were (2.) present, the children behaved properly."

"She disapproved the measure, because it were very improper."

"Though he be high, he hath respect to the lowly."

"Though he were her friend, he did not attempt to justify her conduct."

"Whether he improve or not, I can not determine."

"Though the fact be extraordinary, it certainly did happen."

"Remember what thou wert, and be (3.) humble."

"O that his heart was tender, and susceptible of the woes of others."

"Shall then this verse to future age pretend,
Thou wert my guide, philosopher, and friend?"

1. *Lest* and *that*, annexed to a command preceding, necessarily require the subjunctive mood; as, "Love not sleep, *lest* thou *come* to poverty;" "Reprove not a scorner, *lest* he *hate* thee;" "Take heed *that* thou *speak* not to Jacob."

If, with *but* following it, when futurity is denoted, requires the subjunctive mood; as, "*If* he *do but* touch the hills, they shall smoke;" "*If* he *be but* discreet, he will succeed." But the indicative ought to be used, on this occasion, when future time is not signified; as, "*If*, in this expression, he *does but* jeer, no offence should be taken;" "*If* she *is but* sincere, I am happy." The same distinction applies to the following forms of expression: "If he *do* submit, it will be from necessity;" "Though he *does* submit, he is not convinced;" "If thou *do* not reward this service, he will be discouraged;" "If thou *dost* heartily forgive him, endeavor to forget the offence."

When do *lest* and *that* require the subjunctive mood after them? When does *if* require the subjunctive? When the indicative?

1.

"Despise not any condition, lest it *happens* to be your own."

"Let him that is sanguine take heed lest he *miscarries*."

"Take care that thou breakest not any of the established rules."

"If he does but (4.) intimate his desire, it will be sufficient to produce obedience."

"At the time of his return, if he is but expert in the business, he will find employment."

"If he do but speak to display his abilities, he is worthy of attention."

"If he be but in health, I am content."

"If he does promise, he will certainly perform."

"Though he do praise her, it is only for her beauty."

"If thou dost not forgive, perhaps thou wilt not be forgiven."

"If thou do sincerely believe the truths of religion, act accordingly."

2. In the following instances, the conjunction *that*, expressed or understood, seems to be improperly accompanied with the subjunctive mood: "So much she dreaded his tyranny, *that* the fate of her friend she *dare* not lament;" "He reasoned so artfully, that his friends would listen, and think [*that*] he *were* not wrong."
Will you repeat this Note, and give an example under it?

2.

"His confused behaviour made it reasonable to suppose that he *were* guilty."
"He is so conscious of deserving the rebuke, that he dare not make any reply."
"His apology was so plausible, that many befriended him, and thought he were innocent."

3. The same conjunction governing both the indicative and the subjunctive moods, in the same sentence, and in the same circumstances, seems to be a great impropriety; as in these instances: "*If* there *be* but one body of legislators, it is no better than a tyranny; *if* there *are* only two, there will want a casting voice." "*If* a man *have* a hundred sheep, and one of them is gone astray," &c.
May the same conjunction have both the subjunctive and indicative moods after it in the same sentence? Give an example of this impropriety.

3.

"If one man *prefer* a life of industry, it is because he has an idea of comfort in wealth; if another prefers a life of gayety, it is from a like idea concerning pleasure."
"No one engages in that business, unless he aim at reputation, or hopes for some singular advantage."
"Though the design be laudable, and is favourable to our interest, it will involve much anxiety and labour."

4. Almost all the irregularities in the construction of any language, have arisen from the ellipsis of some words which were originally inserted in the sentence, and made it regular; and it is probable, that this has generally been the case with respect to the conjunctive form of words now in use; which will appear from the following examples: "We shall overtake him, though he *run*;" that is, "though he *should* run." "Unless he *act* prudently, he will not accomplish his purpose;" that is, "unless he *shall* act prudently." "If he *succeed*, and *obtain* his end, he will not be the happier for it;" that is, "If he *should* succeed, and *should* obtain his end." These remarks and examples are designed to show the original of many of our present conjunctive forms of expression; and to enable the student to examine the propriety of using them, by tracing the words in question to their proper origin and ancient connections. But it is necessary to be more particular on this subject, and therefore we shall add a few observations respecting it.

That part of the verb which grammarians call the present tense of the subjunctive mood, has a future signification. This is effected by varying the terminations of the second and third persons singular of the indicative; as will be evident from the following examples: "If thou *prosper*, thou shouldst be thankful." "Unless he *study* more closely, he will never be learned." Some writers, however, would express these sentiments without those variations; "If thou *prosperest*," &c.; "Unless he *studies*," &c.; and, as there is great diversity of practice in this point, it is proper to offer the learners a few remarks, to assist them in distinguishing the right application of these different forms of expression. It may be considered as a rule, that the changes of termination are necessary, when these two circumstances concur: 1st, When the subject is of a dubious and contingent nature; and, 2d, When the verb has a reference to future time. In the following sentences, both these circumstances will be found to unite: "If thou *injure* another, thou wilt hurt thyself." "He has a hard heart; and if he *continue* impenitent, he must suffer." "He will maintain his principles, though he *lose* his estate." "Whether he *succeed* or not, his intention is laudable." "If he be not prosperous, he will not repine." "If a man *smite* his servant, and he *die*," &c. Exod. xxi. 20. In all these examples, the things signified by the verbs are uncertain, and refer to future time. But in the instances which follow, future time is not referred to and therefore a different construction takes place: "If thou *livest* virtuously, thou art happy." "Unless he *means* what he says, he is doubly faithless." "If he *allows* the excellence of Virtue, he does not regard her precepts." "Though he *seems* to be simple and artless, he has deceived us." "Whether virtue *is* better than rank or wealth, admits not of any dispute." "If thou *believest* with all thy heart, thou mayest," &c. Acts viii. 37. There are many sentences, introduced by conjunctions, in which neither contingency nor futurity is denoted; as, "Though he *excels* her in knowledge, she far exceeds him in virtue." "I have no doubt of his principles; but if he *believes* the truths of religion, he does not act according to them."

That both the circumstances of contingency and futurity are necessary, as tests of the propriety of altering the terminations, will be evident, by inspecting the following examples; which show that there are instances in which neither of the circumstances alone implies the other. In the three examples following, contingency is denoted, but not futurity: "If he *thinks* as he speaks, he may safely be trusted." "If he *is* now disposed to it, I will perform the operation." "He acts uprightly, unless he *deceives* me." In the following sentences, futurity is signified, but not contingency. "As soon as the sun *sets*, it will be cooler." "As the autumn *advances*, these birds will gradually emigrate."

It appears, from the tenor of the examples adduced, that the rules above mentioned may be extended to assert, that, in cases wherein contingency and futurity do not concur, it is not proper to turn the verb from its signification of present time, or to vary its form or termination. The verb would then be in the indicative mood, whatever conjunctions might attend it. If these rules, which seem to form the true distinction between the subjunctive and the indicative moods in this tense, were adopted and established in practice, we should have, on this point, a principle of decision simple and precise, and readily applicable to every case that might occur. It will, doubtless, sometimes happen, that, on this occasion, as well as on many other occasions, a strict adherence to grammatical rules would render the language stiff and formal; but when cases of this sort occur, it is better to give the expression a different turn, than violate grammar for the sake of ease, or even of elegance.

Has the present tense of the subjunctive mood a future signification? How is this effected? What two circumstances should concur to render necessary this change of termination? Should the termination be changed when futurity and contingency do not concur? What mood or form will the verb then be in?

4.

"Unless he *learns* faster, he will be no scholar."
"Though he *falls*, he shall not be utterly cast down."
"On condition that he *comes*, I will consent to stay."
"However that affair *terminates*, (1.) my conduct will be unimpeachable."
"If virtue rewards us not so soon as we desire, the payment will be made with interest."
"Till repentance composes his mind, he will be a stranger to peace."
"Whether he confesses or not, the truth will certainly be discovered."
"If thou censurest uncharitably, thou wilt be entitled to no favor."
"Though, at times, the ascent to the temple of virtue appears steep and craggy, be not discouraged."

— Persevere until thou gainest the summit: there, all is order, beauty and pleasure."
"If Charlotte desire to gain esteem and love, she does not employ the proper means."
"Unless the accountant deceive me, my estate is considerably improved."
"Though self-government produce some uneasiness, it is light when compared with the pain of vicious indulgence."
"Whether he think as he speaks, time will discover."
"If thou censure uncharitably, thou deservest no favor."
"Though Virtue appear severe, she is truly amiable."
"Though success be very doubtful, it is proper that he *endeavors* to succeed."

(1.) Or, "may terminate."

5. On the form of the auxiliaries in the compound tenses of the subjunctive mood, it seems proper to make a few observations. Some writers express themselves in the perfect tense as follows: "If thou *have* determined, we must submit;" "Unless he *have* consented, the writing will be void:" but we believe that few authors of critical sagacity write in this manner. The proper form seems to be, "If thou *hast* determined," "Unless he *has* consented," &c., conformably to what we generally meet with in the Bible: "I have surnamed thee, though thou *hast* not known me." Isaiah xlv. 4, 5. "What is the hope of the hypocrite, though he *hath* gained," &c. Job xxvii. 8. See, also, Acts xxviii. 4.

"If thou have determined, we must submit." How should this sentence be altered?

5.

"If thou *have* promised, be faithful to thy engagement."
"Though he have proved his right

to submission, he is too generous to exact it."
"Unless he have improved, he is unfit for the office."

6. In the pluperfect and future tenses, we sometimes meet with such expressions as these; "If thou *had* applied thyself diligently, thou wouldst have reaped the advantage;" "Unless thou *shall* speak the whole truth, we cannot determine;" "If thou *will* undertake the business, there is little doubt of success." This mode of expressing the auxiliaries does not appear to be warranted by the general practice of correct writers. They should be, *hadst, shalt* and *wilt*: and we find them used in this form, in the Sacred Scriptures: "If thou *hadst* known," &c. Luke xix. 47. "If thou *hadst* been here," &c. John xi. 21. "If thou *wilt*, thou canst make me clean." Matt. viii. 2. See, also, 2 Sam. ii. 27; Matt. xvii. 4.

"If thou wilt undertake the business, there is little doubt of success." Is this mode of expression warranted by good authority? How should it be altered?

6.

"If thou *had* succeeded, perhaps thou wouldst not be the happier for it."
"Unless thou shall see the propriety

of the measure, we shall not desire thy support."
"Though thou will not acknowledge, thou canst not deny the fact."

7. The second person singular of the imperfect tense in the subjunctive mood, is also very frequently varied in its termination; as, "If thou *loved* him truly, thou wouldst obey him;" "Though thou *did* conform, thou hast gained nothing by it." This variation, however, appears to be improper. Our present version of the Scriptures, which we again refer to as a good grammatical authority in points of this nature, decides against it: "If thou *knewest* the gift," &c. John iv. 10. "If thou *didst* receive it, why dost thou glory?" &c. 1 Cor. iv. 7. See, also, Dan. v. 22. But it is proper to remark, that the form of the verb *to be*, when used subjunctively in the imperfect tense, is indeed very considerably and properly varied from that which it has in the imperfect of the indicative mood; as the learner will perceive by turning to the conjugation of that verb.

Is the second person singular of the imperfect ever varied in its termination in the subjunctive mood? Will you give an example? Is this variation proper?

7.

"If thou *gave* liberally, thou wilt receive a liberal reward."
"Though thou did injure him, he harbors no resentment."
"It would be well, if the report was only the misrepresentation of her enemies."

"Was he ever so great and opulent, this conduct would debase him."
"Was I to enumerate all her virtues, it would look like flattery."
"Though I was perfect, yet would I not presume."

8. It may not be superfluous also to observe, that the auxiliaries of the potential mood, when applied to the subjunctive, do not change the termination of the second person singular. We properly say, "If thou *mayst* or *canst* go;" "Though thou *mightst* live;" "Unless thou *couldst* read;" "If thou *wouldst*

learn ;"—and not, "If thou *may* or *can* go," &c. It is sufficient, on this point, to adduce the authorities of Johnson and Lowth :—"If thou *shouldst* go;" *Johnson*. "If thou *mayst, mightst*, or *couldst* love ;" *Lowth*. Some authors think that, when *that* expresses the motive or end, the termination of these auxiliaries should be varied; as, "I advise thee, *that* thou *may* beware ;" "He checked thee, *that* thou *should* not presume;" but there does not appear to be any ground for this exception. If the expression of "condition, doubt, contingency," &c. does not warrant a change in the form of these auxiliaries, why should they have it, when a motive or end is expressed? The translators of the Scriptures do not appear to have made the distinction contended for. "Thou buildest the wall, *that* thou *mayst* be their king." Neh. vi. 6. "There is forgiveness with thee, *that* thou *mayst* be feared." Ps. cxxx. 4.

From the preceding observations under this rule, it appears, that, with respect to what is termed the present tense of any verb, when the circumstances of contingency and futurity concur, it is proper to vary the terminations of the second and third persons singular; that without the concurrence of those circumstances, the terminations should not be altered; and that the verb and the auxiliaries of the three past tenses, and the auxiliaries of the first future, undergo no alterations whatever, except the *imperfect* of the verb *to be*, which, in cases denoting contingency, is varied in all the persons of the singular number.

After perusing what has been advanced on this subject, it will be natural for the student to inquire, What is the extent of the subjunctive mood? Some grammarians think it extends only to what is called the present tense of verbs generally, under the circumstances of contingency and futurity, and to the imperfect tense of the verb *to be*, when it denotes contingency, &c.; because in these tenses only, the form of the verb admits of variation; and they suppose that it is variation merely which constitutes the distinction of moods. It is the opinion of other grammarians, (in which opinion we concur,) that, besides the two cases just mentioned, all verbs in the three past and the two future tenses are in the subjunctive mood, when they denote contingency or uncertainty, though they have not any change of termination; and that, when contingency is not signified, the verb, through all these five tenses, belongs to the indicative mood, whatever conjunction may attend it. They think that the definition and nature of the subjunctive mood have no reference to change of termination, but that they refer merely to the manner of the being, action, or passion signified by the verb; and that the subjunctive mood may as properly exist without a variation of the verb, as the infinitive mood, which has no terminations different from those of the indicative. The decision of this point may not, by some grammarians, be thought of much consequence. But the rules which ascertain the propriety of varying or not varying the terminations of the verb, will certainly be deemed important. These rules may be well observed, without a uniformity of sentiment respecting the nature and limits of the subjunctive mood.*

Do the auxiliaries of the potential mood, when applied to the subjunctive, change the termination of the second person singular? When is it proper to vary the terminations of the second and third persons singular of the present tense? Do the verb and auxiliaries of the past tenses, and the auxiliaries of the first future, undergo any alteration? What exception? What is the opinion of some grammarians in regard to the extent of the subjunctive mood? What is the opinion of other grammarians? In which of these opinions does the author concur?

8.

"If thou may share in his labors, be thankful, and do it cheerfully."

"Unless thou can fairly support the cause, give it up honorably."

---

* We have stated, for the student's information, the different opinions of grammarians, respecting the English subjunctive mood ; *First*, that which supposes there is no such mood in our language; *Secondly*, that which extends it no farther than the variation of the verb extend ; *Thirdly*, that which we have adopted, and explained at large, and which, in general, corresponds with the views of the most approved writers on English grammar. We may add a *Fourth* opinion, which appears to possess, at least, much plausibility. This opinion admits the arrangement we have given, with one variation, namely, that of assigning to the first tense of the subjunctive, two forms — 1st, that which simply denotes c. ntingency ; as, "If he *desires* it, I will perform the operation;" that is, if he *now* desires it : 2dly, that which denotes both contingency and futurity ; as, "If he *desire* it, I will perform the operation ;" that is, "If he should *hereafter* desire it." This last theory of the subjunctive mood claims the merit of rendering the whole system of the moods consistent and regular ; of being more conformable than any other to the definition of the subjunctive, and of not referring to the indicative mood forms of expression, which ill accord with its simplicity and nature. Perhaps this theory will bear a strict examination.

SYNTAX. 177

"Though thou might have foreseen the danger, thou couldst not have avoided it."
"If thou could convince him, he would not act accordingly."
"If thou would improve in knowledge, be diligent."
"Unless thou should make a timely retreat, the danger will be unavoidable."
"I have labored and wearied myself that thou may be at ease."
"He enlarged on those dangers, that thou should avoid them."

9. Some conjunctions have correspondent conjunctions belonging to them, either expressed or understood; as,

1st. *Though—yet, nevertheless;* as, " *Though* he was rich, *yet* for our sakes he became poor ;" " *Though* powerful, he was meek."
2d. *Whether—or*; as, " *Whether* he will go *or* not, I cannot tell "
3d. *Either—or ;* as, " I will *either* send it, *or* bring it myself."
4th. *Neither—nor ;* as, " *Neither* he *nor* I am able to compass it."
5th. *As—as ;* expressing a comparison of equality ; as, " She is *as* amiable *as* her sister ; and *as* much respected."
6th. *As—so,* expressing a comparison of equality ; as, " *As* the stars, *so* shall thy seed be. '
7th. *As—so ;* expressing a comparison of quality ; as, " *As* the one dieth, *so* dieth the other ;" " *As* he reads, they read."
8th. *So—as ;* with a verb expressing a comparison of quality ; as, " To see thy glory, *so as* I have seen thee in the sanctuary."
9th. *So—as ;* with a negative and an adjective expressing a comparison of quantity ; as, " Pompey was not *so* great a general *as* Cæsar, nor *so* great a man."
10th. *So—that ;* expressing a consequence ; as, " He was *so* fatigued, *that* he could scarcely move."

The conjunctions *or* and *nor* may often be used, with nearly equal propriety. " The king, whose character was not sufficiently vigorous *nor* decisive, assented to the measure." In this sentence, *or* would, perhaps, have been better ; but, in general, *nor* seems to repeat the negation in the former part of the sentence, and, therefore, gives more emphasis to the expression.

Are there any conjunctions which have correspondent conjunctions belonging to them ? Give examples.

9.

" Neither the cold *or* the fervid, but characters uniformly warm, are formed for friendship."
" They are both praiseworthy, and one is *equally* (1.) deserving as the other."
" He is not *as* diligent and learned as his brother."
' I will present it to him myself, or direct it to be given to him."
' Neither despise or oppose what thou dost not understand."
' The house is not as commodious as we expected it would be."
' I must, however, be so candid to own I have been mistaken."
" There was something so amiable, and yet so piercing in his look, *as* (2.) affected me at once with love and terror."
———" I gained a son ;
And such a son *as* all men hailed me happy."

" The dog in the manger would not eat the hay himself, nor suffer the ox to eat it."
" As far as I am able to judge, the book is well written."
" We should faithfully perform the trust committed to us, or ingenuously relinquish the charge."
" He is not as eminent, and as much esteemed, as he thinks himself to be."
" The work is a dull performance, and is neither capable of pleasing (3.) the understanding, *or* the imagination.
" There is no condition so secure, as cannot admit of change."
" This is an event which nobody presumes upon, or is so sanguine to hope for."
" We are generally pleased with any little accomplishments of body or mind."

10. Conjunctions are often improperly used, both singly and in pairs. The following are examples of this impropriety : " The relations are so uncertain, as that they require a great deal of examination ;" It should be, " *that* they require," &c. " There was no man so sanguine, who did not apprehend

(1.) For " *equally,*" read " *as.*" (2.) " *that it.*" (3.) " *neither One.*"
M

some ill consequences; it ought to be, "so sanguine as not to apprehend," &c.; or, "no man, how sanguine soever, who did not," &c. "To trust in him is no more but to acknowledge his power." "This is no other but the gate of paradise." In both of these instances, *but* should be *than*. "We should sufficiently weigh the objects of our hope; whether they are such as we may reasonably expect from them what they propose," &c. It ought to be, "*that* we may reasonably" &c. "The duke had not behaved with that loyalty as he ought to have done;" "*with which* he ought." "In the order as they lie in his preface;" it should be, "in order as they lie;" or, "in the order *in which* they lie." "Such sharp replies that cost him his life;" "*as* cost," &c. "If he were truly that scarecrow, as he is now commonly painted;" "*such* a scarecrow," &c. "I wish I could do that justice to his memory, to oblige the painters," &c.; "do *such* justice *as* to oblige," &c.

Will you repeat this Note, and give an example under it? What is said of sentences beginning with the conjunctive form of the verb? Give an example. When has *as* the force of a relative pronoun? (1.) Give an example.

There is a peculiar neatness in a sentence beginning with the conjunctive form of a verb. "*Were* there no difference, there would be no choice."
A double conjunctive, in two correspondent clauses of a sentence, is sometimes made use of; as, "*Had* he done this, he *had* escaped;" "*Had* the limitations on the prerogative been, in his time, quite fixed and certain, his integrity *had* made him regard as sacred the boundaries of the constitution." The sentence in the common form would have read thus: "If the limitations on the prerogative had seen," &c. "his integrity would have made him regard," &c.
The particle *as*, when it is connected with the pronoun *such*, has the force of a relative pronoun; as, "Let *such as* presume to advise others, look well to their own conduct;" which is equivalent to, "Let *them who* presume," &c. But when used by itself, this particle is to be considered as a conjunction, or perhaps as an adverb.
Our language wants a a conjunction adapted to a familiar style, equivalent to *notwithstanding*. The words *for all that* seem to be too low. "The word was in the mouth of every one, but, for all that, the subject may still be a secret."
In regard that is solemn and antiquated; *because* would do much better in the following sentence: "It cannot be otherwise, in regard that the French prosody differs from that of every other language."
The word *except* is far preferable to *other than*. "It admitted of no effectual cure other than amputation." *Except* is also to be preferred to *all but*. "They were happy, all but the stranger." In the two following phrases, the conjunction *as* is improperly omitted: "Which nobody presumes, or is so sanguine ^ to hope." "I must, however, be so just ^ to own."

The conjunction *that* is often properly omitted, and understood; as, "I beg you would come to me;" "See thou do it not;" instead of "that you would," "that thou do." But in the following, and many similar phrases, this conjunction were much better inserted: "Yet it is reason the memory of their virtues remain to posterity." It should be, "Yet it is *just that* the memory," &c.

10.

"Be ready to succor such persons *who* (2.) need thy assistance."
"The matter was no sooner proposed, *but* (3.) he privately withdrew to consider it."
"He has too much sense and prudence *than* to become a dupe to such artifices."
It is not sufficient that our conduct *as* far as it respects others, appears to be unexceptionable."
'The resolution was not the less fixed, *that* (4.) the secret was yet communicated to very few."
He opposed the most remarkable corruptions of the church of Rome, so (5.) *as that* his doctrines were embraced by great numbers."

"He gained nothing further by his speech, *but only* (6.) to be commended for his eloquence."
"He has little more of the scholar *besides* the name."
"He has little of the scholar *than* the name."
"They had no sooner risen, but they applied themselves to their studies."
"From no other institution, besides the admirable one of juries, could so great a benefit be expected."
"Those savage people seemed to have no other element but war."
"Such men *that* act treacherously ought to be avoided."

SYNTAX.

"Germany ran the same risk as Italy had done" "No errors are so trivial, but they (1.) deserve to be corrected."

RULE XXIX.
Corresponding with Murray's Grammar,
RULE XX.

When the qualities of different things are compared, the latter noun or pronoun is not governed by the conjunction than or as, but agrees with the verb, or is governed by the verb or the preposition, expressed or understood; as, "Thou art wiser than I;" that is, "than I am." "They loved him more than me;" that is, "more than they loved me." "The sentiment is well expressed by Plato, but much better by Solomon than him;" that is, "than by him."

The propriety or impropriety of many phrases, in the preceding as well as in some other forms, may be discovered, by supplying the words that are not expressed; which will be evident from the following instances of erroneous construction: "He can read better than me." "He is as good as her." "Whether I be present or no." "Who did this? Me." By supplying the words understood, in each of these phrases, their impropriety and governing rule will appear; as, "better than I can read;" "as good as she is;" "present or not present;" "I did it."

"Thou art wiser than I." Will you parse *I*, and repeat the rule for it?

"In some respects, we have had as many advantages as them; but in the article of a good library, they have had a greater privilege than us."
"The undertaking was much better executed by his brother than he."
"They are much greater gainers than me by this unexpected event."

"They know how to write as well as him; but he is a much better grammarian than them."
"Though she is not so learned as him, she is as much beloved and respected."
"These people, though they possess more shining qualities, are not so proud as him, nor so vain as her."

1. By not attending to this rule, many errors have been committed; a number of which is subjoined, as a further caution and direction to the learner: "Thou art a much greater loser than me by his death." "She suffers hourly more than me." "We contributed a third more than the Dutch, who were obliged to the same proportion more than us." "King Charles, and, more than him, the duke and the popish faction, were at liberty to form new schemes." "The drift of all his sermons was, to prepare the Jews for the reception of a prophet mightier than him, and whose shoes he was not worthy to bear." "It was not the work of so eminent an author as him to whom it was first imputed." "A stone is heavy, and the sand weighty; but a fool's wrath is heavier than them both." "If the king give us leave, we may perform the office as well as them that do." In these passages, it ought to be, "*I, we, he, they,*" respectively.

When the relative *who* immediately follows *than*, it seems to form an exception to the 29th Rule; for, in that connection, the relative must be in the objective case; as, "Alfred, *than whom* a greater king never reigned," &c. "Beelzebub, *than whom*, Satan excepted, none higher sat," &c. It is remarkable that, in such instances, if the personal pronoun were used, it would be in the nominative case; as, "A greater king never reigned *than he*," that is, "*than he was*." "Beelzebub *than he*," &c., that is, "*than he sat*." The phrase *than whom* is, however, avoided by the best modern writers.

"She suffers hourly more than me." Will you correct this sentence, and explain why it is wrong?

(1.) "that they do not."

1.

'Who betrayed her companion?" "Not me."
"Who revealed the secrets he ought to have concealed?" "Not him."
"Who related falsehoods to screen herself, and to bring an odium upon others?" "Not me; it was her."
"There is but one in fault, and that is me."

"Whether he will be learned or not, must depend on his application."
"Charles XII. of Sweden, than who (1.) a more courageous person never lived, appears to have been destitute of the tender sensibilities of nature."
"Salmasius (a more learned man than him has seldom appeared) was not happy at the close of life."

RULE XXX.

Corresponding with Murray's Grammar,
RULE XXI.

To avoid disagreeable repetitions, and to express our ideas in a few words, an ellipsis, or omission of some words, is frequently admitted. Instead of saying, "He was a learned man, he was a wise man, and he was a good man," *we make use of the ellipsis, and say,* "He was a learned, wise and good man."

When the omission of words would obscure the sentence, weaken its force, or be attended with an impropriety, they must be expressed. In the sentence, "We are apt to love who love us," *the word* them *should be supplied.* "A beautiful field and trees," *is not proper language; it should be,* "Beautiful fields and trees," *or,* "A beautiful field and fine trees."

Almost all compounded sentences are more or less elliptical; some examples of which may be seen under the different parts of speech.

"I gladly shunned who gladly fled from me." Will you correct this sentence, and repeat the latter part of Rule XXX, by which the correction is made?

"I gladly shunned (2.) who gladly fled from me."
"And this is (3.) it men mean by distributive justice, and is properly termed equity."
"His honor, interest, religion, were all embarked in this undertaking." (4.)
"When so good a man as Socrates fell a victim to the madness of the people, truth, virtue, religion, fell with him." (5.)
"The fear of death, nor hope of life, could make him submit to a dishonest action." (6.)
"An elegant house and furniture were, by this event, irrecoverably lost to the owner." (7.)

1. The ellipsis of the *article* is thus used: "A man, woman, and child;" that is, "a man, a woman, and a child." "A house and garden;" that is, "a house and a garden." "The sun and moon;" that is, "the sun and the moon." "The day and hour;" that is, "the day and the hour." In all these instances, the article being once expressed, the repetition of it becomes unnecessary. There is, however, an exception to this observation, when some peculiar emphasis requires a repetition; as in the following sentence: "Not only the year, but the day and the hour." In this case, the ellipsis of the last article would be improper. When a different form of the article is requisite, the article is also properly repeated; as, "a house and *an* orchard," instead of "a house and orchard."

(1.) "*whom.*"—Note XX. (648.) (2.) "*him who.*" (3.) "*that which.*" (4.) Insert *had twice more.* (5.) "*and*" twice. (6.) "*Neither—nor.*" (7.) "*much costly.*"

SYNTAX. 181

Will you give an example of the ellipsis of the *article ?* Is it necessary to repeat the article in each of these instances ?

1.

"These rules are addressed to none but the intelligent and *the* (1.) attentive."
"The gay and *the* pleasing are, sometimes, the most insidious, and the most dangerous companions."
"Old age will prove a joyless and a dreary season, if we arrive at it with an unimproved, or with a corrupted, mind."
"The more I see of his conduct, I like him better."
"It is not only the duty, but interest, of young persons to be studious and diligent."

2. The *noun* is frequently omitted in the following manner : " The laws of God and man ;" that is, " The laws of God and the laws of man." In some very emphatical expressions, the ellipsis should not be used ; as, " Christ, the power of God, and the wisdom of God ;" which is more emphatical than " Christ the power and wisdom of God."

Will you give an example of the omission of the *noun ?* Should this ellipsis always be used ?

2.

"These counsels were the dictates of virtue, and *the dictates* (2.) of true honor."
"Avarice and cunning may acquire an estate, but avarice and cunning cannot gain friends." (3.)
"A taste for useful knowledge will provide for us a great and noble entertainment, when others leave us." (4.)
"Without firmness, nothing that is great can be undertaken ; that is difficult or hazardous, can be accomplished." (5.)
"The anxious man is the votary of riches ; the negligent of pleasure." (6.)

3. The ellipsis of the *adjective* is used in the following manner : " A delightful garden and orchard ;" that is, " A delightful garden and a delightful orchard." " A little man and woman ;" that is, " a little man and a little woman." In such elliptical expressions as these, the adjective ought to have exactly the same signification, and to be quite as proper, when joined to the latter substantive as to the former ; otherwise the ellipsis should not be admitted.

Sometimes the ellipsis is improperly applied to nouns of different numbers ; as, " A magnificent house and gardens." In this case it is better to use another adjective ; as, " A magnificent house, and fine gardens."

Will you give an example of the ellipsis of the adjective ? What rule is to be observed in the use of this ellipsis ?

3.

"His crimes had brought him into extreme distress and extreme perplexity." (7.)
"He has an affectionate brother, and an affectionate sister, and they live in great harmony." (8.)
"We must guard against too great severity, and facility of manners."(9.)
"We should often recollect what the wisest men have said and written concerning human happiness and vanity." (10.)
"That species of commerce will produce great gain or loss." (10.)
"Many days, and even weeks, pass away unimproved." (10.)
"This wonderful action struck the beholders with exceeding astonishment." (10.) (11.)
"The people of this country possess a healthy climate and soil." (9.)
"They enjoy also a free constitution and laws." (10.)

4. The following is the ellipsis of the *pronoun :* " I love and fear him ;" that is," I love him, and I fear him." " My house and lands ;" that is, " My house, and my lands." In these instances, the ellipsis may take place with propriety ; but if we would be more express and emphatical, it must not be used ; as, " His friends and his foes ;" " My sons and my daughters."

In some of the common forms of speech, the relative pronoun is usually omitted ; as, " This is the man they love," instead of, " This is the man

(1.) Reject " *the.*"   (2.) " *virtue and of true.*"   (3.) Insert " *they*" in the place of two nouns.
(4.) Insert " *entertainments.*"   (6.) Insert " *nothing.*"   (8.) Insert " *man, that.*"   (7.) Reject an adjec
tive.   (8.) Reject two words.   (9.) Insert two words.   (10.) Insert an adjective.   (11.) " *exceedingly.*"

16

whom they love;" "These are the goods they bought," for "These are the goods *which* they bought."

In complex sentences, it is much better to have the relative pronoun expressed; as it is more proper to say, "The posture in which I lay," than "In the posture I lay;" "The horse on which I rode, fell down," than "The horse I rode, fell down."

The antecedent and the relative connect the parts of a sentence together; and, to prevent obscurity and confusion, they should answer to each other with great exactness. "We speak that we do know, and testify that we have seen." Here the ellipsis is manifestly improper, and ought to be supplied; as, "We speak that *which* we do know, and testify that *which* we have seen."

Will you give an example of the ellipsis of the pronoun? Can this ellipsis be properly used at all times?

4.

"His reputation and his estate were both lost by gaming." (1.)

"This intelligence not only excited our hopes, but fears too." (2.)

"His conduct is not scandalous; and *that* is the best can be said of it." (3.)

"This was the person whom calumny had greatly abused, and sustained the injustice with singular patience." (2.)

"He discovered some qualities in the youth of a disagreeable nature, and to him were wholly unaccountable." (2.)

"The captain had several men died in his ship of the scurvy." (2.)

"He is not only sensible and learned, but is religious too." (2.)

"The Chinese language contains an immense number of words; and who would learn them must possess a great memory." (2.)

"By presumption and by vanity, we provoke enmity, and we incur contempt." (1.)

"In the circumstances I was at that time, my troubles pressed heavily upon me." (4.)

"He had destroyed his constitution, by the very same errors *that* so many have been destroyed."

5. The ellipsis of the *verb* is used in the following instances: "The man was old and crafty;" that is, "The man was old, and the man was crafty." "She was young, and beautiful, and good;" that is, "She was young, she was beautiful, and she was good." "Thou art poor, and wretched, and miserable, and blind, and naked." If we would fill up the ellipsis in the last sentence, *thou art* ought to be repeated before each of the adjectives.

If, in such enumeration, we choose to point out one property above the rest, that property must be placed last, and the ellipsis supplied; as, "She is young and beautiful, and she is good."

"I went to see and hear him" that is, "I went to see, and I went to hear him." In this instance, there is not only an ellipsis of the governing verb, *I went*, but likewise of the sign of the infinitive mood, which is governed by it.

Do, did, have, had, shall, will, may, might, and the rest of the auxiliaries of the compound tenses, are frequently used alone to spare the repetition of the verb; as, "He regards his word, but thou dost not;" that is, "dost not regard it." "We succeeded, but they did not;" "did not succeed." "I have learned my task, but thou hast not;" "hast not learned." "They must, and they shall be punished;" that is, "they must be punished."

Will you give an example of the ellipsis of the verb? Suppose we wish to point out one property above the rest? How are the auxiliaries sometimes used?

5.

"He is temperate, he is disinterested, he is benevolent; he is an ornament to his family, and a credit to his profession." (5.)

"Genuine virtue supposes our benevolence to be strengthened, and to be confirmed by principle." (6.)

"Perseverance in laudable pursuits will reward all our toils, and will produce effects beyond our calculation." (7.)

"It is happy for us, when we can calmly and deliberately look back on the past, and can quietly anticipate the future." (7.)

"The sacrifices of virtue will not only be rewarded hereafter, but recompensed even in this life." (1.) All those possessed of any office, resigned their former commission." (2.) 'If young persons were determined to conduct themselves by the rules of virtue, not only would they escape innumerable dangers, but command respect from the licentious themselves." (2.) "Charles was a man of learning, knowledge, and benevolence and, what is still more, a true Christian." (2.)

6. The ellipsis of the *adverb* is used in the following manner: "He spoke and acted wisely;" that is, "He spoke wisely, and he acted wisely." "Thrice I went and offered my service;" that is, "Thrice I went, and thrice I offered my service."

How is the ellipsis of the adverb used?

6.

"The temper of him who is always in the bustle of the world, will be often ruffled, and be often disturbed." (3.) "We often commend imprudently, as well as censure imprudently." (4.) "How a seed grows up into a tree, and the mind acts upon the body, are mysteries which we cannot explain." (5.) "Verily there is a reward for the righteous. There is a God that judgeth in the earth." (5.)

7. The ellipsis of the *preposition*, as well as of the verb, is seen in the following instances: "He went into the abbeys, halls, and public buildings;" that is, "He went into the abbeys, he went into the halls, and he went into the public buildings." "He also went through all the streets and lanes of the city;" that is, "through all the streets, and through all the lanes," &c. "He spoke to every man and woman there;" that is, "to every man and to every woman." "This day, next month, last year;" that is, "On this day, in the next month, in the last year." "The Lord do that which seemeth him good;" that is, "which seemeth *to* him."

Will you give an example of the ellipsis of the preposition and the verb?

7.

"Changes are almost continually taking place, in men and in manners, in opinions and in customs, in private fortunes and public conduct." (5.) (3.) 'Averse either to contradict or blame, the too complaisant man goes along with the manners that prevail." (5.) "By this habitual indelicacy, the virgins smiled at what they blushed before." (5.) "They are now reconciled to what they could not formerly be prompted, by any considerations." (5.) "Censure is the tax which a man pays the public for being eminent." (5.) "Reflect on the state of human life, and the society of men as mixed with good and with evil." (5.)

8. The ellipsis of the *conjunction* is as follows: "They confess the power, wisdom, goodness, and love of their Creator;" that is, "the power, and wisdom, and goodness, and love of," &c. "Though I love him, I do not flatter him;" that is, "Though I love him, *yet* I do not flatter him."

Will you give an example of the ellipsis of a conjunction?

8.

"In all stations and conditions, the important relations take place, of masters and servants, and husbands and wives, and parents and children, and brothers and friends, and citizens and subjects." (6.) 'Destitute of principle, he regarded neither his family, nor his friends, nor his reputation." (4.) "Religious persons are often unjustly represented as persons of romantic character, visionary notions, unacquainted with the world, unfit to live in it." (1.) "No rank, station, dignity of birth, possessions, exempt men from contributing their share to public utility." (7.)

9. The ellipsis of the *interjection* is not very common: it, however, is sometimes used; as, "Oh, pity and shame!" that is, "Oh, pity! oh, shame!"

As the ellipsis occurs in almost every sentence in the English language numerous examples of it might be given; but only a few more can be admitted here.

In the following instance, there is a very considerable one: "He will often argue, that if this part of our trade were well cultivated, we should gain from one nation; and if another, from another;" that is, "He will often argue, that if this part of our trade were well cultivated, we should gain from one nation; and if another part of our trade were well cultivated, we should gain from another nation."

The following instances, though short, contain much of the ellipsis: "Wc is me;" i. e. "wo is to me." "To let blood;" i. e. "to let out blood." "To let down;" i. e. "to let it fall or slide down." "To walk a mile;" i. e. "to walk through the space of a mile." "To sleep all night;" i. e. "to sleep through all the night." "To go a fishing;" "To go a hunting;" i. e. "to go on a fishing voyage or business;" "to go on a hunting party." "I dine at two o'clock;" i. e. "at two of the clock." "By sea, by land, on shore;" i. e. "by the sea, by the land, on the shore."

What is said of the ellipsis of the interjection?

9.

"Oh, my father! Oh, my friend! how great has been my ingratitude!" (1.)

"Oh, piety! virtue! how insensible have I been to your charms!" (2.)

10. The examples that follow are produced to show the impropriety of ellipsis in some particular cases. "The land was always possessed, during pleasure, by those intrusted with the command;" it should be, "those *persons* intrusted;" or, "those *who were* intrusted." "If he had read farther, he would have found several of his objections might have been spared;" that is, "he would have found *that* several of his objections," &c. "There is nothing men are more deficient in, than knowing their own characters;" it ought to be, "nothing *in which* men," and, "than *in* knowing." "I scarcely know any part of natural philosophy would yield more variety and use;" it should be, "*which* would yield," &c. "In the temper of mind he was then;" that is, "*in which* he then was.". "The little satisfaction and consistency to be found in most of the systems of divinity I have met with, made me betake myself to the sole reading of the Scriptures;" it ought to be, "*which are* to be found," and *which* I have met with." "He desired they might go to the altar together, and jointly return their thanks to whom only they were due;" that is, "*to him* to whom," &c.

"There is nothing men are more deficient in, than in knowing their own characters." Will you correct this sentence

10.

"That is a property most men have, or at least may attain." (3.)

"Why do ye that which is not lawful to do on the sabbath days?" (2.)

"The show bread, which is not lawful to eat, but for the priests alone."(2.)

"Most, if not all, the royal family had quitted the place." (2.)

"By these happy labors, they who sow and reap, will rejoice together." (4.)

RULE XXXI.
Corresponding with Murray's Grammar,

RULE XXII.

All the parts of a sentence should correspond to each other: a regular and dependent construction, throughout, should be carefully preserved. The following sentence is, therefore, inaccurate: "He was more beloved, but not so much admired, as Cinthio." *It should be,* "He was more beloved than Cinthio, but not so much admired."

The first example under this rule presents a most irregular construction, namely "he was more beloved as Cinthio." The words *more* and *so much* are very improperly stated as having the same regimen. In correcting such sentences, it is not necessary to supply the latter ellipsis; because it cannot lead to any discordant or improper construction, and the supply would often be harsh or inelegant.

As the 31st rule comprehends all the preceding rules, it may, at the first view, appear to be too general to be useful. But, by ranging under it a number of sentences peculiarly constructed, we shall perceive that it is calculated to ascertain the true grammatical construction of many modes of expression, which none of the particular rules can sufficiently explain.

"This dedication may serve for almost any book, that has, is, or shall be published;" it ought to be. "that has been, or shall be published." "He was guided by interests always different, sometimes contrary to, those of the community;" "different *from*;" or, "always different from those of the community, and sometimes contrary to them." "Will it be urged that these books are as old, or even older than tradition?" the words "as old," and "older," cannot have a common regimen; it should be, "as old as tradition, or even older." "It requires few talents to which most men are not born, or at least may not acquire;" "or which, at least, they may not acquire." "The court of chancery frequently mitigates and breaks the teeth of the common law." In this construction, the first verb is said to mitigate the teeth of the common law, which is an evident solecism. "Mitigates the common law and breaks the teeth of it," would have been grammatical.

"They presently grow into good humor and good language towards the crown;" "grow into good language," is very improper. "There is never wanting a set of evil instruments, who, either out of mad zeal, private hatred, or filthy lucre, are always ready," &c. We say properly, "A man acts out of mad zeal," or, "out of private hatred;" but we cannot say, if we would speak English, "he *acts* out of filthy lucre." "To double her kindness and caresses of me:" the word *kindness* requires to be followed by either *to* or *for*, and cannot be construed with the preposition *of*. "Never was man so teased, or suffered half the uneasiness, as I have done this evening:" the first and third clauses, namely, "never was man so teased," "as I have done this evening," cannot be joined without an impropriety; and to connect the second and third, the word *that* must be substituted for *as;* "or suffered half the uneasiness that I have done;" or else, "half so much uneasiness as I hav suffered."

The first part of the following sentence abounds with adverbs, and those such as are hardly consistent with one another: "*How much soever* the reformation of this degenerate age is *almost utterly* to be despaired of, we may yet have a more comfortable prospect of future times." The sentence would be more correct in the following form: "*Though* the reformation of this degenerate age is *nearly* to be despaired of," &c.

"Oh! shut not up my soul with the sinners, nor my life with the bloodthirsty; in whose hands is wickedness, and *their* right hand is full of gifts." As the passage introduced by the copulative conjunction *and*, was not intended as a continuation of the principal and independent part of the sentence, but of the dependent part, the relative *whose* should have been used instead of the possessive *their;* namely, "and *whose* right hand is full of gifts."

"Eye hath not seen, nor ear heard, neither *have* entered into the heart of man, the things which God hath prepared for them that love him." There seems to be an impropriety in this instance, in which the same noun serves in a double capacity, performing at the same time the offices both of the nominative and objective cases "Neither *hath* it entered into the heart of man to conceive the things," &c. would have been regular.

"We have the power of retaining, altering, and compounding those images which we have once received, into all the varieties of picture and vision." It is very proper to say, "altering and compounding those images which we have once received, into all the varieties of picture and vision;" but we cannot with propriety say, "retaining them into all the varieties;" and yet, according to the manner in which the words are ranged, this construction is unavoidable: for *retaining, altering*, and *compounding* are participles, each of which equally refers to and governs the subsequent noun, *those images;* and that noun, again, is necessarily connected with the following preposition, *into*. The construction might easily have been rectified, by disjoining the participle *retaining* from the other two participles, in this way: "We have the power of retaining those images which we have once received, and of altering and compounding them into all the varieties of picture and vision;" or, perhaps, better thus: "We have the power of retaining, altering, and compounding those images which we have once received, and of forming them into all the varieties of picture and vision."

Why is the first example under this rule inaccurate? "This dedication may serve for almost any book, that has, is, or shall be published." Will you point out the inaccuracies in this sentence, and correct them?

"Several alterations and additions have been made to the work." (1.)

"The first proposal was essentially different, and inferior to the second." (2.)

"He is more bold and active, but not so wise and studious as his companion." (3.)

"Thou hearest the sound of wind, but thou canst not tell whence it cometh, and whither it goeth."

"Neither has he, nor any other persons, suspected so much dissimulation." (4.)

"The court of France or England was to have been the umpire." (5.)

"In the reign of Henry II. all foreign commodities were plenty in England." (6.)

"There is no talent *so* useful towards success in business, or which puts men more out of the reach of accidents, than that quality generally possessed by persons of cool temper, and is, in common language, called discretion." (7.)

"The first project was to shorten discourse, by cutting polysyllables into one." (8.)

"I shall do all I can to persuade others to take the same measures for their cure which I have." (9.)

"The greatest masters of critical learning differ among *one another*."

"Micaiah said, If thou certainly return in peace, then hath not the Lord spoken by me." (10.)

"I do not suppose, that we Britons want a genius, more than the rest of our neighbors." (10.)

"The deaf man whose ears were opened, and his tongue loosened, doubtless glorified the great Physician." (11.)

"Groves, fields, and meadows are, in any season of the year, pleasant to look upon; but never so much as in the opening of the spring." (12.)

"The multitude rebuke them, *because* they should hold their peace."

"The intentions of some of these philosophers, nay, of many, might and probably were good." (13.)

"It was an unsuccessful undertaking; which, although it has failed, is no objection at all to an enterprise so well concerted." (14.)

"The reward is his due, and it has already, or will hereafter be given to him." (15.)

"By intercourse with wise and experienced persons, who know the world, we may improve and rub off the rust of a private and retired education." (16.)

"Sincerity is as valuable, and even more valuable, than knowledge." (17.)

"No person was ever so perplexed, or sustained the mortifications, as he has done to-day." (18.)

"The Romans gave not only the freedom of the city, but capacity for employments, to several towns in Gaul, Spain, and Germany." (19.)

"Such writers have no other standard on which to form themselves, except what chances to be fashionable and popular." (20.)

"Whatever we do secretly, shall be displayed and heard in the clearest light." (21.)

"To the happiness of possessing a person of so uncommon merit, Boethius soon *had* the satisfaction of obtaining the highest honor his country could bestow."

(1.) "*This work has received,*" &c. (2.) "*was inferior to the second, and—from it.*" (3.) "*active than his.*" (4.) Insert "*have.*" (5.) "*or that of.*" (6.) "*plentiful.*" (7.) Insert "*more*" and "*which.*" (8.) "*by reducing—to words of one syllable.*" (9.) Insert a participle. (10.) Reject one word. (11.) Insert two words, and reject one. (12.) Insert "*so.*" (13.) Insert "*have been.*" (14.) "*the failure of which is, however.*" (15.) Insert "*been.*" (16.) End with, "*and rub off its rust.*" (17.) "*as knowledge, and.*" (18.) Insert "*been*" for "*done,*" and end with "*such mortification.*" (19.) "*the inhabitants of.*" (20.) Reject one word. (21.) "*displayed in the clearest.*"

PROSODY.

PROSODY consists of two parts: the former teaches the true PRO-NUNCIATION of words, comprising ACCENT, QUANTITY, EMPHASIS, PAUSE, and TONE; the latter, the laws of VERSIFICATION.

OF PRONUNCIATION.

OF ACCENT.

ACCENT is the laying of a peculiar stress of the voice on a certain letter or syllable in a word, that it may be better heard than the rest, or distinguished from them; as, in the word *presume*, the stress of the voice must be on the letter *u*, and second syllable *sume*, which take the accent.

OF QUANTITY.

The QUANTITY of a syllable is that time which is occupied in pronouncing it. It is considered LONG or SHORT.

A vowel or syllable is long, when the accent is on the vowel, which occasions it to be slowly joined in pronunciation with the following letter; as, *fāll, tāle, mōōd, hōuse, fēature*.

A syllable is short, when the accent is on the consonant, which occasions the vowel to be quickly joined to the succeeding letter; as, *ănt, bŏnĕt, hŭngĕr*.

A long syllable generally requires double the time of a short one in pronouncing it; thus *māte* and *nōte* should be pronounced as slowly again as *măt* and *nŏt*.

OF EMPHASIS.

By EMPHASIS is meant a stronger and fuller sound of voice, by which we distinguish some word or words on which we design to lay a particular stress, and to show how they affect the rest of the sentence. Sometimes the emphatic words must be distinguished by a particular tone of voice, as well as by a greater stress.

OF PAUSES.

PAUSES or RESTS, in speaking and reading, are a total cessation of the voice, during a perceptible, and in many cases, a measurable space of time.

OF TONES.

TONES are different both from emphasis and pauses, consisting in the modulation of the voice, the notes or variations which we employ in the expression of our sentiments.

OF VERSIFICATION.

VERSIFICATION is the arrangement of a certain number and variety of syllables, according to certain laws.

RHYME is the correspondence of the last sound of one verse to the last sound of another.

What is prosody? What is accent? What is the quantity of a syllable? When is a vowel or syllable long? When short? Give examples of each. How much more time does the pronunciation of a long syllable occupy, than a short one? What is emphasis? What are pauses? What are tones? What is versification? What is rhyme?

OF POETICAL FEET.

A certain number of syllables connected form a foot. They are called *feet*, because it is by their aid that the voice, as it were, steps along through the verse in a measured pace.

All feet used in poetry consist either of two, or of three syllables, and are reducible to eight kinds—four of two syllables, and four of three—as follows:

DISSYLLABLE.	TRISYLLABLE.
A Trochee, — ˘	A Dactyl, — ˘ ˘
An Iambus, ˘ —	An Amphibrach, ˘ — ˘
A Spondee, — —	An Anapæst, ˘ ˘ —
A Pyrrhic, ˘ ˘	A Tribrach, ˘ ˘ ˘

A Trochee has the first syllable accented, and the last unaccented; as, "Hāteful, péttish."

An Iambus has the first syllable unaccented, and the latter accented; as, 'Bĕtrāy, cŏnsīst."

A Spondee has both the words or syllables accented; as, "The pāle mōōn."

A Pyrrhic has both the words or syllables unaccented; as, "ŏn thĕ tall tree."

A Dactyl has the first syllable accented, and the two latter unaccented; as, "Lăbŏrĕr, pŏssĭblĕ."

An Amphibrach has the first and last syllables unaccented, and the middle one accented; as, "Dĕlīghtfŭl, dŏméstic."

An Anapæst has the two first syllables unaccented, and the last accented; as, "Cŏntrăvēne, acquiésce."

A Tribrach has all its syllables unaccented; as, "Nŭmĕrăblĕ, conquerable."

Some of these may be denominated *principal* feet, as pieces of poetry may be wholly or chiefly formed of any of them. Such are the Iambus, Trochee, Dactyl, and Anapæst. The others may be termed *secondary* feet, because their chief use is to diversify the numbers, and to improve the verse.

PUNCTUATION.

PUNCTUATION is the art of dividing a written composition into sentences, by points or stops, for the purpose of marking the different pauses which the sense and an accurate pronunciation require.

The *Comma* represents the shortest pause; the *Semicolon*, a pause double that of the comma; the *Colon*, double that of the semicolon; and the *Period*, double that of the colon.

OF THE COMMA.

The Comma usually separates those parts of a sentence which, though very closely connected in sense and construction, require a pause between them.

RULE 1.—With respect to a simple sentence, the several words of which it is composed, have so near a relation to each other, that, in general, no points are requisite, except a full stop at the end of it; as, "The fear of the Lord is the beginning of wisdom." "Every part of nature swarms with living creatures."

A simple sentence, however, when it is a long one, and the nominative case is accompanied with inseparable adjuncts, may admit of a pause immediately before the verb; as, "The good taste of the present age, has not allowed us to neglect the cultivation of the English language." "To be totally indifferent to praise or censure, is a real defect in character."

What constitutes a poetical foot, and why is it so called? Of how many syllables do poetical feet consist? How many kinds of feet are there, and what are they? What is a Trochee? an Iambus? a Spondee? a Pyrrhic? a Dactyl? an Amphibrach? an Anapæst? a Tribrach? Will you give an example of each? Which are called *principal feet?* Which secondary? Why?

What is punctuation? What does the comma represent? the semicolon? the colon? the period? How is the comma used? "The fear of the Lord is the beginning of wisdom." Does this sentence require a pause in it? Will you give the rule for sentences of this kind? "The good taste of the present age has not allowed us to neglect the cultivation of the English language." Does this

RULE 2.—When the connection of the different parts of a simple sentence, is interrupted by an imperfect phrase, a comma is usually introduced before the beginning and at the end of the phrase; as, "I remember, *with gratitude*, his goodness to me." "His work is, *in many respects*, very imperfect." "It is, *therefore*, not much approved." But when the interruptions are slight and unimportant, the comma is better omitted; as, "Flattery is certainly pernicious." "There is *surely* a pleasure in beneficence."

RULE 3.—When two or more nouns occur in the same construction, they are parted by a comma; as, "The husband, wife, and children, suffered extremely" "They took away their furniture, clothes, and stock in trade." From this rule is mostly an exception, with regard to two nouns closely connected by a conjunction; as, "Virtue and vice form a strong contrast to each other." "Libertines call religion bigotry *or* superstition." If the parts connected are not short, a comma may be inserted, though the conjunction is expressed; as, "Romances may be said to be miserable rhapsodies, *or* dangerous incentives to evil."

RULE 4.—Two or more adjectives, belonging to the same substantive, are likewise separated by commas; as, "Plain, honest truth wants no artificial covering." "David was a brave, wise, and pious man." But two adjectives immediately connected by a conjunction, are not separated by a comma; as, "Truth is fair *and* artless." "We must be wise *or* foolish: there is no medium."

RULE 5.—Two or more verbs, having the same nominative case, and immediately following one another, are also separated by commas; as, "Virtue supports in adversity, moderates in prosperity." "In a letter we may advise, exhort, comfort, request, and discuss."

Two verbs immediately connected by a conjunction, are an exception to the rule; as, "The study of natural history expands *and* elevates the mind." Two or more participles are subject to a similar rule and exception.

RULE 6.—Two or more adverbs immediately succeeding each other, must be separated by commas; as, "We are fearfully, wonderfully framed." "We must act prudently, steadily, and vigorously." When two adverbs are joined by a conjunction, they are not parted by a comma; as, "Some men sin deliberately *and* presumptuously."

RULE 7.—When participles are followed by something that depends upon them, they are generally separated from the rest of the sentence by commas; as, "The king, *approving the plan*, put it in execution." "His talents, *formed for great enterprises*, could not fail of rendering him conspicuous."

RULE 8.—When a conjunction is parted by a phrase or sentence from the verb to which it belongs, such intervening phrase has usually a comma at each extremity; as, "They set out early, *and*, before the dawn of day, arrived at the destined place."

RULE 9.—Expressions in a direct address are separated from the rest of the sentence by commas; as, "My son, give me thy heart." "I am obliged to you, *my friends*, for your many favors."

RULE 10.—The case absolute, and the infinitive mood absolute, are separated by commas from the body of the sentence; as, "*His father dying*, he succeeded to the estate." "At length, their ministry performed, and race well run, they left the world in peace." "*To confess the truth*, I was much in fault."

RULE 11.—Nouns in apposition, that is, nouns added to other nouns in the same case, by way of explication or illustration, when accompanied with adjuncts, are set off by commas; as, "Paul, the apostle of the Gentiles, was

---

sentence admit of a pause? If so, where, and what is the rule? "I remember with gratitude his goodness to me." Will you state how this sentence should be pointed, and the rule for it? Will you state the exception to this rule?

"Plain, honest truth wants no artificial covering." Will you state how this sentence should be pointed, and the rule for it? What exception is there to this rule? "Virtue supports in adversity, moderates in prosperity." Will you state how this sentence should be pointed, and the rule for it? State the exceptions to the rule.

"We are fearfully, wonderfully made." Will you

state what points should be placed in this sentence, and the rule for it? State the exceptions.

"The king approving the plan, put it in execution." Will you state how this sentence should be pointed, and the rule for it?

"They set out early and before the dawn of day arrived at the destined place." Will you state the rule for pointing this sentence, and others of a similar kind?

"My son give me thy heart." What is the rule for pointing this sentence?

"Paul the apostle of the Gentiles was eminent for his zeal and knowledge." Will you state how

eminent for his zeal and knowledge.' "The butterfly, child of the summer, flutters in the sun."

But if such nouns are single, or only form a proper name, they are nc divided; as, "Paul the apostle." "The emperor Antoninus wrote an excellent book."

RULE 12.—Simple members of sentences, connected by comparatives, are for the most part distinguished by a comma; as, "*As* the hart panteth after the water-brooks, *so* doth my soul pant after thee." "*Better* is a dinner of herbs with love, *than* a stalled ox and hatred with it."

If the members in comparative sentences are short, the comma is, in general, better omitted; as, "How much *better* is it to get wisdom *than* gold!"

RULE 13.—When words are placed in opposition to each other, or with some marked variety, they require to be distinguished by a comma; as,

"Though deep, yet clear; though gentle, yet not dull;
Strong, without rage; without o'erflowing, full."

"Good men, in this frail, imperfect state, are often found not only in union *with*, but in opposition *to*, the views and conduct of one another."

Sometimes, when the word with which the last preposition agrees, is single, it is better to omit the comma before it; as, "Many states were in alliance *with*, and under the protection *of* Rome."

"The same rule and restriction must be applied when two or more nouns refer to the same preposition; as, "He was composed both under the threatening, and at the approach, *of* a cruel and lingering death."

RULE 14.—A remarkable expression, or a short observation, somewhat in the manner of a quotation, may be properly marked with a comma; as, "It hurts a man's pride to say, I do not know." "Plutarch calls lying, the vice of slaves."

RULE 15.—Relative pronouns are connective words, and generally admit comma before them; as, "He preaches sublimely, *who* lives a sober, righteous, and pious life."

But when two members or phrases are closely connected by a relative, restraining the general notion of the antecedent to a particular sense, the comma should be omitted; as, "Self-denial is the sacrifice which virtue must make."

The fifteenth rule applies equally to cases in which the relative is not expressed, but understood; as, "It was from piety, warm and unaffected, that his morals derived strength."

RULE 16.—A simple member of a sentence, contained within another, or following another, must be distinguished by a comma; as, "To improve time whilst we are blessed with health, will smooth the bed of sickness." "Very often, while we are complaining of the vanity and the evils of human life, we make that vanity, and we increase those evils."

If, however, the members succeeding each other are very closely connected, the comma is unnecessary; as, "Revelation tells us how we may attain happiness."

When a verb in the infinitive mood follows its governing verb, with several words between them, those words should generally have a comma at the end of them; as, "It ill becomes good and wise men, to oppose and degrade one another."

Several verbs in the infinitive mood, having a common dependence, and succeeding one another, are also divided by commas; as, "To relieve the indigent, to comfort the afflicted, to protect the innocent, to reward the deserving, are humane and noble employments."

RULE 17.—When the verb *to be* is followed by a verb in the infinitive mood which, by transposition, might be made the nominative case to it, the former

---

this sentence should be pointed, and the rule for it?
"As the hart panteth after the water-brooks so doth my soul pant after thee." How should this sentence be pointed, and what is the rule for it?
"Though deep yet clear though gentle yet not dull." How should this sentence be pointed, and what is the rule for it? State the exception to this rule. "It hurts a man's pride to say I do not know." How should this sentence be pointed, and what is the rule for it? "He preaches sub-

limely who lives a sober righteous and pious life." Will you state how this sentence should be pointed, and the rule for it? Will you state when the comma should be omitted? Does this rule apply to cases in which the relative is expressed? Give an example.

"To improve time whilst we are blessed with health will smooth the bed of sickness." How should this sentence be pointed, and what is the rule for it? Will you state the exceptions to this rule?

is generally separated from the latter verb by a comma; as, "The most obvious remedy is, to withdraw from all associations with bad men." "The first and most obvious remedy against the infection, is, to withdraw from all associations with bad men."

RULE 18.—When adjuncts or circumstances are of importance, and often when the natural order of them is inverted, they may be set off by commas; as, "Virtue must be formed and supported, not by unfrequent acts, but by daily and repeated exertions." "Vices, like shadows, towards the evening of life, grow great and monstrous."

RULE 19.—Where the verb is understood, a comma may often be properly introduced. This is a general rule, which, besides comprising some of the preceding rules, will apply to many cases not determined by any of them; as, "From law arises security; from security, curiosity; from curiosity, knowledge."

RULE 20.—The words *nay, so, hence, again, first, secondly, formerly, now, lastly, once more, above all, on the contrary, in the next place, in short,* and all other words and phrases of the same kind, must generally be separated from the context by a comma.

OF THE SEMICOLON.

The Semicolon is used for dividing a compound sentence into two or more parts, not so closely connected as those which are separated by a comma, nor yet so little dependent on each other as those which are distinguished by a colon.

The semicolon is sometimes used when the preceding member of the sentence does not of itself give a complete sense, but depends on the following clause; and sometimes when the sense of that member would be complete without the concluding one; as in the following instance: "As the desire of approbation, when it works according to reason, improves the amiable part of our species in every thing that is laudable; so nothing is more destructive to them when it is governed by vanity and folly."

OF THE COLON.

The colon is used to divide a sentence into two or more parts, less connected than those which are separated by a semicolon; but not so independent as separate, distinct sentences.

The colon may be properly applied in the three following cases:—

1. When a member of a sentence is complete in itself, but followed by some supplemental remark, or further illustration of the subject; as, "Nature felt her inability to extricate herself from the consequences of guilt: the gospel reveals the plan of divine interposition and aid."

2. When several semicolons have preceded, and a still greater pause is necessary, in order to mark the connecting or concluding sentiment; as, "A divine Legislator, uttering his voice from heaven; an almighty Governor, stretching forth his arm to punish or reward; informing us of perpetual rest prepared hereafter for the righteous, and of indignation and wrath awaiting the wicked: these are the considerations which overawe the world, which support integrity, and check guilt."

3. The colon is commonly used when an example, a quotation, or a speech is introduced; as, "The Scriptures give us an amiable representation of the Deity, in these words: 'God is love.'"

OF THE PERIOD.

When a sentence is complete and independent, and not connected in construction with the following sentence, it is marked with a Period.

"The most obvious remedy is to withdraw from all associations with bad men." Will you state how this sentence should be pointed, and the rule for it? "Vices like shadows towards the evening of life grow great and monstrous." Will you give the rule for pointing this sentence, and apply it? "From law arises security from security curiosity from curiosity knowledge." How should this sentence be pointed,

and what is the rule for it? "He feared want hence he overvalued riches." Will you state how this sentence should be pointed, and the rule for it? When is the semicolon used? When is the colon used? In what three cases may the colon be properly applied? When is the period used? After abbreviated words what point should be used? Give examples.

The period should be used after every abbreviated word; as, M. S., P S., N. B., A. D., O. S., N. S., &c.

THE DASH.

The Dash, though often used improperly by hasty and incoherent writers, may be introduced with propriety where the sentence breaks off abruptly; where a significant pause is required; or where there is an unexpected turn in the sentiment; as, "If thou art he, so much respected once—but, oh! how fallen! how degraded!"

INTERROGATION.

A Note of Interrogation is used at the end of an interrogative sentence; that is, when a question is asked; as, "Who will accompany me?" "Shall we always be friends?"

EXCLAMATION.

The Note of Exclamation is applied to expressions of sudden emotion, surprise, joy, grief, &c., and also to invocations or addresses; as, "My friend! this conduct amazes me!" "Bless the Lord, O my soul! and forget not all his benefits!"

The interrogation and exclamation points are indeterminate as to their quantity or time, and may be equivalent, in that respect, to a semicolon, a colon, or a period, as the sense may require. They mark an elevation of the voice.

PARENTHESIS.

A Parenthesis is a clause containing some necessary information, or useful remark, introduced into the body of a sentence obliquely, and which may be omitted without injuring the grammatical construction; as,

"Know, then, this truth, (enough for man to know,)
Virtue, alone, is happiness below."

The parenthesis marks a moderate depression of the voice, and may be accompanied with every point which the sense would require if the parenthetical characters were omitted.

Directions respecting the Use of CAPITAL LETTERS.

It is proper to begin with a capital,
1. The first word of every book, chapter, letter, note, or any other piece of writing.
2. The first word after a period, and, if the two sentences are totally independent, after a note of interrogation or exclamation.
3. The appellations of the Deity; as, God, Jehovah, the Almighty, the Supreme Being, the Lord, Providence, the Messiah, the Holy Spirit.
4. Proper names of persons, places, streets, mountains, rivers, ships; as, George, York, the Strand, the Alps, the Thames, the Seahorse.
5. Adjectives derived from the proper names of places; as, Grecian, Roman, English, French, Italian, &c.
6. The first word of a quotation, introduced after a colon, or when it is in a direct form; as, "Always remember this ancient maxim: 'Know thyself.'"
The first word of an example may also very properly begin with a capital.
7. Every substantive and principal word in the titles of books; as, Johnson's Dictionary of the English Language; Thomson's Seasons.
8. The first word of every line in poetry.
9. The pronoun *I* and the interjection *O* are written in capitals

Other words, besides the preceding, may begin with capitals, when they are remarkably emphatical, or the principal subject of the composition.

www.ingramcontent.com/pod-product-compliance
Lightning Source LLC
Chambersburg PA
CBHW020844160426
43192CB00007B/781